Bloom's Modern Critical Interpretations

Alice's Adventures in
   Wonderland
The Adventures of
   Huckleberry Finn
All Quiet on the
   Western Front
As You Like It
The Ballad of the Sad
   Café
Beloved
Beowulf
Billy Budd, Benito
   Cereno, Bartleby the
   Scrivener, and Other
   Tales
Black Boy
The Bluest Eye
Cat on a Hot Tin
   Roof
The Catcher in the
   Rye
Catch-22
The Color Purple
Crime and
   Punishment
The Crucible
Darkness at Noon
Death of a Salesman
The Death of Artemio
   Cruz
The Divine Comedy
Don Quixote
Dubliners
Emerson's Essays
Emma
Fahrenheit 451
Frankenstein

The Grapes of Wrath
Great Expectations
The Great Gatsby
Hamlet
The Handmaid's Tale
Heart of Darkness
I Know Why the
   Caged Bird Sings
The Iliad
Jane Eyre
The Joy Luck Club
The Jungle
Long Day's Journey
   Into Night
Lord of the Flies
The Lord of the Rings
Love in the Time of
   Cholera
Macbeth
The Man Without
   Qualities
The Metamorphosis
Miss Lonelyhearts
Moby-Dick
Night
1984
The Odyssey
Oedipus Rex
The Old Man and the
   Sea
On the Road
One Flew Over the
   Cuckoo's Nest
One Hundred Years of
   Solitude
The Pardoner's Tale
Persuasion

Portnoy's Complaint
A Portrait of the
   Artist as a Young
   Man
Pride and Prejudice
Ragtime
The Red Badge of
   Courage
The Rime of the
   Ancient Mariner
The Rubáiyát of
   Omar Khayyám
The Scarlet Letter
A Separate Peace
Silas Marner
Song of Solomon
The Stranger
A Streetcar Named
   Desire
Sula
The Sun Also Rises
The Tale of Genji
A Tale of Two Cities
The Tempest
Their Eyes Were
   Watching God
Things Fall Apart
To Kill a Mockingbird
Ulysses
Waiting for Godot
The Waste Land
White Noise
Wuthering Heights
Young Goodman
   Brown

Bloom's Modern Critical Interpretations

Zora Neale Hurston's
Their Eyes Were Watching God
New Edition

Edited and with an introduction by
Harold Bloom
Sterling Professor of the Humanities
Yale University

BLOOM'S
LITERARY CRITICISM
An imprint of Infobase Publishing

Bloom's Modern Critical Interpretations:
Their Eyes Were Watching God—New Edition

Copyright © 2008 Infobase Publishing

Introduction © 2008 by Harold Bloom

Bloom's Literary Criticism
An imprint of Infobase Publishing
132 West 31st Street
New York NY 10001

Library of Congress Cataloging-in-Publication Data
Hurston, Zora Neale.
  Zora Neale Hurston's Their eyes were watching God / [edited with an introduction by] Harold Bloom.— New ed.
    p. cm. — (Bloom's modern critical interpretations)
  Includes bibliographical references and index.
  ISBN-13: 978-0-7910-9788-5
  1. Hurston, Zora Neale. Their eyes were watching God. 2. African American women in literature. I. Title: Their eyes were watching God. II. Bloom, Harold. III. Title.
  PS3515.U789T639 2008
  813'.52—dc22
                         2007035378

Contributing Editor: Amy Sickels
Cover designed by Takeshi Takahashi
Cover photo Kuzmin Pavel/Shutterstock.com
Printed in the United States of America
Bang EJB 10 9 8 7 6 5 4 3 2 1

Contents

Editor's Note   vii

Introduction   1
    Harold Bloom

Literacy and Hibernation   5
    Robert B. Stepto

"I Love the Way Janie Crawford Left Her Husbands":
Zora Neale Hurston's Emergent Female Hero   9
    Mary Helen Washington

The Politics of Fiction, Anthropology,
and the Folk: Zora Neale Hurston   23
    Hazel V. Carby

Language, Speech, and Difference
in Their Eyes Were Watching God   41
    Cynthia Bond

Naming and Power in Zora Neale
Hurston's Their Eyes Were Watching God   57
    Sigrid King

Laughin' Up a World: Their Eyes Were
Watching God and the (Wo)Man of Words   71
    John Lowe

"Mink Skin or Coon Hide": The Janus-faced
Narrative of Their Eyes Were Watching God   117
    Susan Edwards Meisenhelder

"The porch couldn't talk for looking":
Voice and Vision in *Their Eyes Were Watching God*   147
    Deborah Clarke

"The Hierarchy Itself": Hurston's
Their Eyes Were Watching God
and the Sacrifice of Narrative Authority   167
    Ryan Simmons

"Some Other Way to Try": From Defiance to
Creative Submission in *Their Eyes Were Watching God*   185
    Shawn E. Miller

Chronology   205

Contributors   209

Bibliography   211

Acknowledgments   215

Index   217

Editor's Note

My Introduction stresses the affinities of Zora Neale Hurston with the heroic vitalism of Theodore Dreiser and D. H. Lawrence.

The distinguished scholar Robert B. Stepto connects *Their Eyes Were Watching God* to Ralph Ellison's *Invisible Man* by the themes of "ascent and immersion."

A more political reading is ventured by Hazel V. Carby, and in linguistic terms by three essayists: Cynthia Bond, Sigrid King, and John Lowe.

Problems of narrative doubling and of the wavering border of the visual and language are the concerns of Susan Edwards Meisenhelder and Deborah Clarke.

Hurston's evasion of narrative directness is studied by Ryan Simmons, after which Shawn E. Miller concludes this volume by analyzing Janie's transition from her bad first marriage to tragic fulfillment in her second.

HAROLD BLOOM

Introduction

I

Extra-literary factors have entered into the process of even secular canonization from Hellenistic Alexandria into the High Modernist Era of Eliot and Pound, so that it need not much dismay us if contemporary work by women and by minority writers becomes esteemed on grounds other than aesthetic. When the High Modernist critic Hugh Kenner assures us of the permanent eminence of the novelist and polemicist Wyndham Lewis, we can be persuaded, unless of course we actually read books like *Tarr* and *Hitler*. Reading Lewis is a rather painful experience, and makes me skeptical of Kenner's canonical assertions. In the matter of Zora Neale Hurston, I have had a contrary experience, starting with skepticism when I first encountered essays by her admirers, let alone by her idolators. Reading *Their Eyes Were Watching God* dispels all skepticism. *Moses: Man of the Mountain* is an impressive book in its mode and ambitions, but a mixed achievement, unable to resolve problems of diction and of rhetorical stance. Essentially, Hurston is the author of one superb and moving novel, unique not in its kind but in its isolated excellence among other stories of the kind.

The wistful opening of *Their Eyes Were Watching God* pragmatically affirms greater repression in women as opposed to men, by which I mean "repression" only in Freud's sense: unconscious yet purposeful forgetting:

> Now, women forget all those things they don't want to remember,
> and remember everything they don't want to forget. The dream
> is the truth. Then they act and do things accordingly.

Hurston's Janie is now necessarily a paradigm for women, of whatever race, heroically attempting to assert their own individuality in contexts that continue to resent and fear any consciousness that is not male. In a larger perspective, should the contexts modify, the representation of Janie will take its significant place in a long tradition of such representations in American and English fiction. This tradition extends from Samuel Richardson to Doris Lessing and other contemporaries, but only rarely has been able to visualize authentically strong women who begin with all the deprivations that circumstance assigns to Janie. It is a crucial aspect of Hurston's subtle sense of limits that the largest limitation is that imposed upon Janie by her grandmother, who loves her best, yet fears for her the most.

As a former slave, the grandmother, Nanny, is haunted by the compensatory dream of making first her daughter, and then her granddaughter, something other than "the mule of the world," customary fate of the black woman. The dream is both powerful enough, and sufficiently unitary, to have driven Janie's mother away, and to condemn Janie herself to a double disaster of marriages, before the tragic happiness of her third match completes as much of her story as Hurston desires to give us. As readers, we carry away with us what Janie never loses, the vivid pathos of her grandmother's superb and desperate displacement of hope:

> "And, Janie, maybe it wasn't much, but Ah done de best Ah kin by you. Ah raked and scraped and bought dis lil piece uh land so you wouldn't have to stay in de white folks' yard and tuck yo' head befo' other chillum at school. Dat was all right when you was little. But when you got big enough to understand things, Ah wanted you to look upon yo'self. Ah don't want yo' feathers always crumpled by folks throwin' up things in yo' face. And Ah can't die easy thinkin' maybe de menfolks white or black is makin' a spit cup outa you: Have some sympathy fuh me. Put me down easy, Janie, Ah'm a cracked plate."

II

Hurston's rhetorical strength, even in *Their Eyes Were Watching God*, is frequently too overt, and theatens an excess, when contrasted with the painful simplicity of her narrative line and the reductive tendency at work in all her characters except for Janie and Nanny. Yet the excess works, partly because Hurston is so considerable and knowing a mythologist. Hovering in *Their Eyes Were Watching God* is the Mosaic myth of deliverance, the pattern of revolution and exodus that Hurston reimagines as her prime trope of power:

But there are other concepts of Moses abroad in the world. Asia and all the Near East are sown with legends of this character. They are so numerous and so varied that some students have come to doubt if the Moses of the Christian concept is real. Then Africa has her mouth on Moses. All across the continent there are the legends of the greatness of Moses, but not because of his beard nor because he brought the laws down from Sinai. No, he is revered because he had the power to go up the mountain and to bring them down. Many men could climb mountains. Anyone could bring down laws that had been handed to them. But who can talk with God face to face? Who has the power to command God to go to a peak of a mountain and there demand of Him laws with which to govern a nation? What other man has ever commanded the wind and the hail? The light and darkness? That calls for power, and that is what Africa sees in Moses to worship. For he is worshipped as a god.

Power in Hurston is always *potentia*, the demand for life, for more life. Despite the differences in temperament, Hurston has affinities both with Dreiser and with Lawrence, heroic vitalists. Her art, like theirs, exalts an exuberance that is beauty, a difficult beauty because it participates in reality-testing. What is strongest in Janie is a persistence akin to Dreiser's Carrie and Lawrence's Ursula and Gudrun, a drive to survive in one's own fashion. Nietzsche's vitalistic injunction, that we must try to live as though it were morning, is the implicit basis of Hurston's true religion, which in its American formulation (Thoreau's), reminds us that only that day dawns to which we are alive. Something of Lawrence's incessant sense of the sun is paralleled by Hurston's trope of solar trajectory, in a cosmos where: "They sat on the boarding house porch and saw the sun plunge into the same crack in the earth from which the night emerged" and where: "Every morning the world flung itself over and exposed the town to the sun."

Janie's perpetual sense of the possibilities of another day propels her from Nanny's vision of safety first to the catastrophe of Joe Starks and then to the love of Tea Cake, her true husband. But to live in a way that starts with the sun is to become pragmatically doom-eager, since mere life is deprecated in contrast to the possibility of glory, or life more abundant, rather than Nanny's dream of a refuge from exploitation. Hurston's most effective irony is that Janie's drive toward her own erotic potential should transcend her grandmother's categories, since the marriage with Tea Cake is also Janie's pragmatic liberation from bondage toward men. When he tells her, in all truth, that she has the keys to the kingdom, he frees her from living in her grandmother's way.

A more pungent irony drove Hurston to end Janie's idyll with Tea Cake's illness and the ferocity of his subsequent madness. The impulse of her own vitalism compels Janie to kill him in self-defense, thus ending necessarily life and love in the name of the possibility of more life again. The novel's conclusion is at once an elegy and a vision of achieved peace, an intense realization that indeed we are all asleep in the outer life:

> The day of the gun, and the bloody body, and the courthouse came and commenced to sing a sobbing sigh out of every corner in the room; out of each and every chair and thing. Commenced to sing, commenced to sob and sigh, singing and sobbing. Then Tea Cake came prancing around her where she was and the song of the sigh flew out of the window and lit in the top of the pine trees. Tea Cake, with the sun for a shawl. Of course he wasn't dead. He could never be dead until she herself had finished feeling and thinking. The kiss of his memory made pictures of love and light against the wall. Here was peace. She pulled in her horizon like a great fish-net. Pulled it from around the waist of the world and draped it over her shoulder. So much of life in its meshes! She called in her soul to come and see.

III

Hurston herself was refreshingly free of all the ideologies that currently obscure the reception of her best book. Her sense of power has nothing in common with politics of any persuasion, with contemporary modes of feminism, or even with those questers who search for a black esthetic. As a vitalist, she was of the line of the Wife of Bath and Sir John Falstaff and Mynheer Peeperkorn. Like them, she was outrageous, heroically larger than life, witty in herself and the cause of wit in others. She belongs now to literary legend, which is as it should be. Her famous remark in response to Carl Van Vechten's photographs is truly the epigraph to her life and work: "I love myself when I am laughing. And then again when I am looking mean and impressive." Walt Whitman would have delighted in that as in her assertion: "When I set my hat at a certain angle and saunter down Seventh Avenue . . . the cosmic Zora emerges. . . . How *can* any deny themselves the pleasure of my company? It's beyond me." With Whitman, Hurston herself is now an image of American literary vitality, and a part also of the American mythology of exodus, of the power to choose the party of Eros, of more life.

ROBERT B. STEPTO

Literacy and Hibernation

I'm not blaming anyone for this state of affairs, mind you; nor merely crying *mea culpa.* The fact is that you carry part of your sickness within you, at least I do as an invisible man. I carried my sickness and though for a long time I tried to place it in the outside world, the attempt to write it down shows me that at least half of it lay within me.

—Ralph Ellison, *Invisible Man*

Anochecí Enfermo. Amanecí bueno (I went to bed sick. I woke up well.)

—Jay Wright, *Dimensions of History*

By the time we travel beyond the major work of Richard Wright, Afro-American literature's narrative tradition is still very much alive—even though the texts are rarely termed "narratives" by writer or reader, or consciously placed in an ongoing artistic continuum. However, after Wright it is also clear that the possibilities for significant revoicings of the ascent and immersion narratives (and their accompanying rhetorics) are virtually exhausted. This is not to say that ascent and immersion narratives do not appear in our recent literature; nor is it to say that Afro-American writers are no longer fascinated with creating rhetorics of racial soulfulness and soullessness. Indeed, in the last decade the abiding fascination with rhetorics of the former type has

From *From Behind the Veil: A Study of Afro-American Narrative*, pp. 163–166. © 1979 by the Board of Trustees of the University of Illinois.

become so pronounced that in some quarters it is seen to be an Artistic Movement, and even an Aesthetic. Be this as it may, the fact remains that, after *Black Boy* in particular, the situation is such that any actual forwarding of the "historical consciousness" of Afro-American narrative must involve some kind of escape from the lockstep imposed by the tradition's dominant and prefiguring narrative patterns. In theory, the logical first stop beyond the narrative of ascent or immersion (a stop which need not be any more generic, in a conventional sense, than were the preceding stops) is one that somehow creates a fresh narrative strategy and arc out of a remarkable combination of ascent and immersion narrative properties. In theory, attempts to achieve such remarkable combinations are possible in Afro-American letters anytime after the appearance of *The Souls of Black Folk* in 1903. In practice, however, very few Afro-American narrativists appear to have comprehended the opportunity before them, let alone fashioned combinations of merit and of a certain energy.

In *The Autobiography of an Ex-Coloured Man*, for example, James Weldon Johnson clearly demonstrates that he has some idea of the symbolic journeys and spaces which the new narrative will require, but his dedication to troping the Du Boisian nightmare of immersion aborted—which, in his hands, is fundamentally a commitment to expressing a new narrative content—precludes his achieving a new narrative arc. In writing *Cane*, Jean Toomer takes further than Johnson did the idea of binding new narrative content to new narrative form; but the success of his effort is questionable, since a new narrative arc never really emerges from his aggressive yet orchestrated display of forms and voices. The absence of such an arc is a further indication of Toomer's inability to detail his persona's final posture outside the realms of ascent and immersion. Without this requisite clarification, *Cane* appears to be an inventive text that can evoke, but not advance, the historical consciousness of its parent forms.

Before *Invisible Man*, Zora Neale Hurston's *Their Eyes Were Watching God* is quite likely the only truly coherent narrative of both ascent and immersion, primarily because her effort to create a particular kind of questing *heroine* liberates her from the task (the compulsion, perhaps) of revoicing many of the traditional tropes of ascent and immersion. Of course, Hurston's narrative is neither entirely new nor entirely "feminine." The house "full ah thoughts" to which Janie ascends after her ritualized journey of immersion with Teacake into the "muck" of the Everglades (recall here Du Bois's swamp in both *The Souls* and *The Quest of the Silver Fleece*) is clearly a private ritual ground, akin in construction if not in accoutrement to Du Bois's study. And Janie's posture as a storyteller—as an articulate figure knowledgeable of tribal tropes (a feature probably overdone in the frame, but not the tale, of *Their Eyes*) and in apparent control of her personal history—is a familiar and valued final siting for a primary voice in an Afro-American narrative. Still, there is much that is new in *Their Eyes*. The narrative takes place in a seemingly ahistorical world: the spanking new all-black town is meticulously bereft of former slave cabins; there are no railroad trains, above or underground, with or without Jim Crow cars; Matt's mule is a bond with and catalyst for distinct tribal memories and rituals, but these do not include the hollow slogan, "forty acres and a mule"; Janie seeks freedom, self-hood, voice, and "living" but is hardly guided—or haunted—by Sojourner Truth or Harriet Tubman, let alone Frederick Douglass. But that world is actually a fresh expression of a history of assault. The first two men in Janie's adult life (Logan Killicks and Jody Starks) and the spatial configurations through which they define themselves and seek to impose definition upon Janie (notably, a rural and agrarian space on one hand and a somewhat urban and mercantile space on the other) provide as much social structure as the narrative requires. Furthermore, the narrative's frame—the conversation "in the present" between Janie and Pheoby—creates something new in that it, and not the tale, is Hurston's vehicle for presenting the communal and possibly archetypal aspects of Janie's quest and final posture. Presentation does not always provide substantiation, and the clanking of Hurston's narrative and rhetorical machinery calls attention to itself when Pheoby offers her sole remark in the final half of the frame: "Lawd! . . . Ah done growed ten feet higher from jus' listenin' tuh you, Janie. Ah ain't satisfied wid mahself no mo.' Ah means tuh make Sam take me fishin' wid him after this. Nobody better not criticize yuh in mah hearin'." But these minor imperfections do not delimit the narrative's grand effort to demystify and site the somewhat ethereal concept of group- and self-consciousness, forwarded especially by *The Souls of Black Folk* and *Cane*. Clearly, Hurston is after a treatment of Janie and Pheoby that releases them from their immediate posture of storyteller and listener, and that propels them to one in which their sisterhood suggests a special kinship among womankind at large.

The one great flaw in *Their Eyes* involves not the framing dialogue, but Janie's tale itself. Through the frame Hurston creates the essential illusion that Janie has achieved her voice (along with everything else), and that she has even wrested from menfolk some control of the tribal posture of the storyteller. But the tale undercuts much of this, not because of its content—indeed, episodes such as the one in which Janie verbally abuses Jody in public abets Hurston's strategy—but because of its narration. Hurston's curious insistence on having Janie's tale—her personal history in and as a literary form—told by an omniscient third person, rather than by a first-person narrator, implies that Janie has not really won her voice and self after all—that her author (who is, quite likely, the omniscient narrating voice) cannot see her way clear to giving Janie her voice outright. Here, I think, Hurston is

MARY HELEN WASHINGTON

"I Love the Way Janie Crawford Left Her Husbands": Zora Neale Hurston's Emergent Female Hero

In the past few years of teaching Zora Neale Hurston's *Their Eyes Were Watching God*,[1] I have become increasingly disturbed by this text, particularly by two problematic relationships I see in the novel: women's relationship to the community and women's relationship to language. *Their Eyes* has often been described as a novel about a woman in a folk community, but it might be more accurately described as a novel about a woman outside of the folk community. And while feminists have been eager to seize upon this text as an expression of female power, I think it is a novel that represents women's exclusion from power, particularly from the power of oral speech. Most contemporary critics contend that Janie is the articulate voice in the tradition, that the novel celebrates a woman coming to self-discovery and that this self-discovery leads her ultimately to a meaningful participation in black folk traditions.[2] Perhaps. But before bestowing the title of "articulate hero" on Janie, we should look to Hurston's first novel, *Jonah's Gourd Vine*, to its main character, Reverend John Pearson, and to the power that Hurston is able to confer on a male folk hero.[3]

From the beginning of his life, John Pearson's relationship to the community is as assured as Janie's is problematic. Living in a small Alabama town and then in Eatonville, where Janie also migrates, he discovers his preaching voice early and is encouraged to use it. His ability to control and

From *Invented Lives: Narratives of Black Women 1860–1960*, © 1987, Doubleday. Reprinted in *Zora Neale Hurston's* Their Eyes Were Watching God: *A Casebook*, pp. 27–40. © 2000 by Oxford University Press.

manipulate the folk language is a source of power within the community. Even his relationships with women help him to connect to his community, leading him to literacy and to speech, while Janie's relationship with men deprive her of community and of her voice. John's friendship with Hambo, his closest friend, is much more dynamic than Janie and Pheoby's because Hurston makes the male friendship a deeper and more complex one, and because the community acknowledges and comments on the men's friendship. In his introduction to *Jonah's Gourd Vine*, Larry Neal describes John Pearson's exalted function in the folk community:

> John Pearson, as Zora notes in her letter to [James Weldon] Johnson is a poet. That is to say, one who manipulates words in order to convey to others the mystery of that Unknowable force which we call God. And he is more; he is the intelligence of the community, the bearer of its traditions and highest possibilities.[4]

One could hardly make such an unequivocal claim for Janie's heroic posture in *Their Eyes*. Singled out for her extraordinary, angelicized beauty, Janie cannot "get but so close to them [the people in Eatonville] in spirit." Her friendship with Pheoby, occurring apart from the community, encapsulates Janie and Pheoby in a private dyad that insulates Janie from the jealousy of other women. Like the other women in the town, she is barred from participation in the culture's oral tradition. When the voice of the black oral tradition is summoned in *Their Eyes*, it is not used to represent the collective black community but to invoke and valorize the voice of the black *male* community.[5]

As critic Margaret Homans points out, our attentiveness to the possibility that women are excluded categorically from the language of the dominant discourse should help us to be aware of the inadequacy of language, its inability to represent female experience, its tendency not only to silence women but to make women complicitous in that silence.[6] Part of Janie's dilemma in *Their Eyes* is that she is both subject and object—both hero and heroine—and Hurston, apparently could not retrieve her from that paradoxical position except in the frame story, where she is talking to her friend and equal, Pheoby Watson. As object in that text, Janie is often passive when she should be active, deprived of speech when she should be in command of language, made powerless by her three husbands and by Hurston's narrative strategies. I would like to focus on several passages in *Jonah's Gourd Vine* and in *Their Eyes* to show how Janie is trapped in her status as object, as passive female, and to contrast the freedom John Pearson has as subject to aspire to a heroic posture in his community.

In both *Their Eyes* and *Jonah's Gourd Vine* sexuality is established in the early lives of Janie and John as a symbol of their growing maturity. The symbol of Janie's emerging sexuality is the blossoming pear tree being pollinated by the dust-bearing bee. Early in the text, when Janie is about fifteen, Hurston presents her stretched out on her back beneath a pear tree, observing the activity of the bees:

> She saw a dust-bearing bee sink into the sanctum of a bloom; the thousand sister-calyxes arch to meet the love embrace and the ecstatic shiver of the tree from root to tiniest branch creaming in every blossom and frothing with delight. So this was marriage! She had been summoned to behold a revelation. Then Janie felt a pain remorseless sweet that left her limp and languid.

She leaves this scene of the pear tree looking for "an answer seeking her" and finds that answer in the person of Johnny Taylor who, in her rapturous state, looks like a golden glorious being. Janie's first sexual encounter is observed by her grandmother and she is summarily punished.[7] To introduce such a sexual scene at the age when Janie is about to enter adulthood, to turn it into romantic fantasy, and to make it end in punishment certainly limits the possibility of any growth resulting from that experience.

John's sexual encounters are never observed by any adult and thus he is spared the humiliation and the punishment Janie endures for her adolescent experimentation. In an early scene, when he is playing a game called "Hide the Switch" with the girl in the quarters where he works, he is the active pursuer, and, in contrast to Janie's romantic fantasies, John's experience of sexuality is earthy and energetic and confirms his sense of power:

> ... when he was "it" he managed to catch every girl in the quarters. The other boys were less successful but girls were screaming under John's lash behind the cowpen and under sweet-gum trees around the spring until the moon rose. John never forgot that night. Even the strong odor of their sweaty bodies was lovely to remember. He went in to bed when all of the girls had been called in by their folks. He could have romped till morning.

A recurring symbol Hurston uses to represent John's sexuality is the train, which he sees for the first time after he meets Lucy, the woman destined to become his first wife. A country boy, John is at first terrified by the "panting monster," but he is also mesmerized by this threatening machine whose sides "seemed to expand and contract like a fiery-lunged monster." It looks frightening, but it is also "uh pretty thing" and it has as many destinations as

John in his philandering will have. As a symbol of male sexuality, the train suggests power, dynamism, and mobility.[8]

Janie's image of herself as a blossom waiting to be pollinated by a bee transforms her figuratively and literally into the space in which men's action may occur.[9] She waits for an answer and the answer appears in the form of two men, both of whom direct Janie's life and the action of the plot. Janie at least resists her first husband, Logan, but once Jody takes her to Eatonville, he controls her life as well as the narrative. He buys the land, builds the town, makes Janie tie up her hair, and prescribes her relationship with the rest of the town. We know that Hurston means for Janie to free herself from male domination, but Hurston's language, as much as Jody's behavior, signifies Janie's status as an object. Janie's arrival in Eatonville is described through the eyes and speech of the men on the front porch. Jody joins the men, but Janie is seen "through the bedroom window getting settled." Not only are Janie and the other women barred from participation in the ceremonies and rituals of the community, but they become the objects of the sessions on the porch, included in the men's tale-telling as the butt of their jokes, or their flattery, or their scorn. The experience of having one's body become an object to be looked at is considered so demeaning that when it happens to a man, it figuratively transforms him into a woman. When Janie launches her most devastating attack on Jody in front of all the men in the store, she tells him not to talk about her looking old because "When you pull down yo' britches you look lak de change uh life." Since the "change of life" ordinarily refers to a woman's menopause, Janie is signifying that Jody, like a woman, is subject to the humiliation of exposure. Now that he is the object of the gaze, Jody realizes that other men will "look" on him with pity: "Janie had robbed him of his illusion of irresistible maleness that all men cherish."

Eventually Janie does speak, and, interestingly, her first speech, on behalf of women, is a commentary on the limitations of a male-dominated society.

> Sometimes God gits familiar wid us womenfolks too and talks His inside business. He told me how surprised He was 'bout y'all turning out so smart after Him makin' yuh different; and how surprised y'all is goin' tuh be if you ever find out you don't know half as much 'bout us as you think you do.

Speech does not lead Janie to power, however, but to self-division and to further acquiescence in her status as object. As her marriage to Jody deteriorates she begins to observe herself: "one day she sat and watched the shadows of herself going about tending store and prostrating itself before Jody, while all the time she herself sat under a shady tree with the wind blowing through her hair and her clothes."

In contrast to Janie's psychic split in which her imagination asserts itself while her body makes a show of obedience, John Pearson, trapped in a similarly constricting marriage with his second wife, Hattie, experiences not self-division but a kind of self-unification in which the past memories he has repressed seep into his consciousness and drive him to confront his life with Hattie: "Then too his daily self seemed to be wearing thin, and the past seeped thru and mastered him for increasingly longer periods. He whose present had always been so bubbling that it crowded out past and future now found himself with a memory." In this new state John begins to remember and visit old friends. His memories prompt him to confront Hattie and even to deny that he ever married her. Of course his memory is selective and self-serving, and quite devastating to Hattie, but it does drive him to action.

Even after Janie acquires the power of speech that allows her to stand up to Jody, Hurston continues to objectify her so that she does not take action. Immediately after Jody's death she goes to the looking glass where, she tells us, she has told her girl self to wait for her, and there she discovers that a handsome woman has taken her place. She tears off the kerchief Jody has forced her to wear and lets down her plentiful hair: "The weight, the length, the glory was there. She took careful stock of herself, then combed her hair and tied it back up again." In her first moment of independence Janie is not seen as autonomous subject but again as visual object, "seeing herself seeing herself," draping before herself that "hidden mystery" that attracts men and makes her superior to women. Note that when she turns to the mirror, it is not to experience her own sensual pleasure in her hair. She does not tell us how her hair felt to her—did it tingle at the roots? Did she shiver with delight?—no, she takes stock of herself, makes an assessment of herself. What's in the mirror that she cannot experience without it: that imaginary other whom the mirror represents, looking on in judgment, recording, not her own sensations but the way others see her.

Barbara Johnson's reading of *Their Eyes* suggests that once Janie is able to identify the split between her inside and outside selves, incorporating and articulating her own sense of self-division, she develops an increasing ability to speak.[10] I have come to different conclusions: that Hurston continues to subvert Janie's voice, that in crucial places where we need to hear her speak she is curiously silent, that even when Hurston sets out to explore Janie's internal consciousness, her internal speech, what we actually hear are the voices of men. Once Tea Cake enters the narrative his name and his voice are heard nearly twice as often as Janie's. He walks into Janie's life with a guitar and a grin and tells her, "Honey since you loose me and gimme privilege tuh tell yuh all about mahself. Ah'll tell yuh." And from then on it is Tea Cake's tale, the only reason for Janie's account of her life to Pheoby being to vindicate Tea Cake's name. Insisting on Tea Cake's innocence as well as his central place in her story, Janie tells Pheoby, "Teacake ain't wasted no money of mine, and he ain't left me for no young gal, neither. He give me every consolation in the world. He'd tell 'em so too, if he was here. If he wasn't gone."

As many feminist critics have pointed out, women do get silenced, even in texts by women, and there are critical places in *Their Eyes* where Janie's voice needs to be heard and is not, places where we would expect her as the subject of the story to speak. Perhaps the most stunning silence in the text occurs after Tea Cake beats Janie. The beating is seen entirely through the eyes of the male community, while Janie's reaction is never given. Tea Cake becomes the envy of the other men for having a woman whose flesh is so tender that one can see every place she's been hit. Sop-de-Bottom declares in awe, "wouldn't Ah love tuh whip uh tender woman lak Janie!" Janie is silent, so thoroughly repressed in this section that all that remains of her is what Tea Cake and the other men desire.

Passages that are supposed to represent Janie's interior consciousness begin by marking some internal change in Janie, then gradually or abruptly shift so that a male character takes Janie's place as the subject of the discourse; at the conclusion of these passages, ostensibly devoted to the revelation of Janie's interior life, the male voice predominates. Janie's life just before and after Jody's death is a fertile period for such self-reflection, but Hurston does not focus the attention of the text on Janie even in these significant turning points in Janie's life. In the long paragraph that tells us how she has changed in the six months after Jody's death, we are told that Janie talked and laughed in the store at times and was happy except for the store. To solve the problem of the store she hires Hezikiah "who was the best imitation of Joe that his seventeen years could make." At this point, the paragraph shifts its focus from Janie and her growing sense of independence to Hezikiah and his imitation of Jody, describing Hezikiah in a way that evokes Jody's presence and obliterates Janie. We are told at the end of the paragraph, in tongue-in-cheek humor, that because "managing stores and women storeowners was trying on a man's nerves," Hezikiah "needed to take a drink of liquor now and then to keep up." Thus Janie is not only removed as the subject of this passage but is subsumed under the male-defined category of worrisome women. Even the much-celebrated description of Janie's discovery of her split selves: "She had an inside and an outside now and suddenly she knew how not to mix them" represents her internal life as divided between two men: her outside self exists for Joe and her inside self she is "saving up" for "some man she had never seen."[11]

Critic Robert Stepto was the first to raise the question about Janie's lack of voice in *Their Eyes*. In his critique of Afro-American narrative he claims that Hurston creates only the illusion that Janie has achieved her voice, that Hurston's strategy of having much of Janie's tale told by an omniscient third person rather than by a first person narrator undercuts the development of Janie's "voice."[12] While I was initially resistant to this criticism of *Their Eyes*, my reading of *Jonah's Gourd Vine* suggests that Hurston was indeed ambivalent about giving a powerful voice to a woman like Janie who is already in rebellion against male authority and against the roles prescribed for women in a male-dominated society. As Stepto notes, Janie's lack of voice is particularly disturbing in the courtroom scene, which comes at the end of her tale and, presumably, at a point where she has developed her capacity to speak. Hurston tells us that down in the Everglades "She got so she could tell big stories herself," but in the courtroom scene the story of Janie and Tea Cake is told entirely in third person: "She had to go way back to let them know how she and Tea Cake had been with one another." We do not hear Janie speaking in her own voice until we return to the frame where she is speaking to her friend, Pheoby.[13]

There is a similar courtroom scene in *Jonah's Gourd Vine*, and there is also a silence, not an enforced silence but the silence of a man who deliberately chooses not to speak. John is hauled into court by his second wife, Hattie, on the grounds of adultery. Like the court system in *Their Eyes*, this too is one where "de laws and de cote houses and de jail houses all b'longed tuh white folks" and, as in Janie's situation, the black community is united against John. His former friends take the stand against him, testifying on Hattie's behalf in order to spite John, but John refuses to call any witnesses for his defense. After he has lost the trial, his friend Hambo angrily asks him why he didn't allow him to testify. John's eloquent answer explains his silence in the courtroom, but more than that, it shows that he has such power over his own voice that he can choose when and where to use it, in this case to defy a hypocritical, racist system and to protect the black community:

> Ah didn't want de white folks tuh hear 'bout nothin' lak dat. Dey knows too much 'bout us as it is, but dey some things dey ain't tuh know. Dey's some strings on our harp fuh us tuh play on an sing all tuh ourselves. Dey thinks wese all ignorant as it is, and dey thinks wese all alike, and dat dey knows us inside and out, but you know better. Dey wouldn't make no great 'miration if you had uh tole 'em Hattie had all dem mens. Dey wouldn't zarn 'tween uh woman lak Hattie and one lak Lucy, uh yo' wife befo' she died. Dey thinks all colored folks is de same dat way.

John's deliberate silence is motivated by his political consciousness. In spite of the community's rejection of him, he is still their defender, especially in the face of a common adversary. Hurston does not allow Janie the insight

John has, nor the voice, nor the loyalty to her people. To Mrs. Turner's racial insults, Janie is nearly silent, offering only a cold shoulder to show her resistance to the woman's bigotry. In the courtroom scene Janie is divorced from the other blacks and surrounded by a "protecting wall of white women." She is vindicated, and the black community humbled. Janie is the outsider; John is the culture hero, their "inspired artist," the traditional male hero in possession of traditional male power.

But John's power in the community and his gift for words do not always serve him well. As Robert Hemenway asserts in his critical biography of Hurston, John is "a captive of the community's need for a public giver of words."

> His language does not serve to articulate his personal problems because it is directed away from the self toward the communal celebration. John, the man of words, becomes the victim of his bardic function. He is the epic poet of the community who sacrifices himself for the group vision.[14]

For John, words mean power and status rather than the expression of feeling. When he first discovers the power of his voice, he thinks immediately of how good he sounds and how his voice can be exploited for his benefits:

> Dat sho sound good . . . If mah voice sound *dat* good de first time
> Ah ever prayed in, de church house, it sho won't be de las'.

John never feels the call to preach until the day on Joe Clarke's porch when the men tease John about being a "wife-made man." One of his buddies tells him that with a wife like Lucy any man could get ahead in life: "Anybody could put hisself on de ladder wid her in de house." The following Sunday in his continuing quest for manhood and power, John turns to preaching. The dramatic quality of his preaching and his showmanship easily make him the most famous preacher and the most powerful man in the area. John's inability to achieve maturity and his sudden death at the moment of his greatest insight suggest a great deal about Hurston's discomfort with the traditional male hero, with the values of the community he represents, with the culture's privileging of orality over inward development. Janie Starks is almost the complete antithesis of John Pearson: "She assumes heroic stature not by externals, but by her own struggle for self-definition, for autonomy, for liberation from the illusions that others have tried to make her live by or that she has submitted to herself."[15]

While Janie's culture honors the oral art, "this picture making with words," Janie's final speech in *Their Eyes* actually casts doubt on the relevance of oral speech:

> Talkin' don't amunt tuh uh hill uh beans when you can't do
> nothing else ... Pheoby you got tuh go there tuh know there.
> Yo papa and yo' mamma and nobody else can't tell yuh and show
> yuh. Two things everybody's got tuh do fuh theyselves. They
> got tuh go tuh God, and they got tuh find out about livin' fuh
> theyselves.

Janie's final comment that experience is more important than words is an implicit criticism of the culture that celebrates orality to the exclusion of inner growth. The language of men in *Their Eyes* and in *Jonah's Gourd Vine* is almost always divorced from any kind of interiority. The men are rarely shown in the process of growth. Their talking is a game. Janie's life is about the experience of relationships. Logan, Jody, and Tea Cake and John Pearson are essentially static characters, whereas Pheoby and Janie allow experience to change them. John, who seems almost constitutionally unfitted for self-examination, is killed at the end of the novel by a train, that very symbol of male power he has been seduced by all of his life.[16]

Vladimir Propp, in his study of folklore and narrative, cautions us not to think that plots directly reflect a given social order but "rather emerge out of the conflict, the contradictions of different social orders as they succeed or replace one another." What is manifested in the tensions of plots is "the difficult coexistence of different orders of historical reality in the long period of transition from one to the other ..."[17]

Hurston's plots may very well reflect such a tension in the social order, a period of transition in which the conflictual coexistence of a predominantly male and a more egalitarian culture is inscribed in these two forms of culture heroes. Both novels end in an ambiguous stance: John dies alone, so dominated by the ideals of his community that he is completely unable to understand his spiritual dilemma. And Janie, having returned to the community she once rejected, is left in a position of interiority so total it seems to represent another structure of confinement. Alone in her bedroom she watches pictures of "love and light against the walls," almost as though she is a spectator at a film. She pulls in the horizon and drapes it over her shoulder and calls in her soul to come and see. The language of this section gives us the illusion of growth and development, but the language is deceptive. The horizon represents the outside world—the world of adventure where Janie journeyed in search of people and a value system that would allow her real self to shine. If the horizon is the world of possibility, of journeys, of meeting new people and eschewing materialistic values, then Janie seems to be canceling out any further exploration of that world. In Eatonville she is a landlady with a fat bank account and a scorn for the people that ensures her alienation. Like the heroine of romantic fiction, left without a man she exists in a position of stasis with no suggestion of how she will employ her considerable energies in her now—perhaps temporarily—manless life.

Hurston was obviously comfortable with the role of the traditional male hero in *Jonah's Gourd Vine*, but *Their Eyes* presented Hurston with a problem she could not solve—the questing hero as woman. That Hurston intended Janie to be such a hero—at least on some level—is undeniable. She puts Janie on the track of autonomy, self-realization, and independence. She allows her to put on the outward trappings of male power. Janie dresses in overalls, goes on the muck, learns to shoot—even better than Tea Cake—and her rebellion changes her and potentially her friend Pheoby. If the rightful end of the romantic heroine is marriage, then Hurston has certainly resisted the script of romance by having Janie kill Tea Cake (though he exists in death in a far more mythical and exalted way than in life). As Rachel Blau Du Plessis argues, when the narrative resolves itself in the repression of romance and the reassertion of quest, the result is a narrative that is critical of those patriarchal rules that govern women and deny them a role outside of the boundaries of patriarchy.[18]

While such a critique of patriarchal norms is obvious in *Their Eyes*, we still see Hurston's ambivalence about Janie's role as "hero" as opposed to "heroine."[19] Like all romantic *heroines*, Janie follows the dreams of men. She takes off after Jody because "he spoke for far horizon," and she takes off after Tea Cake's dream of going "on de muck." By the rules of romantic fiction, the *heroine* is extremely feminine in looks. Janie's long, heavy, Caucasian-like hair is mentioned so many times in *Their Eyes* that, as one of my students said, it becomes another character in the novel. A "hidden mystery," Janie's hair is one of the most powerful forces in her life, mesmerizing men and alienating the women. As a trope straight out of the turn-of-the-century "mulatto" novel (*Clotel*, *Iola Leroy*, *The House Behind the Cedars*), the hair connects Janie inexorably to the conventional romantic heroine. Employing other standard devices of romantic fiction, Hurston creates the excitement and tension of romantic seduction. Tea Cake—a tall, dark, mysterious stranger—strides into the novel and wrenches Janie away from her prim and proper life. The age and class differences between Janie and Tea Cake, the secrecy of their affair, the town's disapproval, the sense of risk and helplessness as Janie discovers passionate love and the fear, desire, even the potential violence of becoming the possessed are all standard features of romance fiction. Janie is not the subject of these romantic episodes; she is the object of Tea Cake's quest, subsumed under his desires, and, at times, so subordinate to Tea Cake that even her interior consciousness reveals more about him than it does about her.

In spite of his infidelities, his arrogance, and his incapacity for self-reflection, John Pearson is unambiguously the heroic center of *Jonah's Gourd Vine*. He inhabits the entire text, his voice is heard on nearly every page, he follows his own dreams, he is selected by the community to be its leader, and he is recognized by the community for his powers and chastised for his shortcomings. The preacher's sermon as he eulogized John at his funeral is not so much a tribute to the man as it is a recognition that the narrative exists to assert the power of the male story and its claim to our attention. Janie has, of course, reformed her community simply by her resistance to its values. The very fact of her status as outsider makes her seem heroic by contemporary standards. Unable to achieve the easy integration into the society that John Pearson assumes, she stands on the outside and calls into question her culture's dependence on externals, its lack of self-reflection, and its treatment of women. Her rebellion changes her and her friend Pheoby, and, in the words of Lee Edwards, her life becomes "a compelling model of possibility for anyone who hears her tale."[20]

Notes

1. Zora Neale Hurston, *Their Eyes Were Watching God* (Urbana: University of Illinois Press, 1978).

2. Robert Hemenway, *Zora Neale Hurston: A Literary Biography* (Urbana: University of Illinois Press, 1977), 239. Hemenway says that Janie's "blossoming" refers personally to "her discovery of self and ultimately to her meaningful participation in black tradition." But at the end of *Their Eyes*, Janie does not return to an accepting community. She returns to Eatonville as an outsider, and even in the Everglades she does not have an insider's role in the community as Tea Cake does.

3. Zora Neale Hurston, *Jonah's Gourd Vine* (Philadelphia: J. B. Lippincott,1971).

4. Ibid., 7.

5. Henry Louis Gates, Jr., "Zora Neale Hurston and the Speakerly Text," in *The Signifying Monkey* (New York: Oxford University Press, 1987). Gates argues that *Their Eyes* resolves the implicit tension between standard English and black dialect, that Hurston's rhetorical strategies create a kind of new language in which Janie's thoughts are cast—not in black dialect per se but a colloquial form of standard English that is informed by the black idiom. By the end of the novel this language (or free indirect discourse) makes Janie's voice almost inseparable from the narrator's—a synthesis that becomes a trope for the self-knowledge Janie has achieved. While Gates sees the language of *Their Eyes* representing the collective black community's speech and thoughts in this "dialect-informed" colloquial idiom that Hurston has invented, I read the text in a much more literal way and continue to maintain that however inventive this new language might be it is still often used to invoke the thoughts, ideas, and presence of men.

6. Margaret Homans, "Her Very Own Howl," *SIGNS* 9 (Winter 1983): 186–205.

7. One of the ways women's sexuality is made to seem less dignified than men's is to have a woman's sexual experience seen or described by an unsympathetic observer. A good example of the double standard in reporting sexual behavior occurs in Ann Petry's "In Darkness and Confusion," in *Black Voices: An Anthology of Afro-American Literature*, ed. Abraham Chapman (New York: New American Library 1968), 161–191. The young Annie Mae is observed by her uncle-in-law who reports that her sexual behavior is indecent. In contrast, his son's sexual adventures are alluded to respectfully as activities a father may not pry into.

8. The image of the train as fearsome and threatening occurs in Hurston's autobiography, *Dust Tracks on a Road: An Autobiography*, ed. Robert Hemenway (Urbana: University of Illinois Press, 1984). When she is a young girl on her way to Jacksonville, Zora, like John Pearson, is at first terrified of its "big, mean-looking eye" and has to be dragged on board "kicking and screaming to the huge amusement of everybody but me." Later when she is inside the coach and sees the "glamor of the plush and metal," she calms down and begins to enjoy the ride, which, she says "didn't hurt a bit." In both *Dust Tracks* and *Jonah's Gourd Vine* the imagery of the train is clearly sexual, but, while Zora sees the train as something external to herself, something that is powerful but will not hurt her, John imagines the train as an extension of his own power.

9. Teresa De Lauretis, *Alice Doesn't: Feminism, Semiotics, Cinema* (Bloomington: Indiana University Press, 1984), 143. De Lauretis notes that the movement of narrative discourse specifies and produces the masculine position as that of mythical subject and the feminine position as mythical obstacle, or, simply "the space in which that movement occurs."

10. I am indebted to Barbara Johnson for this insight which she suggested when I presented an early version of this paper to her class of Afro-American women writers at Harvard in the fall of 1985 I was struck by her comment that Jody's vulnerability makes him like a woman and therefore subject to this kind of attack.

11. Barbara Johnson, "Metaphor, Metonymy, and Voice in *Their Eyes Were Watching God*," in *Black Literature and Literary Theory*, ed. Henry-Louis Gates, Jr. (New York: Methuen, 1984), 204–219. Johnson's essay probes very carefully the relation between Janie's ability to speak and her ability to recognize her own self-division. Once Janie is able "to assume and articulate the incompatible forces involved in her own division," she begins to achieve an authentic voice. Arguing for a more literal reading of *Their Eyes*, I maintain that we hear precious little of Janie's voice even after she makes this pronouncement of knowing that she has "an inside and an outside self." A great deal of the "voice" of the text is devoted to the men in the story even after Janie's discovery of self-division.

12. Robert Stepto, *From Behind the Veil: A Study of Afro-American Narrative* (Urbana: University of Illinois Press, 1979), 164–167.

When Robert Stepto raised this issue at the 1979 Modern Language Association Meeting, he set off an intense debate. While I do not totally agree with his reading of *Their Eyes* and I think he short-changes Hurston by allotting so little space to her in *From Behind the Veil*, I do think he is right about Janie's lack of voice in the courtroom scene.

13. More accurately the style of this section should be called *free indirect discourse* because both Janie's voice and the narrator's voice are evoked here. In his *Introduction to Poetics: Theory and History of Literature*, vol. 1 (Minneapolis: University of Minnesota Press, 1982), Tzvetan Todorov explains Gerard Genette's definition of free indirect discourse as a grammatical form that adopts the indirect style but retains the "semantic nuances of the 'original' discourse."

14. Hemenway, *Zora Neale Hurston*, 198.

15. Mary Helen Washington, "Zora Neale Hurston: A Woman Half in Shadow," in *I Love Myself When I Am Laughing ... And Then Again When I Am Looking Mean and Impressive: A Zora Neale Hurston Reader*, ed. Alice Walker (Old Westbury, N.Y.: Feminist Press, 1979), 16. In the original version of this essay, I showed how Joseph Campbell's model of the hero, though it had been applied to Ralph Ellison's invisible man, could more appropriately be applied to Janie, who defies her status as the mule of the world, and, unlike Ellison's antihero, does not end up in an underground hideout.

Following the pattern of the classic mythological hero, defined by Campbell in *The Hero with a Thousand Faces* (Princeton, NJ: Princeton University Press, 1968), Janie leaves her everyday world to proceed to the threshold of adventure (leaves Nanny and Logan to run off with Jody to Eatonville); she is confronted by a power that threatens her spiritual life (Jody Starks and his efforts to make her submissive to him); she goes beyond that threat to a world of unfamiliar forces some of which threaten her and some of which give aid (Tea Cake, his wild adventures, and his ability to see her as an equal); she descends into an underworld where she must undergo the supreme ordeal (the journey to the Everglades; the killing of Tea Cake and the trial); and the final work is that of the return when the hero reemerges from the kingdom of dread and brings a gift that restores the world (Janie returns to Eatonville and tells her story to her friend Pheoby who recognizes immediately her communion with Janie's experience: "Ah done growed ten feet higher from jus' listenin' tuh you, Janie").

16. Anne Jones, "Pheoby's Hungry Listening: Zora Neale Hurston's *Their Eyes Were Watching God*" (paper presented at the National Women's Studies Association, Humboldt State University, Arcata, California, June 1982).

17. De Lauretis, *Alice Doesn't*, 113. In the chapter "Desire in Narrative," De Lauretis refers to Vladimir Propp's essay "Oedipus in the Light of Folklore," which studies plot types and their diachronic or historical transformations.

18. Rachel Blau Du Plessis, *Writing Beyond the Ending: Narrative Strategies of Twentieth-Century Women Writers* (Bloomington: Indiana University Press, 1985). Du Plessis asserts that "it is the project of twentieth-century women writers to solve the contradiction between love and quest and to replace the alternate endings in marriage and death that are their cultural legacy from nineteenth-century life and letters by offering a different set of choices."

19. Du Plessis distinguishes between *hero* and *heroine* in this way: "the female hero is a central character whose activities, growth, and insight are given much narrative attention and authorial interest." By *heroine* she means "the object of male attention or rescue" (*Writing Beyond the Ending*, n. 22), 200, Hurston oscillates between these two positions, making Janie at one time a conventional romantic heroine, at other times a woman whose quest for independence drives the narrative.

20. Lee R. Edwards, *Psyche as Hero: Female Heroism and Fictional Form* (Middletown, CT: Wesleyan University Press, 1984), 212.

HAZEL V. CARBY

The Politics of Fiction, Anthropology, and the Folk: Zora Neale Hurston

The work of Zora Neale Hurston, in particular the novel *Their Eyes Were Watching God*, has been the object of more than a decade of critical attention. But, in addition to the critical consideration of Hurston's writings, her work has received the level of institutional support necessary for Hurston to enter the American literary mainstream. Two examples of this support would be the special Hurston seminar held at the Modern Language Association annual conference in 1975 and the award of two grants from the National Endowment for the Humanities to Robert Hemenway to write Hurston's biography. Hurston's work has also received institutional support from publishers: The rights to reprint *Their Eyes Were Watching God* in a paperback edition were leased to the University of Illinois Press by Harper and Row, but the 1978 Illinois edition has been so profitable that Harper and Row refused to renew leasing contracts and is reprinting *Their Eyes*, *Jonah's Gourd Vine*, *Mules and Men*, and *Tell My Horse* themselves with Henry Louis Gates as series editor. During the years between Hemenway's biography and the new Harper and Row/Gates monopoly of Hurston, there have been a variety of anthologies and collections of Hurston's essays and short stories, and in 1984, a second edition of Hurston's autobiography, *Dust Tracks on a Road*, was published.[1]

As academics we are well aware that we work within institutions that police the boundaries of cultural acceptability and define what is and what

From *New Essays on Their Eyes Were Watching God*, pp. 71–93. © 1990 by Cambridge University Press.

is not "literature": Our work as teachers and as critics creates, maintains, and sometimes challenges boundaries of acceptability. Graduate students tell me that they teach *Their Eyes Were Watching God* at least once a semester; it is a text that is common to a wide variety of courses in African-American Studies, American Studies, English, or Women's Studies. It is frequently the case that undergraduates in the Humanities may be taught the novel as many as four times, or at least once a year during their undergraduate careers. Traditions, of course, are temporal, and are constantly being fought over and renegotiated. Clearly, a womanist- and feminist-inspired desire to recover the neglected cultural presence of Zora Neale Hurston initiated an interest in her work, but it is also clear that this original motivation has become transformed. Hurston is not only a secured presence in the academy; she is a veritable industry, and an industry that is very profitable. The new Harper and Row edition of *Their Eyes* sold its total print run of 75,000 in less than a month.[2] The *New York Times* of February 4, 1990, published an article on Hurston called "Renaissance for a Pioneer of Black Pride" in which it was announced that a play based on Hurston's life and entitled "Zora Neale Hurston: A Theatrical Biography" was opening in New York, and that another play, "Mule Bone," a collaboration with Langston Hughes, is scheduled to open this summer.[3] On February 14, 1990, the Public Broadcasting System, in their prestigious American Playhouse series, broadcast "Zora is My Name" starring Ruby Dee in a dramatization of selections from *Mules and Men* and *Dust Tracks*. Although it could be said that Hurston has "arrived" as a contemporary, national, cultural presence, I await one further development: the announcement of a Hollywood movie.

I am as interested in the contemporary cultural process of the inclusion of Hurston into the academy as I am interested in her writing. I wonder about the relation between the cultural meanings of her work in the 1920s and 1930s and the contemporary fascination with Hurston. How is she being reread, now, to produce cultural meanings that this society wants or needs to hear? Is there, indeed, an affinity between the two discrete histories of her work? Certainly, I can see parallels between the situation of black intellectuals in the 1920s and 1930s, described now as a "Renaissance," and the concerns of black humanists in the academy in the 1980s. Literary histories could doubtless be written about a "renaissance" of black intellectual productivity within the walls of the academy in the post–civil rights era of the twentieth century. *Their Eyes Were Watching God* now, of course, has a cultural existence outside of the realm of African-American Studies and independent of scholars of the field, but how tenuous is this presence? Does the current fascination of the culture industry for the cultural production of black women parallel the white fascination for African-American peoples as representatives of the exotic and primitive in the 1920s?[4] And will the current thirst for the cultural production of black women evaporate as easily? Will the economic crisis of the late 1980s and early 1990s be used, in a future literary history, to mark the demise of the black intellectual presence in the academy in the same way as the 1929 stock market crash has been used by literary historians to mark the death of the Harlem Renaissance? If there is a fragile presence of black peoples in universities, is our cultural presence secure or only temporarily profitable? With or without reference to our contemporary economic conditions, it is startlingly obvious that current college enrollment figures reveal a sharp fall in the numbers of black graduate students, figures which would seem to confirm the tenuous nature of our critical presence. But what I find most intriguing is the relation between a crisis of representation that shaped cultural responses to black urban migration after World War I and the contemporary crisis of representation in African-American humanist intellectual work that determines our cultural and critical responses, or the lack of response, to the contemporary crisis of black urban America.[5]

However, let me make a theoretical intervention here. Edward Said has asserted that it is "now almost impossible ... to remember a time when people were *not* talking about a crisis in representation," and he points to the enormous difficulties of uncertainty and undecidability that are a consequence of transformations "in our notions of formerly stable things such as authors, texts and objects."[6] In an attempt to be as specific as I can about the particular crisis of representation in black cultural production out of which, I am going to argue, Hurston's work emerges, I will try to define some terms.

The subaltern group that is the subject of Hurston's anthropological and fictional work is represented as the rural black folk. However, the process of defining and representing a subaltern group is always a contentious issue, and is at the heart of the crisis of representation in black intellectual thought in both historical moments.[7] The dominant way of reading the cultural production of what is called the Harlem Renaissance is that black intellectuals assertively established a folk heritage as the source of, and inspiration for, authentic African-American art forms. In African-American studies the Harlem Renaissance has become a convention particularly for literary critics, but it is, as is the case with all literary histories, an imagined or created historical perspective that privileges some cultural developments while rendering other cultural and political histories invisible. The dominance of this particular literary history in our work, as opposed to organizing a history around a Chicago Renaissance, for example, has uncritically reproduced at the center of its discourse the issue of an authentic folk heritage. The desire of the Harlem intellectuals to establish and represent African-American cultural authenticity to a predominantly white audience was a mark of a change from, and confrontation with, what were seen by them to be externally imposed cultural representations of black people produced within, and supported by, a racialized social order. However, what was defined as authentic was a debate that was not easily resolved and involved confrontation among black intellectuals themselves. Alain Locke, for example, who attempted to signal a change or a break in conventions of representation by calling his collection of the work of some Harlem intellectuals *The New Negro*, assumed that the work of African-American intellectuals would be to raise the culture of the folk to the level of art.[8] Locke's position has been interpreted by contemporary critics as being very different from, if not antagonistic to, the dominant interpretation of the work of Hurston, who is thought to reconcile the division between "high and low culture by becoming Eatonville's esthetic representative to the Harlem Renaissance."[9]

In 1934, Hurston published an essay called "Spirituals and Neo-spirituals" in which she argues that there had "never been a presentation of genuine Negro spirituals to any audience anywhere." What was "being sung by the concert artists and glee clubs [were] the works of Negro composers or adaptors *based* on the spirituals."

> Glee clubs and concert singers put on their tuxedos, bow prettily to the audience, get the pitch and burst into magnificent song— but not *Negro* song. . . . let no one imagine that they are the songs of the people, as sung by them.[10]

Hurston was concerned to establish authenticity in the representation of popular forms of folk culture and to expose the disregard for the aesthetics of that culture through inappropriate forms of representation. She had no problem in using the term "the people" to register that she knew just who they were. But critics are incorrect to think that Hurston reconciled "high" and "low" forms of cultural production. Hurston's criticisms were not reserved for the elitist manner in which she thought the authentic culture of the people was reproduced. The people she wanted to represent she defined as a rural folk, and she measured them and their cultural forms against an urban, mass culture. She recognized that the people whose culture she rewrote were not the majority of the population, and that the cultural forms she was most interested in reproducing were not being maintained. She complained bitterly about how "the bulk of the population now spends its leisure in the motion picture theatres or with the phonograph and its blues." To Hurston, "race records" were nothing more than a commercialization of traditional forms of music, and she wanted nothing more to do with them.[11]

Understanding these two aspects of Hurston's theory of folk culture is important. When Hurston complained about the ways in which intellectuals transformed folk culture by reproducing and reinterpreting it as high culture, she identified a class contradiction. Most African-American intellectuals were generations removed from the "folk" they tried to represent. Their dilemma was little different from debates over proletarian fiction in the Soviet Union, in Europe, in the Caribbean, and in North America generally: debates that raged over the question of how and by whom should "the people," the masses of ordinary people, be portrayed.[12] Hurston identified herself as both an intellectual and as a representative figure from the folk culture she reproduced and made authentic in her work. However, asserting that she was both did not resolve the contradictions embedded in the social meanings of each category. When Hurston complained about "race records" and the commercialization of the blues, she failed to apply her own analysis of processes of cultural transformation. On the one hand, she could argue that forms of folk culture were constantly reworked and remade when she stated that "the folk tales" like "the spirituals are being made and forgotten every day."[13] But, on the other hand, Hurston did not take seriously the possibility that African-American culture was being transformed as African-American peoples migrated from rural to urban areas.

The creation of a discourse of "the folk" as a rural people in Hurston's work in the 1920s and 1930s displaces the migration of black people to cities. Her representation of African-American culture as primarily rural and oral is Hurston's particular response to the dramatic transformations within black culture. It is these two processes that I am going to refer to as Hurston's discursive displacement of contemporary social crises in her writing. Hurston could not entirely escape the intellectual practice that she so despised, a practice that reinterpreted and redefined a folk consciousness in its own elitist terms. Hurston may not have dressed the spirituals in tuxedos but her attitude toward folk culture was not unmediated; she did have a clear framework of interpretation, a construct that enabled her particular representation of a black, rural consciousness.

Gayatri Spivak has pointed to an important dilemma in the issue of representing the subaltern. She sees "the radical intellectual in the West" as being caught either "in a deliberate choice of subalternity, granting to the oppressed ... that very expressive subjectivity which s/he criticizes (in a post-structuralist theoretical world)" or, instead she faces the possibility of a total unrepresentability.[14] I don't know if the choice is always as bleak as Spivak claims, or is quite so simple and polarized. Langston Hughes, for example, in his use of the blues to structure poetry, represented a communal sensibility embedded in cultural forms and reproduced social meaning rather than individual subjectivity. In his blues poetry, the reader has access to a social consciousness through the reconstruction and representation of nonliterary, contemporary cultural forms that embodied the conditions of social transformation. Hurston, by contrast, assumed that she could obtain access to, and authenticate, an individualized social consciousness through a utopian reconstruction of the historical moment of her childhood in an attempt to stabilize and displace the social contradictions and disruption of her contemporary moment.

The issue of representing the subaltern, then, not only involves the relation of the intellectual to the represented, but also the relation of the intellectual to history. In Hurston's work, the rural black folk become an aesthetic principle, a means by which to embody a rich oral culture. Hurston's representation of the folk is not only a discursive displacement of the historical and cultural transformation of migration, but also is a creation of a folk who are outside of history. Hurston aggressively asserted that she was not of the "sobbing school of Negrohood"—in particular, to distinguish her work from that of Richard Wright—but she also places her version of authentic black cultural forms outside of the culture and history of contestation that informs his work. What the *New York Times* has recently called Hurston's "strong African-American sensibility" and is generally agreed to be her positive, holistic celebration of black life, also needs to be seen as a representation of "Negroness" as an unchanging, essential entity, an essence so distilled that it is an aesthetic position of blackness.

Hurston was a central figure in the cultural struggle among black intellectuals to define exactly who the people were that were going to become the representatives of the folk. Langston Hughes shaped his discursive category of the folk in direct response to the social conditions of transformation, including the newly forming urban working class and "socially dispossessed," whereas Hurston constructed a discourse of nostalgia for a rural community.[15] In her autobiographical writings, Hurston referenced the contradictory nature of the response of the black middle class and urban intellectuals to the presence of rural migrants to cities. In an extract written six months after completion of *Their Eyes Were Watching God*, Hurston describes this response:

> Say that a brown young woman, fresh from the classic halls of Barnard College and escorted by a black boy from Yale, enters the subway at 50th Street. They are well-dressed, well-mannered and good to look at. . . .
> . . . the train pulls into 72nd Street. Two scabby-looking Negroes come scrambling into the coach. . . . but no matter how many vacant seats there are, no other place will do, except side by side with the Yale–Barnard couple. No, indeed! Being dirty and smelly, do they keep quiet otherwise? A thousand times, No! They woof, bookoo, broadcast. . . .
> Barnard and Yale sit there and dwindle and dwindle. They do not look around the coach to see what is in the faces of the white passengers. They know too well what is there. . . . That's just like

a Negro." Not just like *some* Negroes, mind you, no, like all. Only difference is some Negroes are better dressed. Feeling all of this like rock-salt under the skin, Yale and Barnard shake their heads and moan, "My People, My People!"...

Certain of My People have come to dread railway day coaches for this same reason. They dread such scenes more than they do the dirty upholstery and other inconveniences of a Jim Crow coach. They detest the forced grouping.... So when sensitive souls are forced to travel that way they sit there numb and when some free soul takes off his shoes and socks, they mutter, "My race but not My taste." When somebody else eats fried fish, bananas, and a mess of peanuts and throws all the leavings on the floor, they gasp, "My skinfolks but not my kinfolks." And sadly over all, they keep sighing, "My People, My People!"[16]

This is a confrontation of class that signifies the division that the writer as intellectual has to recognize and bridge in the process of representing the people. It is a confrontation that was not unique to Hurston as intellectual, but it was one that she chose to displace in her decision to recreate Eatonville as the center of her representation of the rural folk.

The Eatonville of *Their Eyes Were Watching God* occupies a similar imaginative space to the mountain village of Banana Bottom in Claude McKay's novel of the same name published four years earlier.[17] McKay's Jamaican novel, set in the early 1900s, recreates the village where he grew up. Much of the argument of *Banana Bottom* emerges in the tension between attempts by missionaries to eradicate black cultural forms and the gentler forms of abuse present in white patronage of black culture. Against these forms of exploitation McKay reconstructs black culture as sustaining a whole way of life. But it is a way of life of the past, of his formative years, a place that the intellectual had to leave to become an intellectual and to which he does not return except in this Utopian moment. Eatonville, likewise, is the place of Hurston's childhood, a place to which she returns as an anthropologist. As she states in her introduction to *Mules and Men*, she consciously returns to the familiar,[18] and she recognizes that the stories she is going to collect, the ones she heard as a child, are a cultural form that is disappearing.[19]

In returning to and recreating the moment of her childhood, Hurston privileges the nostalgic and freezes it in time. Richard Wright, in his review of *Their Eyes Were Watching God*, accused Hurston of recreating minstrelsy. Though this remark is dismissed out of hand by contemporary critics, what it does register is Wright's reaction to what appears to him to be an outmoded form of historical consciousness. Whereas Wright attempted to explode the discursive category of the Negro as being formed, historically, in the culture of minstrelsy, and as being the product of a society structured in dominance through concepts of race, Hurston wanted to preserve the concept of Negroness, to negotiate and rewrite its cultural meanings, and, finally, to reclaim an aesthetically purified version of blackness. The consequences for the creation of subaltern subject positions in each of their works are dramatically different. The antagonism between them reveals Wright to be a modernist and leaves Hurston embedded in the politics of Negro identity.

Eatonville, as an anthropological and fictional space, appears in Hurston's work before her first anthropological expedition in 1927.[20] Not all the stories and anecdotes in *Mules and Men* originated from her research, and many appeared in different versions in different texts.[21] Rather than being valued primarily as a mode of scholarly inquiry, anthropology was important to Hurston because it enabled her to view the familiar and the known from a position of scientific objectivity, if not distance. She could not see her culture for wearing it, she said: "It was only when I was off in college, away from my native surroundings, that I could see myself like somebody else and stand off and look at my garment. Then I had to have the spyglass of Anthropology to look through at that."[22] Anthropology, then, is seen by Hurston as providing a professional point of view. Ethnography becomes a tool in the creation of her discourse of the rural folk that displaces the antagonistic relations of cultural transformation.[23]

George Marcus and Michael Fischer have described the ways in which anthropology "developed the ethnographic paradigm" in the 1920s and 1930s. "Ethnographies as a genre," they argue, "had similarities with traveler and explorer accounts, in which the main narrative motif was the romantic discovery by the writer of people and places unknown to the reader."[24] Hurston shares this romantic and, it must be said, colonial imagination. Her representation of Eatonville in *Mules and Men* and in *Their Eyes Were Watching God* is both an attempt to make the unknown known and a nostalgic attempt to preserve a disappearing form of folk culture.[25] Marcus and Fischer argue that there are three dimensions to the criticism that ethnography offered of Western civilization:

> [T]hey—primitive man—have retained a respect for nature, and we have lost it (the ecological Eden); they have sustained close, intimate, satisfying communal lives, and we have lost this way of life (the experience of community); and they have retained a sense of the sacred in everyday life, and we have lost this (spiritual vision).[26]

Whereas the other students of Franz Boas, Margaret Mead and Ruth Benedict, turned to societies outside of Europe and North America to point to what the West had lost but the cultural "other" still retained, Hurston's anthropological work concentrated upon the cultural "other" that existed within the racist order of North America.

In 1935, Ruth Benedict published *Patterns of Culture*, in which she asserted that black Americans were an example of what happens "when entire peoples in a couple of generations shake off their traditional culture and put on the customs of the alien group. The culture of the American Negro in northern cities," she continued, "has come to approximate in detail that of the whites in the same cities."[27] With this emphasis in the school of anthropological thought that most influenced Hurston, anthropology provided her with not only a "spyglass" but with a theoretical paradigm that directed her toward rural, not urban, black culture and folk forms of the past, not the present.

Hurston, like Benedict, was concerned with the relationships among the lives and cultures that she reconstructed and her own search for a construction of the self.[28] She lived the contradictions of the various constructions of her social identity and rewrote them in *Their Eyes Were Watching God*. Her anthropological "spyglass," which she trained on the society that produced her, allowed her to return to that society in the guise of being a listener and a reporter. In her fictional return, Hurston represents the tensions inherent in her position as an intellectual—in particular as a writer—in antagonistic relation to her construction of the folk as community. It is in this sense that I think Hurston is as concerned with the production of a sense of self as she is with the representation of a folk consciousness through its cultural forms. Both, I would argue, are the motivating forces behind the use of anthropological paradigms in Hurston's work. But it is the relation and tension between the two, particularly the intellectual consciousness and the consciousness of the folk, that is present in the fictional world of *Their Eyes Were Watching God*, which is written between her two books of anthropology, *Mules and Men* and *Tell My Horse*. In this novel, we can see how Hurston brings into being a folk consciousness that is actually in a contradictory relation to her sense of herself as an intellectual.

Throughout the 1930s, Hurston is in search of a variety of formal possibilities for the representation of black rural folk culture. She produced three musicals—*From Sun to Sun*, *The Great Day*, and *Singing Steel*—because she was convinced that folk culture should be dramatized. She returned to fiction as a form after a gap of six years when she wrote "The Gilded Six Bits" in 1933, and *Jonah's Gourd Vine*, which was published in 1934. Then Hurston seriously considered pursuing a Ph.D. degree at Columbia in anthropology and folklore. After finalizing all the arrangements for the publication of *Mules and Men*, however, Hurston accompanied Alan Lomax on a trip to collect folk music for the Library of Congress in 1935. That fall she joined the Federal Theatre Project and was prominent in organizing its Harlem unit as well as producing a one-act play, "The Fiery Chariot." Between 1936 and 1938, Hurston spent a major part of her time in the Caribbean collecting material on voodoo practices. She spent six months in Jamaica, and *Their Eyes Were Watching God* was written while she was in Haiti.[29] In *Their Eyes* she reproduces Eatonville from a distance which is both geographical and metaphorical and politically inscribed with issues of gender and class. Hurston's work during this period, then, involves an intellectual's search for the appropriate forms in which to represent the folk and a decision to rewrite the geographical boundaries of representation by situating the southern, rural folk and patterns of migration in relation to the Caribbean rather than the northern states.

Henry Louis Gates, Jr. has explored the great detail matters of voice in *Their Eyes Were Watching God* in relation to a politics of identity by tracing Hurston's construction of a protagonist engaged in a search "to become a speaking black subject."[30] On the other hand, Mary Helen Washington and Robert Stepto have both raised intriguing questions about Janie's lack of voice in the text. Washington relates this silencing of a female protagonist to her reading of *Jonah's Gourd Vine* and concludes that "Hurston was indeed ambivalent about giving a powerful voice to a woman like Janie who is already in rebellion against male authority and against the roles prescribed for women in a male dominated society."[31] However, both sides of this debate about the speaking or silent subject exist within the same paradigm of voice. I wish to introduce an alternative paradigm that suggests ways in which *Their Eyes Were Watching God* is a text concerned with the tensions arising from Hurston's position as writer in relation to the folk as community that she produces in her writing. In other words, I want to concentrate upon the contradictions that arise in the relation between writer, as woman and intellectual, and her construction of subaltern subject positions rather than remain within critical paradigms that celebrate black identity.

The two chapters that frame the story of Janie's life and are central to arguments about the ways in which Hurston prepares the fictional space in which Janie can tell her own story actually detail the antagonistic relation between Janie, as a woman alone, and the folk as community. The community sits "in judgment" as the figure of Janie, the protagonist, walks through the town to her house. This walk can be seen as analogous to crossing a stage and "running the gauntlet." Oral language, as it was embodied in the folktale in *Mules and Men*, was a sign of an authentic culture that enabled a people to survive and even triumph spiritually over their oppression. In the opening chapter of *Their Eyes Were Watching God*, however, oral language is represented as a "weapon," a means for the destruction and fragmentation of the self rather than a cultural form that preserves a holistic personal and social identity. Questions become "burning statements," and laughs are "killing tools" (2). Janie has broken the boundaries of social convention and becomes the accused. She doesn't act appropriately for her age, which is "way past forty" (3). (Hurston was forty-five years old at the time the text was written, but on various occasions took between seven and nineteen years off her age.)[32] Also inappropriate are the class codes that Janie threatens in her behavior and in her dress: As a middle-class widow she should not have associated with the itinerant Tea Cake; and as a middle-class woman, her "faded shirt and muddy overalls" are a comforting sign to the folk as community who can ease their antagonism and resentment with the thought that maybe she will "fall to their level someday" (11).

Hurston increases the tension between her protagonist and the community to which she returns through a series of binary oppositions between the intellect, or mind, and speech. The process of the analysis by the anthropological self in *Mules and Men* is reversed by the creator of fiction in *Their Eyes Were Watching God*. In the former, the oral tale is a sign of a whole healthy culture and community; in the latter, the individual functions of speaking are isolated and lack a center. Janie responds to her victimization through synecdoche. The community is indicted as a "Mouth Almighty," a powerful voice that lacks intellectual direction. Far from being spiritually whole, the folk who are gathered on the porch are reduced to their various body parts: In each, an "envious heart makes a treacherous ear" (5).[33] This is the context that determines Janie's refusal to tell her story directly to the community, a refusal that distinguishes her story from the directly told and shared folktale. In the process of transmitting Janie's story, Hurston requires an instrument of mediation between her protagonist and the folk, and it is Janie's friend Pheoby who becomes this mediator. When Janie decides to tell her story through her friend—"Mah tongue is in mah friend's mouf" (5), she says—Hurston creates a figure for the form of the novel, a fictional world that can mediate and perhaps resolve the tension that exists in the difference between the socially constructed identities of "woman" and "intellectual" and the act of representing the folk.[34]

Hurston's particular form of mediation appears to be an alternative version of the anthropological spyglass that she needed to create a professional point of view between her consciousness of self and the subjects she was reproducing. Janie's definite refusal to tell her tale directly, as in a folktale, distinguishes not only her story from other stories that are communally shared, but also her position from that of the folk as community. Hurston's position as intellectual is reproduced as a relation of difference, as an antagonistic relationship between Janie and the folk. The lack in the folk figures, the absence of mind, or intellectual direction in the porch sitters, is symbolically present when Janie mounts her own porch.

In *Mules and Men*, the porch is the site for the expression of the folktale as an evocation of an authentic black culture. In *Their Eyes Were Watching God*, the porch is split and transformed. Whereas in *Mules and Men* the anthropological self is positioned on a figuratively unified porch, primarily as a listener and a recorder, in *Their Eyes Were Watching God* the anthropological role of listener is embedded in the folk as community and the role of recorder situated in the mediator—Pheoby/the text. In the novel, then, a listening *audience* is established for the narrative self, whereas in *Mules and Men* Hurston constructs a listening *anthropological subject*. It is Janie who can address and augment the lack in the folk as community and Janie who can unify the division between mind and mouth. Janie, of course, is placed in the subject position of intellectual and has the desire to "sit down and tell [the folk] things." Janie, as intellectual, has traveled outside of the community and defines herself as "a delegate to de big 'ssociation of life" (6); her journey is the means by which knowledge can be brought into the community. As intellectual she creates subjects, grants individual consciousness, and produces understanding—the cultural meanings without which the tale is useless to the community—"taint no use in me telling you somethin' unless Ah give you de understandin' to go 'long wid it," Janie tells Pheoby. The conscious way in which subjectivity is shaped and directed is the act of mediation of the writer; it is this sense in which Pheoby becomes both Hurston's instrument of mediation and her text in an act of fictionalization.

The second part of the frame in the last chapter of *Their Eyes Were Watching God* opens with the resolution of the tension, division, and antagonism that are the subject of the opening chapter. The pattern of division of the first part of the frame is repeated: Janie is verbally condemned by the folk as community because she killed Tea Cake. The folk "lack" the understanding of the reasoning behind Janie's actions, but this deficiency is compensated for only through Janie's defense of herself in a court of law. The folk on the muck finally end their hostility to Janie when Sop explains that Tea Cake went crazy and Janie acted to protect herself. Reconciliation, then, between the position of intellectual and the folk as community takes place through acts of narration. The discursive unity that is maintained in the framing of the text prefigures the possibility for reconciliation between the position of Janie, as both intellectual and woman, and the folk as community when Pheoby provides them with the understanding of Janie's life through what will be another act of narration. *Their Eyes Were Watching God*, as such an act of narration itself, offers a resolution to the tension between Hurston, as intellectual, as writer, and the people she represents. In a paragraph that reproduces the tension in relation of the intellectual to the folk Hurston specifies the source of antagonism between Janie and the community as being a lack of knowledge.

Now, Pheoby, don't feel too mean wid de rest of 'em 'cause dey's parched up from not known' things. Dem meatskins is *got* tuh rattle tuh make out they's alive. Let 'em consolate theyselves wid talk. 'Course, talkin' don't amount tuh uh hill uh beans when yuh can't do nothin' else. And listenin' tuh dat kind uh talk is jus' lak openin' yo' mouth and lettin' de moon shine down yo' throat. It's uh known fact, Pheoby, you got tuh go there tuh *know* there. Yo' papa and yo' mama and nobody else can't tell yuh and show yuh. Two things everybody's got tuh do fuh theyselves. They got tuh go tuh God, and they got tuh find out about livin' fuh theyselves. (183)

The passage that I have quoted here is the final paragraph in Janie's story. It gains authority from claiming the tone of the preacher and the pedagogue, and at the same time it evokes the dilemma of the intellectual. Hurston's journey away from the community that produced her and that she wants to reproduce has provided her with a vision of an alternative world. Although it is not actually present in the text, the novel ends with the possibility that that history could be brought into the community and suggests that Pheoby/ the text is the means for accomplishing the transformation necessary to reconcile difference. However, as a woman and as an intellectual, Hurston has to negotiate both gendered and classed constructions of social identity and subjectivities.

Critics often forget that Janie is a protagonist whose subject position is defined through class, that she can speak on a porch because she owns it. The contradictions between her appearance in overalls, a sign of material lack, and the possession of nine hundred dollars in the bank are important. Hurston's anthropological trips for *Mules and Men* were financed by a patron, Mrs. Osgood Mason, to whom she dedicates the text. The folklore material that Hurston had collected she could not freely utilize as she wished: Mason had made it abundantly clear that she claimed proprietary ownership of all that ethnographic material. Hurston traveled to Jamaica and Haiti on her own Guggenheim grant, and, when she was writing *Their Eyes*, she must have pleasured in the sense that no one else could claim ownership of her words and her work. However, the problem is that providing her protagonist with the financial independence that Hurston herself must have found necessary in order to occupy a position from which to write reinforces the division between Janie and her community. The text here echoes Janie's grandmother's demand for a place like the white woman's, a place on high. The fact that Janie does indeed mount and own her porch enables the story, but also permeates it with a bourgeois discourse that differentiates her from the folk as community.

But this intellectual and property owner is also a woman, and thus the problem of representation here is also a question of how a woman can write her story within a site that is male-dominated and patriarchally defined. In *Mules and Men*, Hurston addresses the social constitution of gender roles in particular tales and through brief narratives that describe the relations among the tale-tellers on the porch, but she does not inscribe a concern with gender within the terms of the professional role of the anthropologist itself.[35] However, the role of listener had its limitations. Hurston's conscious reversal of the role of anthropologist reveals the contradictions inherent in the processes through which an intellectual, an intellectual who is also a woman, can instruct a community about what is outside of its social consciousness. This is the problem that frames the novel. The final metaphor of the horizon as a "great fish-net" with "so much of life in its meshes" (184) that Janie pulls in and drapes around herself is an appropriate image for a writer who can recreate and represent a social order in her narrative. But what this metaphor also confirms is the distance between the act of representation and the subjects produced through that act of representation. The assertion of autonomy implicit in this figuration of a discourse that exists only for the pleasure of the self displaces the folk as community utterly and irrevocably.

I have suggested ways in which the narrative strategies of *Mules and Men* and *Their Eyes Were Watching God* are different and yet similar in that they both evoke the romantic imagination so characteristic of ethnography in the 1930s. If, as Marcus and Fischer suggest, the main narrative motif of ethnography is the "romantic discovery by the writer of people and places unknown to the reader," then *Mules and Men* both discovers the rural folk and acts to make known and preserve a form of culture that embodies a folk consciousness. The folk as community remain the "other" and exist principally as an aesthetic device, a means for creating an essential concept of blackness. The framing of that novel is the process of working out, or mapping, a way of writing and discovering the subject position of the intellectual in relation to what she represents.

Hurston's journey to Jamaica and two trips to Haiti produced *Tell My Horse*, a text that Robert Hemenway has dismissed as Hurston's "poorest book." Hemenway argues that Hurston "was a novelist and folklorist, not a political analyst or traveloguist."[36] I would agree that Hurston's overtly political comments in *Tell My Horse* are usually reactionary, blindly patriotic, and, consequently, superficial. The dominant tendency in Hurston scholarship has been to ignore or dismiss as exceptional some of her more distasteful political opinions but, as Marcus and Fischer have explained, the ethnology and travelogue share a romantic vision (and I would add a colonial or imperial vision), making *Tell My Horse* not an exception to Hurston's work at this moment in her life but an integral part of it. In the second chapter of Part Two of *Mules and Men*, the section entitled

"Hoodoo," Hurston shifts away from a concern to record and preserve a particular form of black culture, the folktale, and toward a desire to create the boundaries of a cultural world in a relation of difference to the dominant culture. The geographical boundaries of Hurston's black folk are rural, but their Southernness is not defined through a difference to Northernness as much as it is related to cultural practices and beliefs of the Caribbean. This shift is clear when Hurston, the anthropologist, moves from Florida to New Orleans and seeks to become a pupil of a "hoodoo doctor."[37]

In her introduction to *Mules and Men*, Hurston explains that she chose Florida as a site for the collection of folklore not only because it was familiar, but because she saw Florida as "a place that draws people ... Negroes from every Southern state ... and some from the North and West. So I knew it was possible for me to get a cross section of the Negro South in one state."[38] In the section of *Mules and Men* that is situated in Louisiana, we can see a shift in Hurston's work to a stress on a continuity of cultural beliefs and practices with beliefs and practices in the Caribbean. In *Their Eyes Were Watching God* this system of reference is continued through the way in which Hurston discursively displaces the urban migration of black people in the continental United States. In her novel, as in *Mules and Men*, migration is from the Southern states further south to Eatonville, Florida. Migration in a northerly direction is undertaken only by the Barbadians who join Janie and Tea Cake on the "muck." After the completion of her novel, Hurston continued her search for an appropriate vehicle for the expression of black culture in *Tell My Horse*—a first-person account of her travels in Jamaica and Haiti. Part Three of *Tell My Horse* completes the journey, initiated in *Mules and Men*, in search of the survival of the ritual and practices of Vodoun.[39]

The geographic boundaries that enclose *Their Eyes Were Watching God* enlarge our understanding of the metaphoric boundaries of self and community. The discourse of the folk, which I have argued is irrevocably displaced in the figuration of a discourse of individualized autonomy existing only for the pleasure of the self, is dispersed and fragmented in a narrative of Hurston's personal initiation into African religious practices in the diaspora. Hurston does not return again to a romantic vision of the folk. Her next book, *Moses, Man of the Mountain*, is an extension of her interest in the relations between and across black cultures because it rewrites in fictional terms the worship of Moses and the worship of Damballah that had first interested her in Haiti.[40] This figuration of Moses/Damballah also transforms questions about the relation of the intellectual to the folk as community into an exploration of the nature of leaders and leadership. The intricate inquiry into the construction of subject positions, as writer, as woman, and as intellectual, is also not repeated. In *Dust Tracks on a Road*, an apparently autobiographical act, Hurston ignores her earlier attempts to represent the complexity of the relationship between public and private constructions of the self. She continues, however, to displace the discourse of a racist social order and maintains the exclusion of the black subject from history. This is the gesture that eventually wins her the recognition and admiration of the dominant culture in the form of the Anisfield-Wolf Award for the contribution of *Dust Tracks on a Road* to the field of race relations.[41]

We need to return to the question why, at this particular moment in our society, *Their Eyes Were Watching God* has become such a privileged text. Why is there a shared assumption that we should read the novel as a positive, holistic, celebration of black life? Why is it considered necessary that the novel produce cultural meanings of authenticity, and how does cultural authenticity come to be situated so exclusively in the rural folk?

I would like to suggest that, as cultural critics, we could begin to acknowledge the complexity of our own discursive displacement of contemporary conflict and cultural transformation in the search for black cultural authenticity. The privileging of Hurston at a moment of intense urban crisis and conflict is, perhaps, a sign of that displacement: Large parts of black urban America under siege; the number of black males in jail in the 1980s doubled; the news media have recently confirmed what has been obvious to many of us for some time—that one in four young black males are in prison, on probation, on parole, or awaiting trial; and young black children face the prospect of little, inadequate, or no health care. Has *Their Eyes Were Watching God* become the most frequently taught black novel because it acts as a mode of assurance that, really, the black folk are happy and healthy?

Richard Wright has recently been excluded from contemporary formations of the African-American canon because he brought into fictional consciousness the subjectivity of a *Native Son* created in conditions of aggression and antagonism,[42] but, perhaps, it is time that we should question the extent of our dependence upon the romantic imagination of Zora Neale Hurston to produce cultural meanings of ourselves as native daughters.

Notes

1. I would like to thank Richard Yarborough for his helpful suggestions and corrections made to an earlier version of this manuscript. The editions cited in the text are as follows: Robert E. Hemenway, *Zora Neale Hurston: A Literary Biography* (Urbana: University of Illinois Press, 1977); Zora Neale Hurston, *Their Eyes Were Watching God* (New York: Harper and Row, 1990); Hurston, *Dust Tracks on a Road* (New York: Harper and Row, 1990); Hurston, *Mules and Men: Negro Folktales and Voodoo Practices in the South* (New York: Harper and Row, 1990); Hurston, *Tell My Horse* (New York: Harper and Row, 1990).

2. Personal communication with Henry Louis Gates, Jr. (February 1990).

3. Rosemary L. Bray, "Renaissance for a Pioneer of Black Pride," *New York Times* (February 4, 1990).

4. A more detailed consideration of this parallel would need to examine what Nelson George calls "selling race." The ability of the record industry to market and make a profit from "black talent performing black music" in the 1920s could be interestingly compared to the highly profitable publishing of the work of black women writers, the Book of the Month Club's distribution of Alice Walker's novel, *The Color Purple*, and the subsequent film of the same name, and the success of Spike Lee's *She's Gotta Have It* and *School Daze*. See Nelson George, *The Death of Rhythm and Blues* (New York: Pantheon, 1988), pp. 8–9.

5. Hazel V Carby, *Reconstructing Womanhood: The Emergence of the Afro-American Woman Novelist* (New York: Oxford University Press, 1987), pp. 163–6.

6. Edward W Said, "Representing the Colonized: Anthropology's Interlocutors," *Critical Inquiry* 15 (Winter 1989): 205–6.

7. See Gayatri Chakravorty Spivak, *In Other Worlds: Essays in Cultural Politics* (New York: Methuen, 1987), pp. 197–221. Spivak identifies and elaborates upon the concern of the work of subaltern studies with change as "confrontations rather than transition" and the marking of change through "function changes in sign systems." This rather awkward phrase, "function changes in sign systems," becomes in the process of Spivak's analysis the somewhat shorter phrase "discursive displacements."

8. See, for example, Hemenway, *Zora Neale Hurston*, p. 50.

9. Ibid., p. 56.

10. Hurston, "Spirituals and Neo-spirituals," in *The Sanctified Church* (Berkeley, CA: Turtle Island, 1981), pp. 80–1.

11. Hemenway, *Zora Neale Hurston*, p. 92.

12. See Hazel V. Carby, "Proletarian or Revolutionary Literature: C. L. R. James and the Politics of the Trinidadian Renaissance," *South Atlantic Quarterly* 87 (Winter 1988): 39–52.

13. Hurston, "Spirituals and Neo-spirituals," p. 79.

14. Spivak, *In Other Worlds*, p. 209.

15. See Ralph Ellison, "Recent Negro Fiction," *New Masses* 40 (August 5 1941) : 22–6.

16. Hurston, *Dust Tracks on a Road*, pp. 292–4.

17. Claude McKay, *Banana Bottom* (New York: Harper & Row, 1933).

18. Hurston, *Mules and Men*, pp. 17–19.

19. Ibid., p. 24.

20. See Hurston, "The Eatonville Anthology," *Messenger* 8 (Sept., Oct., Nov, 1926): 261–2, 297, 319, 332.

21. See Arnold Rampersad's comments in his introduction to the new edition of *Mules and Men* (New York: Harper and Row, 1990), pp. xxii–xxiii.

22. Hurston, *Mules and Men*, p. 17.

23. See Hemenway, *Zora Neale Hurston*, p. 221, who calls this reconstruction of Eatonville idealized but feels that Hurston chose to assert positive images "because she did not believe that white injustice had created a pathology in black behavior." I remain unconvinced by this argument because it simplifies to a level of binary oppositions between positive and negative images what are very complex processes of representation. It is interesting that Hemenway seems to realize this inadequacy in the next paragraph when he raises but cannot resolve the problem of "professional colonialism" in Hurston's anthropological stance.

24. George E. Marcus and Michael E. Fischer, *Anthropology as Cultural Critique: An Experimental Moment in the Human Sciences* (Chicago: University of Chicago Press, 1986), pp. 129, 24.

25. Hurston's desire to make black people and culture known is evident in letters she wrote to James Weldon Johnson. See Zora Neale Hurston to James Weldon Johnson,

January 22, 1934, in which she complains that the J. B. Lippincott Company is "not familiar with Negroes"; and May 8, 1934, in which she says about the review of *Jonah's Gourd Vine* in the *New York Times* that she "never saw such a lack of information about us." Both letters are in the James Weldon Johnson Collection, Beinecke Library, Yale University.

26. Marcus and Fischer, *Anthropology as Cultural Critique*, p. 129.

27. Ruth Benedict, *Patterns of Culture* (Boston: Houghton Mifflin, 1934), p. 13.

28. See Margaret Mead's introduction to *Patterns of Culture*, written in 1958, which opens the 1959 edition, p. ix.

29. Hemenway, *Zora Neale Hurston*, pp. 184–5, 202–27, 230.

30. Henry Louis Gates, Jr., *The Signifying Monkey: A Theory of Afro-American Literary Criticism* (New York: Oxford University Press, 1988), pp. 170–216.

31. Mary Helen Washington, *Invented Lives: Narratives of Black Women 1860–1960* (New York: Doubleday, 1987), p. 245. Washington's re-reading of *Their Eyes Were Watching God* is an admirable analysis of the ways in which this text has been romanticized, and initiates the important work of comparative analysis across texts. It was this essay that first encouraged and inspired me to follow her lead and think seriously of the relations between Hurston's texts. See also Robert Stepto, *From Behind the Veil: A Study of Afro-American Narrative* (Urbana: University of Illinois Press, 1979), pp. 164–7.

32. See Hemenway's introduction to the second edition of *Dust Tracks on a Road*, p. xi.

33. I am grateful to Richard Yarborough for pointing out to me that of course, this aphorism is itself drawn from oral tradition. My emphasis is that in its application at this point in the novel, it stresses division.

34. I am implicitly arguing, therefore, that it is necessary to step outside questions of voice and issues of third-person (as opposed to first-person) narration in order to understand why Hurston needs an instrument of mediation between the teller of the tale and the tale itself.

35. This may have been because other women like Mead and Benedict were also using the role of anthropologist as a position from which to accumulate knowledge that was both authoritative and scientific. But this is just a guess. The relations among these three anthropologists have not been explored, as far as I know, but a comparative examination of the nature of their work would seem to be an interesting area for future study.

36. Hemenway, *Zora Neale Hurston*, pp. 248–9.

37. Hurston, *Mules and Men*, p. 239.

38. Ibid., p. 17.

39. It would be fruitful to explore the relationship between Hurston's interest in and use of the Caribbean in these years with the cultural production of intellectuals who turned to the Caribbean, in particular the island of Haiti, as a source for an alternative revolutionary black history. I am thinking here, among other works, of the production of the play *Touissant L'Ouverture* by C. L. R. James, which opened in London in March 1936 starring Paul Robeson, and the publication, in 1938, of *Black Jacobins*; Jacob Lawrence's series of paintings on Touissant L'Ouverture, 1937–8; Langston Hughes's *Troubled Island* written for, but never produced by, the Federal Theatre; and the New York Negro Federal Theatre production of *Macbeth*, often referred to as the "voodoo" *Macbeth*, directed by Orson Welles in 1936. Other black units in the Federal Theatre performed *Black Empire* by Christine Ames and Clarke Painter, and *Haiti* by William Du Bois, a journalist for the *New York Times*.

40. Hurston, *Tell My Horse*, pp. 139–40.

41. Hemenway, "Introduction" to Hurston, *Dust Tracks*, p. ix.

42. See Henry Louis Gates, Jr., *The Signifying Monkey: A Theory of Afro-American Literary Criticism*, pp. 118–20 and 181–4.

CYNTHIA BOND

Language, Speech, and Difference in Their Eyes Were Watching God

One of the major problems that faces a reader of so-called marginalized texts, reading within the culture that has marginalized the authors of such texts, is the definition and recognition of a literary tradition. What is the nature of a text that presents itself within a language and ideology that necessarily excludes and even represses that text's cultural context. This concern is problematized in different ways for different minority literatures. For Afro-Americans, the literate tradition began as a crime, as we know it was illegal for black slaves to be taught to read and write. Yet throughout the history of blacks in America, this "crime" has been successfully committed over and over again: from the earliest slave narratives, up through the tremendously powerful twentieth century voices of Hughes, Wright, Hurston; Ellison, Baraka and Reed to name a few. It is the textual voice—a concept both irrevocably and richly oxymoronic— which has been problematized by Afro-American literature, situated as it is within complex African and American oral traditions. In describing the significance of this tradition for black textual production, Henry Louis Gates suggests the "Speakerly Text" as a particularly appropriate category in black literary history: "The 'Speakerly Text,' by which I mean a text whose rhetorical strategy is designed to represent an oral literary history."[1] Gates marks Zora Neale Hurston's *Their Eyes Were Watching God* as the beginning in black literature of a self-reflexive understanding of speech and its relationship to written figural language. He argues that it is this linguistic self-reflexivity that is the very best of the black textual tradition. Gates appropriates the signifier of stucturalist poetics and establishes a relational tension with black "signifyin(g)" rituals. Black authors "signify" on texts that precede them and signal this by celebrating and privileging the representation of speech within their own texts.

Their Eyes Were Watching God is a text which addresses the black linguistic tradition, but within the frame of female difference. Janie's grandmother tells her:

> Ah wanted to preach a great sermon about colored women sittin' on high, but they wasn't no pulpit for me. Freedom found me wid a baby daughter in mah arms ... She would expound what Ah felt. But somehow she got lost offa de highway ... So whilst Ah was tendin' you of nights Ah said Ah'd save de text for you.[2]

*   *   *

It is this potential text of women and language which Hurston presents in *Their Eyes*. Janie's ability to narrate her life arises initially from her self-conscious entrance into the performance of figural language. As a child, Hurston had listened to the adults' "signifyin'" rituals on the porch of Eatonville's general store with great interest. These linguistic battles were male dominated, and in *Their Eyes* Hurston makes room on the porch for the female voice's employment of figural language. By the end of the events described in the novel, which is the beginning of Janie's narrative, Janie walks past the voices on the porch, identifying figurative rhetoric as insufficient. She condemns the tropological aspect of language despite the complex understanding of the constitution of figures of speech which she reveals earlier in the novel's narrative. What Janie comes to recognize is the strategic importance of the deployment of figures within the sphere of language spoken "for its own sake," which she distinguishes from, and rejects for, the referential potential of language within the sphere of communicable meaning.

Hurston's expertise at dialect writing is indisputable, and her recognition of the cultural significance of the black oral tradition is central to her work. However, Hurston does not present this tradition without critique. She did, after all, *write*; we are not to hear her as an ethnographic tape recorder. As mentioned above, Gates reads Hurston's representations of dialect and multi-levelled voices as a valorization of the speakerly, and thus an historical recuperation of the oral black linguistic tradition. However, *Their Eyes* encloses a forceful critique of an essentially male signifying tradition, and a pointed critique of figural speech specifically. In *Their Eyes*, Hurston writes herself into, and then back out of, the speakerly tradition.

In beginning an analysis of *Their Eyes*, Hurston's opening is an irresistible starting point; the parable which defines the nature of sexual difference described within the novel:

> Ships at a distance have every man's wish on board. For some they come in with the tide. For others they sail forever on the horizon, never out of sight, never landing until the Watcher turns his eyes away in resignation, his dreams mocked to death by Time. That is the life of men.

Reading this first paragraph, one recognizes a recurrent literary figure; the ship as hope. The "Watcher," the "every man," seems a universal character, a figure of human desire. But the allegorical universality of this parable is collapsed in the next paragraph:

> Now, women forget all those things they don't want to remember, and remember everything they don't want to forget. The dream is the truth. Then they act and do things accordingly.
> So the beginning of this was a woman and she had come back from burying the dead.

These opening paragraphs, in the appositive nature of the bifurcated parable, announce the novel's concern with sexual difference. Men's aspirations are projected out of themselves, often are tied up with commerce and often are frustrated. Women, on the other hand, possess their dreams and will what they desire. The chiasmatic statement preceding "The dream is the truth" leaves a residual negative that suggests the validity of the inverse statement, "The truth is the dream." This suggested equivalence implies a specific female potential for existential and linguistic integration, and the following paragraph justifies this reading: "So the beginning of this was a woman," a statement that follows *necessarily* if we read "so" as a conjunction of necessary consequentiality. That is, women have a distinct opportunity for self-reflective integration and are therefore more reliable subjects for narratives than men. The biblical resonance of this line is important; in the beginning is not the engendering voice of a male deity, but a woman. By the novel's end (which is also its beginning) the figure of woman becomes the figure of textual creation, the voice made material. The prefatory parable suggests a metalinguistic project. And indeed, what follows is a representation and critique of various figures of speech—figures which, as they are employed by men, involve a play for power. Janie appropriates and subverts the male use of figural language and then rejects it for a notion of linguistic meaning as constituted by truth.

One of the text's most important recurrent images is that of the blossoming pear tree. This figure, as it is created by Janie and as it is used by the text, stands in important opposition to the specifically male rhetorical signifying rituals. It is a more directly mimetic figure, appropriated from the pear tree outside of Janie's girlhood home:

> She had been spending every minute that she could steal from her chores under that tree for the last three days . . . It had called her to come and gaze on a mystery. From barren brown stems to glistening leaf-buds; from the leaf-buds to snowy virginity of bloom. It stirred her tremendously. How? Why? It was like a flute song forgotten in another existence and remembered again . . . This singing she heard that had nothing to do with her ears.

Women remember what they don't want to forget, and the pear tree marks the beginning of Janie's figural memory: a "singing"—a "signing"—that is not received by the ears. It is a figure which is never given vocal status but instead remains a material fact of the text. Janie internalizes the image of the pear tree, using it over and over again to figure her life. "Oh to be a pear tree—*any* tree in bloom" she thinks as a girl; and in her maturity, when she begins the narration of her story, her experience is described as equal to the status of the tree but with the added understanding of figural distance: "Janie saw her life *like* a great tree in leaf with the things suffered, things enjoyed, things done and undone" (emphasis added). The internalization of this metaphor is framed by an awakening self-love, allusively an act of masturbation:

> She saw a dust-bearing bee sink into the sanctum of a bloom; the thousand sister-calyxes arch to meet the love embrace and the ecstatic shiver of the tree from root to tiniest branch creaming in every blossom and frothing with delight. So this was a marriage! . . . Then Janie felt a pain remorseless sweet that left her limp and languid.

It is the "sister-calyxes" which "cream with delight," indicating a self-referentiality that mirrors, and facilitates, the "marriage" of reality and image. This marriage is not only a local metaphor but has linguistic implications for the text as a whole.

Quite distinct from Janie's privatized self-figuration, male tropes occur in "lying," or signifying sessions. As mentioned above, these figurative battles of figuration occur for the most part in social contexts; episodes on the general store porch, the lamp-lighting ceremony, and the burial of the mule are the most notable occasions in the novel. The citizens of Eatonville display a great respect for the importance of figural language in any proper signifying. When Jody and Janie first set up their store in Eatonville, Tony Taylor takes it upon himself to make a welcoming speech, and is subsequently booed down:

> "Brother Starks, we welcomes you and all dat you have seen fit tuh bring amongst us—yo' beloved wife, yo' store, yo' land—"
> A big-mouthed burst of laughter cut him short.
> "Dat'll do, Tony," Lige Moss yelled out. "Mist' Starks is uh smart man, we'se all willin' tuh acknowledge tuh dat, but de day he comes waggin' down de road wid two hund'ed acres of land over his shoulder, Ah wants tuh be dere tuh see it."

Tony then attempts to protect his effort from derision:

> "All yall know whut wuz meant. Ah don't see how come—"
> "'Cause you jump up tuh make speeches and don't know how," Lige said.

Lige proceeds to instruct Tony in the correct method to present a speech, which is to employ analogy:

> "... You can't welcome uh man and his wife 'thout you make comparison about Isaac and Rebecca at de well, else it don't show de love between 'em if you don't."
> Everybody agreed that that was right. It was sort of pitiful for Tony not to know he couldn't make a speech without saying that.

Lige understands that communicating what is "meant" is not the object of speeches, figurative rhetoric is the object of speeches. He demonstrates Tony's rhetorical inadequacy by turning his trope back onto him and then suggests the proper trope to be used. The importance of figures is similarly indicated when Janie speaks herself for the first time in the speakerly tradition by delivering an oration on Joe's benevolence in freeing the mule:

> "Freein' dat mule makes uh mighty big man outa you. Something like George Washington and Lincoln. Abraham Lincoln, he had de whole United States tuh rule so he freed de Negroes. You got uh town so you freed uh mule. You have tuh have power tuh free things and dat makes you lak uh king uh something."

Janie's use of the figures of Washington and Lincoln elicit pleasure and appreciation from her audience: "Hambo said, 'Yo' wife is uh born orator, Starks. Us never knowed dat befo'. She put jus' de right words tuh our thoughts."Janie's command of language is described as natural—that is, one that is an *essential* rhetorical facility. Not only does she use analogy effectively, but she puts the "right" ("authentic") words to the thoughts of others. She not only knows how to say, she knows what is "right" to say. The referential importance of language is foregrounded later in the novel when Janie makes a decisive distinction between rhetoric and truth. Janie's articulateness upsets Joe. It is he who had aspired to being a "big voice," a status dependent on the submissive silence of his wife. It is significant that Janie makes reference to the "founding fathers" in her speech, for she is entering into an essentially male tradition of signifying. The fate and fame of men are ships on the horizon, forces that manifest themselves in the outside world. Janie deploys the male symbols of Washington and Lincoln in her speech because she speaks in a male context. Her sexually distinct figure at this point remains the interiorized image of the pear tree.

Male signifying is specifically grounded in competition, and in the mastery of women. After meeting Janie and Joe for the first time, two Eatonville residents discuss the merits of metaphorical facility in the courtship of women:

> ... But dat wife uh hisn'! Ah'm uh son of uh combunction if Ah don't go tuh Georgy and git me one just like her."
> "Whut wid?"
> "Wid mah talk, man."
> "It takes money tuh feed pretty women. Dey gits uh lavish uh talk."
> "Not lak mine. Dey loves to hear me talk because dey can't understand it. Mah co-talking is too deep. Too much co to it."

Rhetorical sophistication is here defined as a dazzling deployment of figural language. The very exclusion of women from signifying ensures that they will be taken in by it when it is deployed by men.

In the space of rhetorical rivalry, women are always recognized as the object of such signifying. One evening on Starks' porch the men are engaged in what the narrator calls "acting-out courtship" with three local women when Daisy Blunt, the town beauty, walks by. They proceed to "act out their rivalry":

> David said, "Jim don't love Daisy. He don't love yuh lak Ah do."
> Jim bellowed indignantly, "Who don't love Daisy? Ah know you ain't talkin' 'bout me."

Dave: "Well all right, less prove dis thing right now who love dis gal de best."

They go on to "prove" their love rhetorically, vying with each other for the most extreme images of devotion:

". . . Ah'd buy Daisy uh passenger train and give it tuh her."
"Humph! Is dat all? Ah'd buy her uh steamship and then Ah'd have some men's tuh run it fur her."
"Daisy, don't let Jim fool you wid his talk. He don't aim tuh do nothin' fur yuh. Uh lil ole steamship! Daisy, Ah'll take uh job cleanin' out de Atlantic Ocean fuh you any time you say you so desire."

The rhetorical logic behind this competition is that the more unactualizable the imagery, the more "truthfully" it represents the speaker's devotion. Dave warns Daisy that Jim's declaration is empty talk but then proceeds to produce the most implausible scenario of wooing yet delivered in the game. That the signifying game takes women as its object and excludes them as speakers is underscored when Jody admonishes Janie to wait on customers, thereby forcing her to miss the rest of the play-acting. Her exclusion is further underscored by Joe's outburst over the empty barrel of pig's feet:

". . . All you got tuh do is mind me. How come you can't do lak Ah tell yuh?"
[Janie:] "You sho loves to tell me whut to do, but Ah can't tell you nothin' Ah see!"
"Dat's cause you need tellin'," he rejoined hotly. "It would be pitiful if Ah didn't. Somebody got to think for women and children and chickens and cows. I god, they sho don't think none theirselves."

Joe's outburst leads Janie to examine the "inside" of her marriage, an examination which reveals important information:

The spirit of the marriage left the bedroom and took to living in the parlor. It was there to shake hands whenever company came to visit, but it never went back inside the bedroom again. So she put something in there to represent the spirit like a Virgin Mary image in a church.

Just as Janie sets up an image to represent her transformed marriage, she similarly recognizes her Joe as an image she once constructed:

She stood there until something fell off the shelf inside her. Then she went inside there to see what it was. It was her image of Jody tumbled down and shattered. But looking at it she saw that it never was the flesh and blood figure of her dreams. Just something she had grabbed up to drape her dreams over. In a way she turned her back upon the image where it lay and looked further. She had no more blossomy openings dusting pollen over her man, neither any glistening your fruit where the petals used to be.

Barbara Johnson marks this point in Janie's understanding as an entrance into the creation of figural language: ". . . she has stepped irrevocably into the necessity of figurative language, where inside and outside are never the same. It is from this point on in the novel that Janie, paradoxically, begins to speak."[3] However, Janie has successfully used figurative language at an earlier point in the novel, in the speech on Jody quoted above. In addition, her self-figuring through the pear tree begins with her adolescence. However, Johnson is correct in marking this revelation as a turning point. It is not that Janie first enters figurative language here, but that she generates a sophisticated conceptualization of representation which is transmuted into the moment of power when she signifies on Jody later in the novel. Essentially what Janie understands here is the displacing power of figures in the external, social world; a power that she herself can deploy for mastery. While Joe's image is "false," she can institute an image to represent her true feelings in its place—the virginal Mary. When she looks further than Joe's fallen image, she looks to her own image, the "blossomy openings." The image of the pear tree bridges the gap between the inside and outside of figures in Janie's life. It is the essentialized figure, the mimetic metaphor internalized yet responsive to external conditions. Janie's installation of images of her marriage is a recognition of *represented* power, a "bow to the outside of things"; while the pear tree remains the privileged image of an inherent yet undeployed power.

While the notion that figurative language empowers its deployer is critiqued later in the novel, the forcefulness of tropes *within signifying sessions* is symbolized in the text as a reification of figures into physical objects. Joe wishes to become a "big voice" in Eatonville; a voice like the voice of God whose word becomes physical in the act of creation. When Joe delivers the mock eulogy for the mule, the narrator says the oration, ". . . made him more solid than building the schoolhouse had done." Rhetoric assumes the integrity of physical objects. The signifying sessions themselves are described as a kind of alchemic process whereby figures are transmuted into objects. The porch talkers pass "nations" through their mouths, they use "a side of the world for a canvas," they "paint" thoughts as "pictures" and pass them around, etc. The mule Joe buys becomes a walking mythological figure which remains present even after its death by virtue of the "lies" told on the porch of Starks' store: "The yaller mule was gone from the town except for the porch talk, and for the children visiting his bleaching bones now and then in the spirit of adventure." While the "content" of the mule is gone, his "form" remains—in bones and figures of speech. It is the "physicalization" of figures that initially marks Janie's rhetorical freedom. She signifies on Joe: "When you pull down yo' britches, you look lak de change uh life." Joe is stunned and asks Janie to repeat the figure, to which one of the store customers replies, "You heard her, you ain't blind." The verbal figure Janie cuts is so powerful that it is described as an object perceivable by sight. This is the highest achievement of rhetoric in signifying; its figurative reification in space. Janie's "telling" on Joe is her first (and last) entrance into male signifying; that is, signifying which is used explicitly for the purposes of domination. It is significant that she uses as image which in its application simultaneously implies a *de*-sexing, and an androgyny which is essentially sexless for it is by her female passage into male linguistic territory that she is able to free herself from the hierarchical sexual difference prescribed within the roles of her marriage. She figures both the appropriation of male signifying power and the obliteration of sexual difference. Her performance of the image represents a castration, the figurative correlate of male power. And, (as Gates notes) she kills Joe rhetorically.

Their Eyes is indeed a polyphonic text. Hurston weaves among various narrative dictions: the lyrical "standard english" voice of the opening parable; the dialect representation of characters' dialogue; and what Gates identifies as the "free, indirect discourse" of the characters' thoughts. The tension between these modes is similarly manifest in *Tell My Horse*, where Hurston vacillates between the scientific voice of the ethnographer and the passionate voice of the engaged participant. It is this difference that constitutes the text and the very category of text in Hurston's writing. It will be remembered that while Hurston grew up in the middle of the Southern black oral tradition, she was distanced within it by her sexual difference and her literary appetite. Stated reductively, "Hurston was struggling with two concepts of culture . . . She enjoyed Keats, but recognized the poetry in her father's sermons; she read Plato, but told stories of Joe Clarke's wisdom."[4] This struggle is preserved in her work. Hurston's relationship to the speakerly tradition is in essence ambivalent. *Their Eyes* does not wholeheartedly privilege the speakerly as Gates suggests. Hurston's sense of the recuperation of experience potential in texts is suggested in the narrator's statement about Janie at one point: "She didn't read books so she didn't know that she was the world and the heavens boiled down to a drop. Man attempting to climb to painless heights from his dung hill." And in the course of Janie's vocal ascendancy, she comes to reject speakerly rhetoric as an insufficient positing of identity.

Janie ends her narrative attempting to distance herself from figurality. Her relationship with Tea Cake plays a large role in this. Gates points out that Tea Cake's first name "Vergible" is a vernacular form of "veritable": "Vergible Tea Cake Woods, is a sign of verity, one who speaks the truth, one genuine and real, one not counterfeit or spurious, one not false or imaginary but the thing that in fact has been named."[5] Janie moves from her marriage to the "big voice" to a marriage to "verity." The nature of these marriages in relation to Janie's search for identity is perhaps best understood in their negativity—in Janie's "murder" of both Joe and Tea Cake. As mentioned above, the moment of Joe's demise is correlative to Janie's entrance into competitive, figurative speech. She "kills" him rhetorically, by deploying a vicious trope. Joe's death brings Janie the physical and financial freedom of movement which allows her to be with Tea Cake. Her relationship with Tea Cake represents the burgeoning reconciliation of the inside and outside she had so scrupulously separated to live false emotions with Joe. The pear tree symbol drops away in the novel's narrative of Tea Cake's and Janie's life together, precisely because her metaphorical figure of fulfillment has been collapsed into veritable fulfillment. Janie's sense of disjunctive representation is resolved as she experiences with Tea Cake the reconciliation of "inside" and "outside" which is figured by the tree metaphor.

Tea Cake's death initially seems unnecessary to the novel's development; the dynamic of his relationship with Janie does not lose its narrative charm. A cursory biographical note may be of some use here. Hurston had just ended a relationship with a man when she went to Jamaica, where she wrote *Their Eyes*. In her autobiography she wrote, "The plot was far from the circumstances, but I tried to embalm all the tenderness of my passion for him in *Their Eyes Were Watching God*."[6] She left this lover to preserve her work, of which he was jealous. This suggests one reason why Hurston might have "killed off" Tea Cake in the novel. The text must "sacrifice" and subsume its own emblems of lived experience in establishing its material identity outside of that experience.

Obviously, a biographical reading does not explain the structural significance of Tea Cake's death within the novel. Briefly, the events of his demise are as follows: Tea Cake saves Janie from a rabid dog during the flood, but not without being fatally bitten. He catches rabies, detected too late to save him, and is transformed. In his delirium, Tea Cake pulls a pistol on Janie. She recognizes that Tea Cake is no longer Tea Cake at this point; that it is his "suffering brain urging him to kill," that the "fiend in him" fires the gun. Tea Cake is no longer veritable but possessed. She shoots and kills him just as he fires at her. It is not Tea Cake Janie seeks to kill, but the "fiend" inhabiting him.

The trial marks a significant turn in Janie's establishment of a vocal identity. Like the signifying rituals, the courtroom presents a highly social rhetorical occasion. But in the courtroom, Janie seeks to suppress the devices of rhetoric in order to communicate the context of her relationship with Tea Cake. It is precisely her voice that is on trial:

> The court set and Janie saw the judge who had put on a great robe to listen about her and Tea Cake. And twelve more white men had stopped whatever they were doing to listen and pass on what happened between Janie and Tea Cake Woods.

The emphasis on the activity of listening in this paragraph is crucial, for it is Janie's statement which is her only defense, and she is the only one who can speak it. In the courtroom, the guilty subject's voice is constituted as an identity only as it transcends the "artifice" of speech. Janie is faced with the necessity of clear referentially accurate speech; she is to speak ". . . the truth, the whole truth and nothing but the truth. So help her God." She recognizes the distinct nature of this speakerly occasion:

> First thing she had to remember was she was not at home. She was in the Courthouse fighting something and it wasn't death. It was worse than that. It was lying thoughts. She had to go way back to let them know how she and Tea Cake had been with one another so they could see she could never shoot Tea Cake out of malice.

This passage is a statement of rhetorical strategy. Janie realizes that she must build a narrative rather than deny the facticity of the evidence. She must reply affirmatively rather than negatively. She must create "fictional," narrative, evidence—but fiction that constitutes "truth" rather than the rhetorical facility prized at home. At the trial Janie fears "misunderstanding" more than death and her narrative is an attempt to communicate the true nature of her relationship with Tea Cake. Janie's courtroom speech marks her conscious separation of talk and action, figurality and truth. At the beginning of the novel when she begins telling Pheoby her story, she stresses communicable meaning over formal rhetorical skill. When Pheoby questions her own ability to follow Janie's narrative, Janie reassures her:

> [Pheoby] "It's hard for me to understand what you mean, de way you tell it.

And then again, Ah'm hard of understandin' at times."
[Janie] "Now, 'taint' nothin' lak you might think. So 'taint' no use
in telling you somethin' unless Ah give you de understandin' to
go 'long wid it."

Janie has moved beyond an admiration of performative language for its own
sake—the figurative language of the signifying rituals—to a privileging of
language as a means to communicate truth, "de understandin'." As previously
suggested, her evolution in thought is figured by her progression from her
marriage to Joe (the "big voice" of empty rhetoric) to her marriage to Tea
Cake (the veritable language of affirmation).

The trial scene is the only episode in the novel in which whites figure
prominently as the source of law. Janie reaches out to them in her testimony,
specifically the women, without hostility. It is this type of gesture with its
apparent lack of overt racial critique which led Richard Wright and others to
condemn Hurston's work as too personal and politically reactionary. The scene
is undeniably disturbing. For the first time in the novel, blacks are overtly
silenced. This suppression is particularly jarring given the preceding displays
of verbal facility. When Sop-de-Bottom speaks up at the trial, he is coldly
silenced by the white District Attorney, Mr. Prescott: "We are handling this
case. Another word out of *you*; out of any of you niggers back there, and I'll
bind you over to the big court." While Hurston is clearly not complicitous with
the sentiments of this character, she nevertheless undermines the powerful
rhetoric of signifying by pointing up the impotence that contextualizes such
rituals:

> They [the black audience] were there with their tongues cocked
> and loaded, the only real weapon left to weak folks. The only
> killing tool they are allowed to use in the presence of white
> folks.

This passage is similar to an earlier description of the porch-sitters watching
Janie on her return to Eatonville: "They made burning statements with
questions, and killing tools out of laughs. It was mass cruelty. A mood
come alive. Words walking without masters...." Here, black verbal skill is
denigrated as mean-spirited and ineffectual. The tropes of signifying rituals
do not constitute verbal mastery but instead master their speakers. The
identification of the racial problem as an essentially black problem is perhaps
politically redeemable if we theorize Hurston's development of black identity
in terms of the Deleuzian reformation of the Master–Slave dialectic.[7] In
Their Eyes and in her essays specifically on black identity, Hurston gestures
to a politics of human dignity. Empowerment must be distinguished from

represented power. Blacks must resist an automatic assumption of weakness in the face of manifested white power; they must resist, in Nietzschean terms, the dialectical slave mentality. At the time, Hurston's critique was seen as callous and racist.[8] This critique also filters into Janie's rejection of the folk of Eatonville:

> "Dem meatskins is got tuh rattle tuh make out they's alive. Let 'em consolate theyselves wid talk. 'Course, talkin' don't amount tuh uh hill uh beans when yuh can't do nothin' else ... It's uh known fact, Pheoby, you got tuh go there tuh *know* there."

Speech is described here as a futile attempt to posit existence, a substitution for genuine empowerment. It is action that Janie privileges over speech, or at least the kind of "active" speech represented by her testimony at the trial. Janie's defense speech seeks to suppress the figural aspect of language in favor of a language that posits meaning as truth and ultimately secures salvation.

Hurston's distinction between true and represented mastery is further evidenced by her repeated use of anthropomorphic images. The most striking example of this in *Their Eyes* is the recurrent figure of the mule. In the novel's opening pages, she describes the bestiality of black life: "These sitters had been tongueless, earless, eyeless conveniences all day long. Mules and other brutes had occupied their skins. But now, the sun and the bossman were gone, so the skins felt powerful and human. They became lords of sounds and lesser things." The deprecating irony of this statement is clear. While Hurston references the oppression that brutalizes blacks, she does not posit their refined verbal technique as true empowerment, but merely a self-deluded mastery of "lesser things." It is Janie, ostracized from white and black male culture alike, who walks past the porch rejecting figural, speakerly mastery in favor of a privatized sense of self-determination and action. Mule imagery is used later in the novel to similarly express the impotence of figural language. After Joe frees the mule, the porch voices construct numerous myths about his activities, all of them anthropomorphic in character:

> How he pushed open Lindsay's kitchen door and slept in the place one night and fought until they made coffee for his breakfast ... he ran Mrs. Tully off of the croquet ground for having such an ugly shape; he ran and caught up with Becky Anderson on the way to Maitland so as to keep his head out of the sun under her umbrella ...

The men use the mule to figure activities they themselves would like to perform but can only do rhetorically. For Janie, verbal skill—if not constitutive of identity—is only represented mastery, delusively embraced by men as a means to power. Throughout the signifying rituals in the test, the only power accessible to the man with rhetorical skill is a kind of crude domination and subordination of the immediate opponent. As figures of speech are used to dominate, domination will only be figurative.

Janie's progress is cast in the terms of a search for truth, for a horizontal knowledge that can only be obtained through action, defined distinctly from rhetoric. In the novel's opening, Janie passes the opportunity to share feats of oration with the porch sitters, preferring to narrate her tale to one close female friend. While it includes many voices, this narration's unfolding is essentially *textual*—the text of *Their Eyes Were Watching God*. Janie's initial conversation with Pheoby acts as a preface to the textually transmuted experience of Janie's life. The various voices and dictions which constitute the novel's progress are subsumed as a rendering of Janie's life, which is the novel's text. The novel's structure casts linguistic power and identity as a textual recuperation of speakerly rhetoric rather than a valorization of the speakerly as a sufficient, figurally self-reflexive linguistic presence.

At the very end of the novel, Janie defines herself as the material system, the "text" which preserves Tea Cake: "Of course he wasn't dead. He could never be dead until she herself had finished feeling and thinking." This statement echoes Hurston's "embalming" her affection for her lover in the text of *Their Eyes*. Negativity—the death of Tea Cake and the failure of Hurston's love—is ignored and re-figured by the fact of Janie's existence and the material text of the novel. This rejection of negativity is predicated on the reconciliation of interiority and exteriority. Janie reunites her inside and outside in the last paragraph of the novel: "She pulled in her horizon like a great fish-net. Pulled it from around the waist of the world and draped it over her shoulder. So much of life in its meshes! She called in her soul to come and see." Her dreams are no longer draped over the image of Joe, incarnation of the "big voice," but are instead draped over her self, uniting the dream and truth of the opening parable. While existential integration is achieved, the figure that clothes it maintains the ambivalence of representation. For a fishnet both culls vast experience and restrains it. It is both of one piece and riddled with holes. The fishnet as an image of integration figurally maintains the ultimate disjunction of sign and referent. As Johnson suggests, Hurston does indeed recognize disjunction as the irrevocable condition of metaphor. However, the maintenance of a sense of linguistic disjunction is not the enabling force which constitutes the identity of a speaking subject. The privileging of tropes which mean most "meaningfully" among themselves is identified with the rhetorically would-be power of oppressive male speakers. It is the distinction between verbal and textual representation which Hurston offers as a crucial linguistic disjunction, a fruitful gap which leads to the articulation of identity. Janie achieves a soul by positing a self that masters and transcends its own figuration in constituting identity. In the case of the novel, identity is contingent upon the recognition of linguistic sufficiency as constituted by communicable meaning that is textual rather than by performative rhetorical skill.

I began this essay by suggesting the metaphor of criminality to describe the generation of black literature. This metaphor is rich in potential as a description of the black textual tradition because it illustrates one thematization of absence and presence in marginalized literature. Black authors initially had to appropriate a language which excluded them from textual linguistic production. Through this "theft" the presence of a textual voice, a textual tradition, is posited. The means must be stolen, and is stolen, for a preservation which equals survival. Writers like Hurston were faced with the necessity of fortifying a black *literature*, of creating cultural artifacts that would go beyond the temporality of a human voice, a voice whose very existence was threatened by cultural ephemerality. The means of literate expression was necessarily posited within the context of a rich oral tradition, but sought to establish a more permanent, textual tradition. In the case of black literature, the text may be constituted as a sufficient "presence" above the speakerly since it is the black *textual* existence which is "absented" by the larger cultural milieu. It is the *text* of speech that Janie's grandmother wants to pass on to her, but must be satisfied with an oral narration of the days of slavery. Janie in turn must "orate" her history, but is textually substantiated by Hurston's *Their Eyes Were Watching God*.

NOTES

1. Henry Louis Gates, Jr., *The Signifying Monkey*. Quoted from manuscript with the permission of the author.

2. *Their Eyes Were Watching God* (Urbana, Illinois: University of Illinois Press, 1978), p. 32.

3. Barbara Johnson, "Metaphor, Metonymy and Voice in *Their Eyes Were Watching God*," *Black Literature and Literary Theory* (New York: Methuen, 1984), p. 212.

4. Hemenway, p. 99.

5. Gates, p. 427.

6. Hurston, *Dust Tracks on a Road* (Urbana: Univ. of Illinois Press, 1984), p. 260.

7. Gilles Deleuze, *Nietzsche & Philosophy* (New York: Columbia University Press, 1983). See especially "Against the Dialectic," pp. 8–10.

8. Hurston's political beliefs are notoriously contradictory. For more information on her problematic loyalties, see *Dust Tracks on a Road* and Hemenway's *Literary Biography*.

SIGRID KING

Naming and Power in Zora Neale Hurston's
Their Eyes Were Watching God

The women say, unhappy one, men have expelled you from the world of
symbols and yet they have given you names, they have called you slave,
you unhappy slave. Masters, they have exercised their rights as masters.
—Monique Wittig, *Les Guerilleres*

Naming has always been an important issue in the Afro-American tradition
because of its link to the exercise of power. From their earliest experiences
in America, Afro-Americans have been made aware that those who name
also control, and those who are named are subjugated. Slaves were forced to
abandon their African identities when they were captured, and were renamed
with their masters' identities when they arrived in America. In *Orality and
Literacy*, Walter Ong points out that for primarily oral cultures (such as the
early slave communities) naming conveyed a power over things, for without
learning a vast store of names, one was simply "powerless to understand" (33).
This sense of powerlessness could extend beyond the individual to include an
entire community of "unnamed" people. Naming is tied to racial as well as
individual identity: "To have a name is to have a means of locating, extending,
and preserving oneself in the human community, so as to be able to answer
the question 'who?' with reference to ancestry, current status, and particular
bearing, with reference to the full panoply of time" (Cooke 171). William
Halsey in his essay "Signify(cant) Correspondences" further emphasizes the

From *Critical Essays on Zora Neale Hurston*, pp. 115–127. © 1998 by G. K. Hall and Co.

importance of naming for Afro-Americans, saying that names and naming are "a heavily ritualized rite (or is that right?) of passage and theme prevalent in African culture" (259).

This concern with naming in Afro-American culture is evident in black literature from the earliest slave narratives to more contemporary works. The titles of many of these works, such as *Black Boy*, *Invisible Man*, and *Nobody Knows My Name*, indicate their authors' awareness of the correspondence between namelessness and lack of power. Ralph Ellison, in "Hidden Name and Complex Fate" stressed that "our names, being the gift of others, must be made our own" (147). Taking possession of one's own name and thus claiming sovereignty over one's self is an act of power. In his article "'I Yam What I Am': Naming and Unnaming in Afro-American Literature," Kimberly Benston defines language in a way which is particularly relevant to a discussion of naming and power:

> Language—that fundamental act of organizing the mind's encounter with an experienced world—is propelled by a rhythm of naming. It is the means by which the mind takes possession of the named, at once fixing the named as irreversibly Other and representing it in crystallized isolation from all conditions of externality. (3)

Benston's use of the phrase *take possession* shows clearly the underlying text in the naming of slaves by their masters. Fixing the named as "Other" also implies an interpretation of the named as an object, rather than a subject— something which cannot be part of the namer's self. The objectification of slaves is a well-documented method used by slave owners to distance themselves enough from their slaves to treat them as non-human. The namer has the power; the named is powerless. For the powerless, being named carries with it the threat of limitation, reduction, and destruction.

In order to break away from this sense of powerlessness, Afro-Americans have historically "unnamed" or renamed themselves. As Benston points out, renaming can be a means of self-creation and reformation of a fragmented familial past. Former slaves discarded their masters' names and created new names for themselves. Self-designation indicated social and economic freedom, the birth of a truly new self (3). Benston points out that unnaming has a particular significance for the questing hero or heroine in much of Western literature. Many questing literary characters come to the realization that names are fictions, that no particular name can satisfy the energy of the questing self. So long as the questing character seeks a name through a prescribed social role, he or she discovers only limitation, whereas, when a character is unnamed, he or she can have limitless designations which disrupt the function of social labeling and deny the applicability of words' topical function to his or her unfolding experience (7–9).

Benston's essay is an important introduction to the relationship between naming and power, but his examples only explore this issue in the literature of men. Naming has a double importance in the tradition of Afro-American women writers. One of the crucial issues for women writing within the Western tradition is the dichotomy between woman's command of language as opposed to language's command of woman (Gilbert and Gubar 236). Gilbert and Gubar point out that "the female need to achieve a command over language has, to begin with, been most practically expressed through strategies of unnaming and renaming, strategies that directly address the problem of woman's patronymically defined identity in western culture" (237). Black women have experienced a "double dispossession" (238). Lorraine Bethel discusses the two ways in which black women are oppressed: "The codification of Blackness and femaleness by whites and males is contained in the terms 'thinking like a woman' and 'acting like a nigger . . .'" (178). To counterbalance this, black women writers often focus on connection rather than separation, transforming silence into speech, and giving back power to the culturally disenfranchised (Pryse 5).

One of the most important and innovative Afro-American women writing in this tradition is Zora Neale Hurston. Hurston was a pioneer in the attempt to define the totality of Afro-American women in literature and anthropological studies, rather than their being defined by others (Bush 1035). Hurston's novel *Their Eyes Were Watching God* focuses on the character Janie, whose quest for the "horizons" of herself finally leads her to a place where she defines herself, despite a society which wants to deny her power because she is a black woman. The importance of naming and unnaming in Hurston's novel fixes it firmly within the tradition of Afro-American women writers. As Janie develops in the novel, she experiences the oppressive power of those who name her, the growing potential of being renamed, and finally the freeing experience of being unnamed.

Near the start of the novel, Janie has no name when she returns to Eatonville: "So the beginning of this was a woman" (9). The sentence places her within the larger context of the women mentioned in the book's second paragraph: "Now, women forget all those things they don't want to remember, and remember everything they don't want to forget" (9). As Janie walks into town she remains nameless; in fact, it is not until several pages into the novel that she is finally named by the townspeople on the porch. Ironically, when they say her name, they do so incorrectly; since she had married for a third time, her name is no longer "'Janie Starks'" (12). Naming is clearly a source of power for the watchers on the porch, yet their power cannot affect Janie. Because the townspeople have been under the "bossman's" eye all day, they now need to exercise some power in the only way they can—within their oral tradition. "They became lords of sounds and lesser things. They passed nations through their mouths. They sat in judgment" (10). The metaphors used to describe their words equate them with weapons. Janie recognizes the negative relationship between her neighbors' sense of power and naming. Speaking to Pheoby later, she calls them collectively "'Mouth-Almighty'" (16), and Pheoby comments that "so long as they get a name to gnaw on they don't care whose it is, and what about, 'specially if they can make it sound like evil" (17).

According to Hortense Spillers, it is important that Hurston chose to name her character Janie because it differentiates her from a literary type (such as the women found in literature by Larsen and Fauset) whose life possibilities have been circumscribed and prescribed by preconditions (253). Janie's name gives her an identifiable status, yet it does not limit her to one role or life experience.

As Janie and Pheoby talk, Janie begins to trace the experiences that have brought her back to Eatonville. Starting with her years as a little girl, Janie makes it clear that naming was used as a limiting or prescribing force by people around her and that, at a young age, she adopted their views of naming as her own. Janie relates how she was raised by her grandmother, Nanny, in the home of a wealthy white family, the Washburns. Because of her protected environment, Janie did not know she was black until she was six years old. As she explains the event in which she discovered her racial heritage, Janie mentions that the white family named her "Alphabet": "'Dey all useter call me Alphabet 'cause so many people had done named me different names'" (21). As "Alphabet," Janie seems to be no more than a character (like a letter of the alphabet) who signifies nothing for herself while facilitating the "circulation of signs" that reinforces communication among those who exercise power (Gilbert and Gubar 238).

Elizabeth Meese feels that Janie, at the beginning of her life, "receives her sense of definition from others. She is woman as object in a racist, patriarchal culture. Failing to recognize herself as the one black child in a photograph, she begins her story without name or color" (61–62). It is interesting that Hurston begins both the narrative frame and Janie's narrative with Janie as a nameless character. The effect is one more of contrast than of resonance, though, since Janie as an adult is well-defined and does not need to be named to identify herself, as she did as a girl.

Janie's first lessons about naming come from a woman whose name, Nanny, exemplifies her place within the white patriarchal structure. One of Nanny's responsibilities was to look after the four white grandchildren who lived in the Washburn house. Janie says, "'Days how come Ah never called mah Grandma nothin' but Nanny, 'cause days what everybody on de place called her'" (20). Nanny lived under the naming system of the white slave owners who used force to teach her the connection between names and power. Nanny relates an incident to Janie in which the mistress of the plantation where she was enslaved confronted her in the slave cabins. The mistress, angry over Nanny's illegitimate child, tells her, "'"Look lak you don't know who is Mistis on dis plantation, Madam. But Ah aims to show you"'" (33). The white woman invokes her own name, Mistress, and ties it to the brutal power of the whip which she will use to "show" Nanny.

Nanny teaches Janie the same lessons she learned about naming: Names are bound within the white male power structure, and the most a black woman can hope for is to endure within them. Nanny's explanation of the power hierarchy places black women on the bottom as "'de mule[s] uh de world'" (29). Nanny's naming of all black women, including Janie, as "mules" will haunt Janie for the next twenty years. She will be identified with the work animal first by Logan Killicks and then by Joe Starks when he buys a mule many years later in Eatonville. Janie will not be free of the mule name until Joe's mule finally dies.

In her adolescence, Janie tries her own hand at naming. As she is stretched on her back beneath the pear tree in Nanny's back yard one afternoon, she has an intense sensory experience of delight and responds by naming it "marriage" (24). By misinterpreting her own deepening sense of her self as a sign of possible joy with another, Janie limits the thing she names. Missy Dehn Kubitschek states that this identification of marriage with total fulfillment reflects Janie's immature consciousness, and that her interpretation of the tree is essentially static, focused on a prescribed social institution (22).

Because Janie associates marriage with her experience under the pear tree, she allows Nanny to arrange for her first legal name change to Mrs. Logan Killicks. Killicks's name is ironic, for his relationship to Janie quickly "kills" her definition of marriage: "She knew now that marriage did not make love. Janie's first dream was dead, so she became a woman" (44). With Killicks, Janie also learns more about the power associated with names. When they argue about her doing outside work in their yard, she calls him "'Mist' Killicks,'" a name which ironically reflects his attempt to be her master. He, on the other hand, calls her "'LilBit,'" a name which reveals her position of powerlessness in his mind. Logan Killicks finally goes too far when he associates Janie with a second mule for working in the fields. Janie knows from Nanny's narrative that the mule has the least powerful position, and she knows that is not what she wants.

Janie finds her way out when Joe Starks appears. The first thing Joe does after asking for a drink of water is to name himself: "Joe Starks was the name, yeah Joe Starks from in and through Georgy" (47). Hurston's naming of

Starks is ironic for several reasons. The word *stark* is often used as a synonym for barren, and Joe Starks and Janie never have any children. Hurston hints at sexual problems that develop between the pair because of their separate beds and Janie's eventual verbal "castration" of Joe in the store. Starks's name is also ironic because of his focus on capitalistic pursuits. Starks's wealth gives him a false sense of power because the townspeople resent him and the things he does to gain his wealth. Starks's name could also be seen as a comment on his desire to be a "big voice." As Janie eventually finds out, there is not much behind the big voice; it is a façade for the starkness inside Joe.

Hurston provides some hints about Joe's true nature through the limiting and subjugating names he calls Janie when they first meet. He calls her "'lil girl-chile'" and "'pretty doll-baby'" (48–49), indications of the role that he will want her to play once he becomes mayor of Eatonville. When Jody names her in the socially prescribed role of "wife," he says, "'Ah wants to make a wife outa you'" (50). He clearly places himself in the position of power by his naming Janie. When Janie tries to name him, substituting the more affectionate "Jody" for "Joe," he is pleased, but still controls the naming. He asks her to "'Call me Jody lak you do sometime,'" and after she starts a sentence with his new name, he cuts her off with "'Leave de s'posin' and everything else to me'" (50). Janie is satisfied to stop "'s'posin'" for the time being. As she rides away with Joe Starks, she realizes that "her old thoughts were going to come in handy now, but new words would have to be made and said to fit them" (54).

Although Joe seems better than Logan at first, once he and Janie are together, he quickly assumes the "master" role. Janie unconsciously associates him with the white patriarchal system from the beginning. When she first sees him coming down the road, she notes that "he was a seal-brown color but he acted like Mr. Washburn or somebody like that to Janie" (47). When Joe and Janie are on the train the day after their marriage, she proudly describes him as "kind of portly like rich white folks" (56). When they arrive in Eatonville, Joe begins to use a habitual expression "I god," which ironically sounds as though he is naming himself God. Joe's association of naming with power is apparent when he finds out that Eatonville has no mayor: "'Ain't got no Mayor! Well, who tells y'all what to do?'" (57). The name *mayor* connotes control over others to Joe. Hurston's synthesis of the name *mayor* with the phrase *I god* may have come from her own life, since her father was a minister and mayor of the all-black Eatonville when she was born (Bloom, "Chronology" 115).

Once Joe finds out there is no named authority, he sets himself up in the town's highest position of power. He gathers the men around him and asks, "'Whut is de real name of de place?'" (59). Ironically, Eatonville is named for Captain Eaton, a white landowner who has exercised power over the small, black community. Joe replaces Captain Eaton as the power broker when he uses his capital literally to "buy" Eatonville for his own. Once he has bought the town, Joe sets himself up as God; he creates new buildings and names them and brings light to Eatonville in the form of the lamp post.

Once Joe is officially named mayor, Janie becomes "Mrs. Mayor Starks." Unfortunately, the power that Joe readily adopts with his new name is not meant to be shared with Janie. Her name simply becomes a reflection of the new power of Joe. When the townspeople ask "Mrs. Mayor Starks" to make a speech, Joe cuts in: "'Thank yuh fuh yo' compliments, but mah wife don't know nothin' 'bout no speech-makin'. Ah never married her for nothin' lak dat. She's uh woman and her place is in de home'" (69). John Callahan points out that Joe views Janie as his "appendage" (102). Joe says, "'Ah told you in de very first beginnin' dat Ah aimed tuh be uh big voice. You oughta be glad, 'cause dat makes uh big woman outa you'" (74). Joe reasons that because he loves being Mr. Mayor, Janie should gratefully accept the name and identity of Mrs. Mayor (Callahan 102). Joe does not understand that Janie can make a "'big woman outa'" herself. This relationship of power with Joe "t[a]k[es] the bloom off of things" (70) for Janie, and "a feeling of coldness and fear" takes hold of her (74).

Janie's fears are well-founded, for the role of the mule returns to haunt her in her second marriage. When Joe first met Janie, he protested against Logan Killicks's treatment of her as a beast of burden: "'You behind a plow! You ain't got no mo' business wid uh plow than uh hog is got wid uh holiday!'" (49). After Joe's store and house are completed, though, he comes increasingly to treat her like an animal obliged to work his property. One day as she is working in the store, she sees some of the men tormenting Matt Bonner's mule outside. Her thoughts reveal an unconscious identification of her situation with that of the mule:

> She snatched her head away from the spectacle and began muttering to herself. "They oughta be shamed uh theyselves! Teasin dat poor brute lak they is! Done been worked tuh death; done had his disposition ruint wid mistreatment, and now they got tuh finish devilin''im tuh death. Wisht Ah had mah way wid 'em all." (89)

Janie feels as powerless as Matt's mule; she's being mistreated and "worked to death" by Joe. As she turns away from the window, "a little war of defense for helpless things" goes on inside her, and she thinks, "People ought to have some regard for helpless things" (90). When Joe overhears what Janie has muttered, he buys the mule from Matt, pretending that "freeing" the mule is his idea. In front of the others, Janie delivers an ironic speech in which she compares Joe to George Washington and Abraham Lincoln:

> "Abraham Lincoln, he had de whole United States tuh rule so he freed de Negroes. You got uh town so you freed uh mule. You have tuh have power tuh free things and dat makes you lak uh king uh something." (92)

Janie's juxtaposition of the freeing of slaves with the freeing of the mule shows the ironic contrast between the importance of what Joe has done and what Lincoln did. It also links servitude to the state of the mule; thus, Janie's servitude to Joe is clearly less important to him than the "servitude" of the mule.

After this incident, Janie begins to feel a stronger desire for freedom and a greater dissatisfaction with her relationship with Joe. One night, Joe hits her because her dinner does not please him. After that, Janie's image of Joe "tumble[s] down and [is] shattered," and her association of him with the pear tree ideals is ruined (112). He becomes "'nothin ... in [her] mouth'" (118), and she starts to use words to fight back at him. Janie finally defeats Joe with her words, during their fight in the store, and the "big voice" of Joe is silenced. When Joe hears Janie expose the truth about his sexuality, he feels humiliation and rage: "Joe Starks didn't know the words for all this, but he knew the feeling. So he struck Janie with all his might" (124). When this happens, Janie's power relationship with Joe is reversed. For Janie, "new thoughts had to be thought and new words said" (125). Joe becomes ill and retreats from contact with Janie. His last attempt to control her is to name her as his murderer. When Janie finds out he is spreading this rumor, she tearfully tells Pheoby, "'Tuh think Ah been wid Jody twenty yeahs and Ah just now got tuh bear de name uh poisonin him'" (127). Joe's final actions toward her make Janie sad, but she refuses to be controlled by him.

When she realizes that Joe is about to die, she ignores his order for her to stay out of the sick room and confronts him one last time. When she faces her oppressor, she reverses the seat of power; Janie becomes the one who names. Janie sees that "Jody, no Joe, gave her a ferocious look. A look with all the unthinkable coldness of outer space. She must talk to a man who was ten immensities away" (130). Janie recognizes the difference between the man she affectionately named "Jody" twenty years ago and the man named "Joe Starks," the "big voice." Janie tells him, "'Listen, Jody, you ain't de Jody ah run off down de road wid. You'se whut's left after he died'" (133). Starks protests against the truth, but then Death, "the square-toed one," takes him. Janie muses for a while on the transformation of her Jody into Joe Starks, "the making of a voice out of a man" (134), and then she calls in the community to mourn.

Janie takes on a new name at this stage in her life; she becomes the "widow of Joe Starks," a woman of property. It is readily apparent that the attraction associated with her new name is still linked to Joe Starks. She sees the difference between her state as a "widow" and the status of the other widows in town; men will woo her because she has Joe Starks's money and property. John Callahan feels that with his "big voice" Joe Starks, in effect, became Nanny's successor, and so it is appropriate that after his death and burial Janie discovers her true feelings about Nanny (105). Nanny's dream for Janie has been realized in the security offered by Joe's wealth, but for Janie, Nanny's definition of happiness is not enough:

> ... Nanny had taken the biggest thing God ever made, the horizon—for no matter how far a person can go the horizon is still way beyond you—and pinched it in to such a little bit of a thing that she could tie it about her granddaughters neck tight enough to choke her. She hated the old woman who had twisted her so in the name of love. (138)

What Nanny had named "love" Janie renames as "mis-love" (138). Janie recognizes that she must define her own horizons now. Maria Tai Wolff states that Janie knows that another's ideas are never adequate; the only truths she will now accept are those derived from her own experience (31).

As soon as Janie has this realization, she imagines her own creation. Missy Dehn Kubitschek says that Hurston underscores Janie's rebirth by associating her reflections on her marriages with a creation myth (24). Janie finds a "jewel" within herself and opposes that image to "tumbling mud-balls" (139). Janie has a new sense of strength and identity which comes from within herself rather than from her association with someone else.

Tea Cake's entrance into Janie's life and his relationship to naming foreshadow the kind of relationship they will share. Whereas Joe Starks's first words were to name himself ("Joe Starks was the name"), Tea Cake's first words call Janie by name, "'Good evenin', Mis' Starks,'" (144). Janie tells him that he has "'all de advantage 'cause Ah don't know yo' name'" (144), but Tea Cake does not view his name as important. "'People wouldn't know me lak dey would you,'" he tells her (145). Janie finds herself relaxed and laughing as she talks to Tea Cake because he uses his words to entertain her. John Callahan says that Tea Cake "revivifies" names (106): Instead of asking Janie for a match, he says, "'You got a lil piece uh fire over dere, lady?'" (145). When Janie finally learns his name, she finds that he has been renamed from Vergible Woods to Tea Cake. Janie likes the renaming and asks Tea Cake if it suits his nature: "'Tea Cake! So you sweet as all dat?'" (149). Tea Cake does not name to gain power; he names to explore the true nature of a thing.

As their relationship develops, Janie finds that naming no longer holds the limiting power that it manifested in her relationships with Logan and Joe. She explains to Pheoby that the age difference between her and Tea Cake does not affect them because they "'thinks de same'" (173). Janie forms a new relationship to language, but this time she has power over it rather than its having power over her: "'So in the beginnin' new thoughts had tuh be thought and new words said. After Ah got used tuh dat, we gits 'long jus' fine. He done taught me de maiden language all over'" (173). Tea Cake's use of language is positive and creative, rather than limiting and destructive.

Soon after this, Janie and Tea Cake are married. This time, her name change does not bring about a relationship of unequal power. Instead, she and Tea Cake move away from Eatonville and form a new life in the "'Glades." Their trust and love for each other develop so far that Janie can finally feel free to say to Tea Cake, "'All right then, you name somethin' and we'll do it'" (250). She knows that, because she and Tea Cake think "the same," he will never use his naming as a source of power over her.

Although their move away from Eatonville provides them with a place where they can create their own relationship to language, it also places them in a larger world, a world which is not racially segregated and which brings them face to face with the forces they name "God" and "Death." The issues of race and name are, however, inextricably combined by Mrs. Turner, Janie and Tea Cake's neighbor in the "'Glades." Mrs. Turner's use of naming falls into the Western literary tradition described by Benston. The privileging of "white" over "black" and the reduction of a human being to the word nigger are methods used by Mrs. Turner to give her a sense of power. She tells Janie:

> "Ah can't stand black niggers. Ah don't blame de white folks
> from hatin' 'em 'cause Ah can't stand 'em mahself. 'Nother thing,
> Ah hates tuh see folks lak me and you mixed up Add 'em. . . . If
> it wuzn't for so many black folks it wouldn't be no race problem.
> De white folks would take us in wid dem. De black ones is holdin'
> us back." (210)

Mrs. Turner names people by their skin color rather than their individual names. Her rejection of "black niggers" is a complete denial of her Afro-American heritage.

Mrs. Turner is not Janie's only exposure to the destructive naming based on skin color. After the hurricane, when Tea Cake and Janie are recovering in Palm Beach, Tea Cake is approached by two white men with guns. He is concerned because they do not know him, but he soon discovers that they are not interested in his real name:

"Hello, there, Jim," the tallest one called out. "We been lookin'
fuh you.

"Mah name ain't no Jim," Tea Cake said watchfully. 'Whut
you been lookin' fuh me fuh? Ah ain't done nothin.'" (251)

The men's generic misnaming demeans Tea Cake by grouping him with all
black men, denying him a separate identity. Tea Cake is forced to go with
the men to bury the dead, and again he sees the denial of identity based on
skin color. The white men have the workers separate the bodies according
to color and save the white bodies for burial in a box, whereas the black
bodies will be covered in a mass grave. Tea Cake remarks ironically on the
fact that, with the shape these bodies are in, he "'can't tell whether dey's
white or black'" (253).

When he escapes back to Janie, he tells her, "'It's bad bein' strange
niggers wid white folks. Everybody is aginst yuh'" (255). Because the white
people of Palm Beach do not know Tea Cake and Janie by name, he feels,
they are not safe there. Janie comments further on the naming according to
race: "'Dat sho is de truth. De ones de white man know is nice colored folks.
De ones he don't know is bad niggers'" (255). Janie and Tea Cake decide to
return to their former home in the "Muck" where they control the naming,
and through their naming maintain a sense of control.

It is on the "Muck" that Janie comes up against two powerful forces
which she cannot control: the force which causes the hurricane and the force
which she describes as the "being with . . . square toes" (129). Janie names
these abstractions to try to understand them. The first force, the one she and
Tea Cake encounter in the hurricane, she names "God." Janie has already
used the name *God* in association with Tea Cake. She describes him earlier
in the novel as "a glance from God," bringing him together with her vision of
the pear tree blossoming in the spring (161). During the storm, she reiterates
Tea Cake's connection to the force she names "God" when she explains her
love for him:

"We been tuhgether round two years. If you kin see de light at
daybreak, you don't keer if you die at dusk. Its so many people
never seen de light at all. Ah wuz fumblin' round and God
opened de door." (236)

For Janie, then, *God* is a name for what she has learned through her own
growth and through her relationship with Tea Cake. *God* is the unexplainable
force which is located somewhere beyond the horizon, the goal which Janie
is constantly seeking. As Janie and Tea Cake sit together in the darkened
shanty, they become aware of their connection with this unknown force:

They sat in company with the others in other shanties, their eyes straining against crude walls and their souls asking if He meant to measure their puny might against His. They seemed to be staring at the dark, but their eyes were watching God. (236).

Hurston's use of the final clause as the title of her novel emphasizes its importance. The name *God* is not defined by Hurston in the way that it is used in the Western literary tradition. Hurston's renaming of this force (or potential) places her novel outside the white male literary canon, and creates a powerful new place for black women writers to rename their experience.

Along with her re-signification of the name *God*, Hurston also re-signifies the name *Death*. When Joe Starks is dying, Janie personifies Death as the "strange being with the huge square toes" who has been standing in his high house since "before there was a where or a when or a then" (129). Janie's renaming of death as a being identified by the shape of his toes (tombstones) helps her understand the phenomenon of death and helps her control her fear of it. She describes the time after the hurricane like a reprieve after the visitation of a dreaded neighbor or relative:

And then again Him-with-the-square-toes had gone back to his house. He stood once more and again in his high flat house without sides to it and without a roof with his soulless sword standing upright in his hand. . . .. The time of dying was over. It was time to bury the dead. (249)

By naming death, Janie gains an understanding of it. It is this understanding of death that enables Janie to shoot Tea Cake when she is forced by his illness to become an instrument of death. Although she is filled with sorrow at the thought of killing him, she recognizes that she must do it for her own life to continue.

When Janie kills Tea Cake, she becomes once again unnamed. She has actively ended her role as his wife, which leaves her an option to name her own roles. She easily overcomes the last attempt by someone in the novel to name her when she is tried for Tea Cake's murder. The white lawyers designate her "'the defendant,'" rather than Janie (279). In their arguments, the lawyers offer the jury a variety of other names: "'poor broken creature,'" "'devoted wife,'" or "'wanton killer.'" Janie knows that the assignment of any of these names to her would be untrue and would limit the "horizon" she has come to know. The assignment of one of these names to Janie would result in a misunderstanding of her relationship with Tea Cake, and Janie fears such a misunderstanding more than death (279). To counter this last attempt at naming, Janie tells her own story to the jury.

Her words hold more power than the names: "She just sat there and told and when she was through she hushed. She had been through for some time before the judge and the lawyer and the rest seemed to know it" (278). The jury comes to an understanding of Janie through her own words, and so she is freed.

Janie has been to the horizon and back (284), as she tells Pheoby. Her return to Eatonville is not a defeat, as the watchers on the porch interpret it to be. Instead, Janie returns full of new knowledge and power, able to rename her surroundings because she has unnamed herself. She tells Pheoby, "'Dis house ain't so absent of things lak it used tuh be befo' Tea Cake come along. It's full uh thoughts, 'specially dat bedroom'" (284). Janie transforms her experiences with renaming: Tea Cake becomes the "son of Evening Sun" (281), and the lamp in Janie's hand is a "spark of sun-stuff washing her face in fire" (285). Janie Crawford Killicks Starks Woods has survived a succession of marital and other identities, and at the end of the novel, empowered to tell her own story, she has become a sort of goddess who pulls "in her horizon like a great fish-net" (Gilbert and Gubar 238–39).

Janie's last act is an invocation of her self: "She called in her soul to come and see" (286). Janie is the final one who names in Hurston's novel, and with her call to herself, Janie becomes a model of powerful self-identification for later Afro-American women writers.

Works Cited

Benston, Kimberly W. "'I Yam What I Am': Naming and Unnaming in Afro-American Literature." *Black American Literature Forum* 16 (1982): 3–11.

Bethel, Lorraine. "'This Infinity of Conscious Pain': Zora Neale Hurston and the Black Female Literary Tradition." *But Some of Us Are Brave.* Ed. Gloria Hull, Patricia Bell Scott, and Barbara Smith. New York: Feminist, 1982. 176–88.

Bloom, Harold. "Chronology." Bloom, *Zora* 115–18.

———, ed. *Zora Neale Hurston's Their Eyes Were Watching God.* New York: Chelsea, 1987.

Bush, Trudy. "Transforming Vision: Alice Walker and Zora Neale Hurston." *Christian Century* 105 (1988): 1035–38.

Callahan, John F. "'Mah Tongue Is in Mah Friend's Mouf': The Rhetoric of Intimacy and Immensity in *Their Eyes Were Watching God.*" Bloom, *Zora* 87–113.

Cooke, Michael G. "Naming, Being, and Black Experience." *Yale Review* 67.2 (1977): 167–86.

Ellison, Ralph. "Hidden Name and Complex Fate." *Shadow and Act.* New York: Random, 1964. 144–66.

Gilbert, Sandra, and Susan Gubar. *No Man's Land.* 2 vols. New Haven: Yale UP, 1988. Vol 1.

Halsey, William. "Signify(cant) Correspondences." *Black American Literature Forum* 22 (1988): 257–61.

Hurston, Zora Neale. *Their Eyes Were Watching God.* 1937. Urbana: U of Illinois P, 1978.

Kubitschek, Missy Dehn. "'Tuh de Horizon and Back': The Female Quest in *Their Eyes Were Watching God.*" Bloom, *Zora* 19–34.

Meese, Elizabeth. "Orality and Textuality in *Their Eyes Were Watching God*." Bloom, *Zora* 59–72.

Ong, Walter J. *Orality and Literacy: The Technologizing of the Word*. London: Methuen, 1982.

Pryse, Marjorie. "Zora Neale Hurston, Alice Walker, and the 'Ancient Power' of Black Women." Pryse and Spillers 1–24.

Pryse, Marjorie, and Hortense Spillers, ed. *Conjuring: Black Women, Fiction, and Literary Tradition*. Bloomington: Indiana UP, 1985.

Spillers, Hortense. "Cross-Currents, Discontinuities: Black Women's Fiction." Pryse and Spillers 249–61.

Wittig, Monique. *Les Guerilleres*. Trans. David Le Vay. Boston: Beacon, 1985.

Wolff, Maria Tai. "Listening and Living: Reading and Experience in *Their Eyes Were Watching God*." *Black American Literature Forum* 16 (1982): 29–33.

JOHN LOWE

Laughin' Up a World:
Their Eyes Were Watching God
and the (Wo)Man of Words

[The] ability of a person to use active and copious verbal performance
to achieve recognition within his group is observable throughout Afro-
American communities in the New World. It has given rise to an
observable social type ... called "the man-of-words." His performances
are typified by his willingness to entertain and instruct anywhere and
anytime, to make his own occasions. In all he does, he attempts to dazzle
as well as amuse. And in each performance he must incessantly call
attention to himself as an unexcelled speaker or singer.

—Roger D. Abrahams

There is no such thing as a Negro tale which lacks point. Each tale
brims over with humor. The Negro is determined to laugh even if he
has to laugh at his own expense. By the same token, he spares nobody
else. His world is dissolved in laughter. His "bossman," his woman, his
preacher, his jailer, his God, and himself, all must be baptized in the
stream of laughter.

—Zora Neale Hurston

*J*onah provided Hurston a great rehearsal for the issues she would raise in
her masterwork, *Their Eyes Were Watching God.* In some ways, Janie's story
resurrects Lucy, now free, to go forward and preach the great sermon that

From *Jump at the Sun: Zora Neale Hurston's Cosmic Comedy,* pp. 156–204. © 1997 by the
Trustees of the University of Illinois.

71

her social role in the earlier novel denies her. Janie, child-free, financially secure, leaves one husband, buries two others, and finds the "pulpit" Lucy always deserved. She does so, as her predecessor attempted without success, by using that fearful weapon John alludes to in *Jonah*: "'Jes' cause women folks ain't got no big muscled arm and fistes lak jugs, folks claims they's weak vessels, but dass uh lie. Dat piece uh red flannel she got hung 'tween her jaws is equal tuh all de fistes God ever made and man ever seen. Jes' take an ruin a man wid they tongue, and den dey kin hold it still and bruise 'im up jes' ez bad'" (158).

Janie, however, will go far beyond this description, for she learns that humor can be constructive, supportive, and joyous, and that it can create personal and communal harmony as well as discord. She also seems to understand that even language has its limits, however, and that the search to express many of life's mysteries must be ultimately surrendered to the "inaudible voice of it all" (24).

Although the text signals Janie's achievement of voice to the reader in various ways, the most telling lies in her overarching transmission of her story to her friend Pheoby, who learns and grows from her sister-in-the-spirit's tale. Pheoby then tells the story to others, taking in her turn the expression so key to the novel, "mah tongue is in mah friend's mouf" (17).

This phrase appears in Swift's *Gulliver's Travels* during the voyage to Laputa. In the kingdom of Luggnagg, Gulliver has been taught, without understanding the words themselves, the local way to say to the king, "My tongue is in the mouth of my friend"; Gulliver tells us that "by this expression was meant that I desired leave to bring my interpreter" (Swift 166). Whether Hurston took the expression from Swift or directly from folk culture seems less interesting than Swift's own recognition of the need for linguistic bridges, be they between people or cultures, and the usefulness of "translators" and "friends"; above all, however, Swift, like Hurston, understood the great role humor could play in that endeavor.[1] Accordingly, the tongue Janie wields in *Their Eyes* is honed by humor and the ability to "talk that talk," for she achieves maturity, identity, and independence through the development of a voice, one that treats narrative as a repository and display piece for her hard-won, humorously expressed wisdom.

The book's justly famous opening leans more to the cosmic than the comic, but even here the two realms merge: "Ships at a distance have every man's wish on board. For some they come in with the tide. For others they sail forever on the horizon, never out of sight, never landing until the Watcher turns his eyes away in resignation, his dreams mocked to death by Time. That is the life of men" (9). Thus we see right away the possibility of God the joker, an idea everywhere in Hurston's works; for Time/God, Watcher/Man, and the promise of life itself are all subject to interpretation as a series of cosmic jokes, a race that must be run but never won. This somewhat ominous opening should be borne in mind by those who see the book as a "simple" and joyous" tale and nothing else.[2]

Their Eyes describes a woman's quest for identity and, like most quests, ends with the heroine's returning to the community for reintegration; she thereby achieves wholeness while enriching the community with her newfound insights.[3] Most critics have quite rightly concentrated on this search for a voice; as the second paragraph tells us, for women "the dream is the truth. Then they act and do things accordingly" (9). It takes Janie more than a little while (over twenty years) to find her dream, but she does indeed "act accordingly" once she finds it, concordantly with a voice. While criticism focusing on this aspect of the book has been quite persuasive and illuminating,[4] most scholars have entirely neglected Janie's skills as a narrator who entertains, indeed, mesmerizes, and much of this comes from her considerable gifts as a humorist. Rewarding, reciprocal love with Tea Cake and self-expression come from the mastery of laughter and its language, which subsequently becomes a bond between Janie and her community.

Henry Louis Gates, Jr., in *The Signifying Monkey* provides an intriguing reading of *Their Eyes*, demonstrating Hurston's success in creating what he calls a "speakerly text," which introduces free indirect discourse into African American narration. Doing so enables her to gradually annul the distance between her own authorial voice and those of her characters, especially Janie's, a device that enables the intimacy of first person narration while avoiding its restrictions. The speakerly text privileges its own folk-centered, vernacular mode of narration over all other structural elements. Gates does especially well in linking signification with the pattern of play and gaming in the novel, although after touching on this he goes on to his real interest, Hurston's narrative play. I would add that humor constitutes a key ingredient in Hurston's craft and especially in the play aspect that so intrigues Gates. Dialect, after all, finds its shape and form from folk content, and humor functions as the heart and soul of both Hurston's idiomatic prose and presentations of play.

Hurston signals the importance of Janie's linguistic maturity by emphasizing through the frame story the verbal tools she bears within her as she marches back into Eatonville at the opening of the novel. In this respect she proves fortuitously armed, for the community has an arsenal of scorn waiting for her: "Seeing the woman as she was made them remember the envy they had stored up and swallowed with relish. They made burning statements with questions, and killing tools out of laughs" (10). This returns us with a vengeance to Freud's concept of humor as an aggressive force. Their cruel laughter has a base in presumed dichotomies, always a rich source of mirth; the blue satin dress of her departure against the overalls of her return, the

money left by Jody and the money now presumed squandered, the woman of
forty with the loose hair of "some young gal," but most of all, the woman of
forty alone, not the woman who left with "dat young lad of a boy." Janie, they
hope, will turn out to be a comic script they know well and hope to use, for
they intend their humor to "uncrown" Janie, as Bakhtin would say, to make
her "fall to their level" (11). The women hoard up this image, knowing they
might need it, for their men are also "reading" this text, seeing Janie's "firm
buttocks like she had grape fruits in her hip pockets" and her "pugnacious
breasts trying to bore holes in her shirt" (11). A comic contrast develops
between the men's richly appreciative and sly appraisal of the body and the
women's smugly snickering scorn, but both depersonalize her. After Janie
wordlessly enters her gate and slams it behind her, "Pearl Stone opened her
mouth and laughed real hard because she didn't know what else to do" (11).
Like Hester Prynne in the opening pages of *The Scarlet Letter*, Janie will be
the victim of cruel, unthinking humor until she silences it, and unlike Hester,
she must cap the discussion by having the last laugh herself.

The figuration of Janie's buttocks and breasts as grapefruits and weapons
would seem to be mere significations upon the object of desire, but in fact
meld and reverse traditional associations. The breasts would ordinarily be
associated with food, but here become weapons; the buttocks, traditionally
associated with ridicule (the "butt" of jokes) become not only food, but local
food (grapefruit), and thus a sign of bounty, as they literally "grow on trees"
all around. Thus Janie, potentially nutritive and destructive, represents both
promise and threat. She embodies, in short, mystery. A concentration on her
buttocks and breasts in this particular way suggests both possibilities of her
return. She will either become a recurring victim of men's lust, the way the
pathetic Mrs. Tyler has been with her succession of young male lovers, or she
will be revealed as someone who actually learned from her absence, thereby
presumably strengthening her preexisting separation from the community. If
she is set apart because of her class, her breasts cannot be sexually enjoyed,
and thus nutritive to the male ego, but taunting, inaccessible weapons. Janie's
overalls would seem to signal the "fall" the women wish, but they actually
make even her sexual identity puzzling, feeding into a general air of mystery
that the town feels as she reenters their world. By treating her humorously,
they attempt to reduce her mystery to a mere riddle that may be solved.

Janie wants to refamiliarize herself with the town, to use her narrative
to annul the differences separation and absence create. In her case, however,
her mystery goes further, as her name suggests, for "Jan(ie)" stems from
Hurston's birth month, January. Janus was a god unique to the Romans;
he has no Greek equivalent. Even the Romans were unable or unwilling
to assign him a specific meaning; like Janie's all-purpose tabula rasa status
among the white Washburn children, who appropriately name her Alphabet,

Janus was a god whose sign could be created by his worshippers, yet he was seen and worshipped as one of the "oldest, holiest, and most exalted of gods" (Seyffert, Nettleship, and Sandys 328). At sacrifices, he was invoked first; prayers to him preceded even those to Jupiter. Originally, he was the god of sun and light who opened up the gates of paradise when he went out in the morning and closed them when he returned at night. Eventually, he was termed the god of going out and coming in and identified with all doors and gates, which were holy to him and often dedicated to him. Indeed, his image, remembered by us as merely his doubled head, was also a gatekeeper with a staff and a key in his hands. His face was not just looking forward and backward, but also in and out, signifying his governance over time. Therefore, the beginnings and ends of things were sacred to him. His chief festival date was January 1, when he was honored with cakes of meal. Gifts of sweets were exchanged between celebrants. Furthermore, the origin of all life was associated with him and he was also known as the "sower." More generally, however, he was known as the "Custodian of the Universe."[5]

Hurston's strong identification with and interest in folklore and myth influenced her work continuously. Hurston's particular attraction to the Janus myth, however, may have affected decisions about her personal life. According to the family Bible, Hurston was born on January 15, 1891, although census records indicate she was born on January 7 of that year. All during her life, however, she often listed her birthday as January 1, 3, or 7 and the year of her birth as 1901 or 1903, even on official identification such as her driver's license. Furthermore, her religious sensibility, particularly after her hoodoo research, was always multicultural, syncretic, and personal. *Moses* demonstrates her brilliant conflation of the title figure and Damballah, the West African God. Janus, with his two heads, his mystery, his depiction as both laughing and serious, and the obvious parallel this forms with the masks of attic tragedy and comedy would make him a double of the two-headed man, the conjurer, and an associate of the trickster in folk comedy as well. An African parallel exists; Henry Louis Gates, Jr., has pointed out that the Fon people's primal god has two sides; these represent male and female divinities, Lisa and Mawu, whose eyes respectively form the sun and the moon. This mode of characterization also appears in certain depictions of Esu, reconciling the opposite poles of discourse (*Signifying* 23, 29, 34).

In *Jonah* Hurston had already played on the Janus imagery. The entire book rings with the comedy of initiation and of the greenhorn, which shows Janus's obvious link with liminality. Hurston made the central couple, Lucy and John, radically different people who nevertheless live together—an obvious manifestation of Janus's opposed identities. As we saw, Lucy's birthday, December 31, contrasts dramatically with John's, January 1. She represents the traditional, the tried, the true, home and hearth, while he stands for the new, the forbidden, the uncharted.

Hurston provides obvious references to Janus throughout *Their Eyes*. Janie repeatedly gets associated with doors, thresholds, gates, and gateposts, and we know from *Dust Tracks* that Hurston's favorite picture of herself was that of a young girl leaning over the gatepost looking down the glistening shell road and dreaming of horizon (36, 45). It was also an image she associated with freedom, for in a 1932 letter to Godmother anticipating the day in which she would be financially independent, she says only then will Godmother be able to see her again as "the Zora of the Eatonville Gatepost."[6] And Janie begins her story by deciding "her conscious life had commenced at Nanny's gate" (13). She must have seen the intersection of the actual road and the cosmic horizon and related it to her internal dreams. Tea Cake several times tells Janie she has "the keys to the kingdom," reminding us of the black woman's role as gatekeeper and Hurston's constant reference to the folktale concerning woman's domestic "keys."

Food continues the overt Janus references throughout the novel. Janie's decision to leave Jody comes as she flips a hoe-cake onto its other side. The two faces of the cake sacred to Janus of course augur a new beginning, and Janie soon darts out the door, tossing her apron on a bush. Similarly, in the frame tale, Pheoby comes bearing a gift of mulatto rice (red and white rice, or beans and rice), a "sweet-meat" appropriate for exchange among celebrants of Janus, and indeed, in the South, January 1 can begin a string of bad luck unless one eats a goodly quantity of black-eyed beans and rice seasoned with hog's jowl (significantly, meat from the mouth). Pheoby's gift, also referred to as a "covered bowl" (13), could have another, darker, classical allusion as well, the gifts for the dead mentioned in the title of Aeschylus's *The Libation Bearers*.

More often, however, Janus plays a less direct but more significant role. The narrative itself, for instance, begins Janus-like, looking forward and backward, as the townspeople and readers try to piece together Janie's past in an effort to predict her future. Appropriately, for a book that will repeatedly focus on humorous modes of address and description, Pheoby presents Janie's case to the other women with a scornful humor: "'De way you talkin' you'd think de folks in dis town didn't do nothin' in de bed 'cept praise de Lawd'" (13). She greets Janie's arrival more positively: "'Gal, you sho looks *good*. You looks like youse yo' own daughter.' They both laughed" (14). The irony and therefore the doubling of the joke lies in the fact that Janie, in a metaphorical sense, is her own daughter, in that she has created a new persona out of the woman who left town with Tea Cake. Pheoby's joke fits with her entrance to Janie's yard through the "intimate" gate, for her humor, always useful in establishing intimacy, brings the two old friends together quickly.

Janie exuberantly expresses her appreciation for the dish Pheoby has brought her: "'Gal, it's *too* good! you switches a mean fanny round in a kitchen'" (15). This inaugurates her in the reader's mind as a woman versed in folk wisdom and humor and signals that, like Pheoby, she knows how to use a joke to initiate warmth and welcome.[7] The dish itself, mulatto rice, constitutes a joke too, since Janie's white blood relates her to the food and causes jealousy within the community. Hurston extends the food/eating metaphor further; as Janie eats, she comments that "'people like dem wastes up too much time puttin' they mouf on things they don't know nothin' about. Now they got to look in to me loving Tea Cake and see whether it was done right or not! They don't know if life is a mess of corn-meal dumplings, and if love is a bed-quilt! . . . If they wants to see and know, why they don't come kiss and be kissed? Ah could then sits down and tell 'em things. Ah been a delegate to de big 'ssociation of life. Yessuh! De Grand Lodge, de big convention of livin' is just where Ah been dis year and a half y'all ain't seen me'" (17–18). People "like dem" can be heard laughing up the road, and Janie immediately comments, "'Well, Ah see Mouth-Almighty is still sittin in de same place. And Ah reckon they got *Me* up in they mouth now,'" a cogent comment on the judgmental, rigidly righteous neighbors (16).

Although Janie jokes that "'if God don't think no mo' 'bout 'em then Ah do, they's a lost ball in de high grass,'" she knows she has an interest in the social game, and the ensuing story of her wanderings told to Pheoby appears meant to bring the players together again (16). As John Callahan has demonstrated, Janie tells her story to Pheoby because, unlike the community as a whole at this point, Pheoby eagerly listens, responds, and urges on the narrative. As Hurston states, "Pheoby's hungry listening helped Janie to tell her story" (23). Callahan usefully points to the way this structural device, taken from the modes of black discourse in general and the black church in particular, supports the achievement of what he calls a rhetoric of "intimacy and immensity" throughout the entire book (115–49). Although Callahan does not discuss the role of humor, his terms here are similar to those I have identified as key to Hurston's comedic world: the systolic system she creates by recognizing the "co(s)mic," humor's paradoxically central role in the cosmos, but also its ability to cancel voids by the achievement of intimacy. As I see it, the intimacy Callahan traces so diligently comes from the humor of the characters and the culture in addition to the structural device of call and response.

The retrospective narrative of Janie's life significantly begins with a joke she remembers was played on her as a child. Raised with the white Washburn children, she doesn't identify herself as black until all the children view a group photograph. When she exclaims, "'Where is me?'" Janie's distinguishing question throughout the book, the assembled group laughs at her. "'Miss Nellie . . . said, "Dat's you, Alphabet, don't you know yo' ownself?" . . . Ah said: "Aw, aw! Ah'm colored!" Den dey all laughed real hard. But before Ah seen de picture Ah thought Ah wuz just like de rest'" (29). Here laughter, although loving, also becomes isolating. Conversely, the black children at school tease Janie about "livin' in de white folks backyard." Although Hurston doesn't see fit to stress the fact, Janie's octoroon status causes her to catch comic venom from both sides throughout the book. A "knotty head gal name Mayrella" teases her relentlessly because the white Mis' Washburn favors Janie and dresses her beautifully. Mayrella incites others, so their play forestalls Janie's, significantly pushing her out of "de ring plays," the African-derived circle games that here obviously signify membership in African American society.

The frame story of the novel repeats this situation, for once again Janie's identity becomes a burning issue for a circle of questioning faces, but this time Janie herself provides the answers, fighting the firestorm of cruel, aggressive laughter with narrative, uniting, communal laughter, refusing to let the circle of fellowship become broken. Her voice, multiplied by those of the characters who have shaped and been shaped by her life, does indeed become an alphabet at last, one that spells out the human comedy and condition.

Hurston's narratives are replete with tragedy as well, but virtually everyone in the book has some comic lines. Nanny offers no exception to this, but she can only joke after Janie has been safely married off. In some ways, we may posit Nanny's mode of narration as generated by her harsh experiences and thus representative of both slave narratives and what would become known as "protest literature" after Richard Wright exploded on the literary scene.[8] Hurston ingeniously presents us with this representative history and then has the text ask, through Janie, will a tragic history (as expressed through Nanny and Leafy) take the pleasure out of present black life (Janie's)? For a time, the answer seems to be yes.

In her desire to provide Janie "security" before her own death, Nanny marries her to Logan Killicks, a work-deadened but decent older man who appears to be almost as imprisoned by sharecropping as his ancestors were by slavery. His stunted manhood finds its symbol in the metaphor Janie chooses to describe his farm, "a lonesome place like a stump in the middle of the woods where nobody had ever been" (39). The stump imagery links Logan with Nanny's despair; she wears dead palma christi leaves (thought to be poisonous by rural communities) around her head for coolness and refers to black people as "branches without roots" (31). The amputated stump suggests Logan's notably unadorned speech as well. Hurston said "Negro expression" is always characterized by the "will to adorn," which "satisfies the soul of the creator" ("Characteristics" 39). Nanny's and Logan's barren signifiers stand in stark contrast to Janie's glorious flowering pear tree, where she dreams of love and eternity.

When Janie's expectation of falling in love with Logan is not met, she seeks advice from Nanny, who erupts in revealing, dialect-driven, comic invective. She employs "black on black" signification and a telling malapropism: "'Ah know dat grass-gut, liver-lipted nigger ain't done took and beat mah baby already! Ah'll take a stick and salivate 'im!'" (40). This does not indicate surprise at Janie's being beaten, but that she has been beaten so soon. The "liver-lipted" reference is part of black-on-black humorous tradition, and the reference to his "grass-gut" transforms him into a cow and thus feminizes him. Her previously unstated reservations about Logan find further expression when Janie adds, to be fair, that Logan draws water and chops wood for her. "'Humph! don't 'spect all dat tuh keep up. He ain't kissin' yo' mouf when he carry on over yuh lak dat. He's kissin' yo' foot and 'tain't in uh man tuh kiss foot long. Mouf kissin' is on uh equal and dat's natural but when dey got to bow down tuh love, dey soon straightens up.'" Nanny offsets her comic skepticism, however, with her respect for material things: "'If you don't want him, you sho oughta. Heah you is wid de onliest organ in town, amongst colored folks, in yo' parlor. Got a house bought and paid for and sixty acres uh land right on de big road and . . . Lawd have mussy! Dat's de very prong all us black women gits hung on. Dis love!'" (41–42). Nanny's discourse has two embedded sexual jokes in it. Janie has an "organ" in her parlor now, but neither she nor Logan can make "music" with it. And clearly the "prong" women get "hung on" is more than just "dis love."

Nanny thus correctly reads Janie's sexual frustration, seen most prominently in the young bride's cry, "'Ah hates de way his head is so long one way and so flat on de sides and dat pone uh fat back uh his neck. . . . His belly is too big too, now, and his toe-nails look lak mule foots. And 'tain't nothin' in de way of him washin' his feet every evenin' before he comes tuh bed'" (42). This signifying address affords a fine example of a technique we have seen before, where a character may speak in deadly earnest, even in pain, but Hurston sees to it that the dialogue is comically adorned for the reader's benefit. This suggests (as we saw in the conversations between Amy and Ned in *Jonah*) that comic expression of the most painful things somehow eases heavy psychic burdens, even if the characters speaking and listening do not necessarily seem amused at the utterance.

The drama of Jody's explosion onto the scene profits from his contrast with Logan, a figure notably lacking in many traits, but especially humor. After Nanny's death, Logan decides to quit hauling wood and drawing water for Janie, as Nanny predicted; he even wants his wife to start plowing. This draws a comic tirade from Janie, a play on words that nevertheless sends a message: "'Scuse mah freezolity, Mist' Killicks, but Ah don't mean to chop de first chip'" (44). Her "freezolity" combines a sense of iciness and frivolity, expressing both the way she feels and how she knows he will interpret her emotion.

Logan's response to her supposition that she might leave him represents his only comic moment, and he uses humor aggressively, to hurt. "'You won't git far and you won't be long, when dat big gut reach over and grab dat little one. . . . Ah'm sleepy. Ah don't aim to worry mah gut into a fiddle-string wid no s'posin'"" (52). When he demands that Janie come out and help him shovel manure the next day, that is the final straw. Logan doesn't know that Janie thinks he looks at this moment "like a black bear doing some clumsy dance on his hind legs" (52); the reader goes further, and sees that Logan is figuratively as well as literally "shoveling shit."

It thus comes as no surprise when Janie falls for the flashy, ambitious, and apparently fun-loving Jody Starks, even though he "did not represent sun-up and pollen and blooming trees, but he spoke for horizon. He spoke for change and chance" (50). He comes into the novel audibly first, through his cheerful whistle. Because he does not look her way, Janie labors furiously at the pump to get his attention, which (accidentally?) causes her hair, always mentioned as her sexual glory, to fall down. Jody's immediate interest and his request for a drink of water provides us with yet another biblical woman-at-the-well scenario. Moreover, "It had always been his wish and desire to be a big voice," and he intends to develop it in Eatonville, an all-black town where a man can have a chance. His abundant humor adds an ingredient; he makes Janie laugh: "'You behind a plow! You ain't got no mo' business wid uh plow than uh hog is got wid uh holiday! . . . A pretty doll-baby lak you is made to sit on de front porch and rock and fan yo'self'" (49). Over the next twenty years, however, this joke pales, fob it proves grimly prophetic. His appellation of "doll-baby" falls alarmingly close to Logan's pet name for her, "L'il Bit."

Jody's entry into Eatonville with Janie on his arm leads to his first comic deflation, following a discussion with two men "sitting on their shoulderblades" who "almost" sit upright at "the tone of his voice," which he characteristically raises in demand: "'I god, where's de Mayor.'" This question doubles as an assertion—he's God, so the mayor, if there is one, must be lesser, and if no one has been elected, he's an obvious candidate. His posture, however, as so often happens later in the book, instantly collapses, as one of the men slyly asks, "'You and yo' daughter goin' tuh join wid us in fellowship?'" (57).

Up until now we have largely drawn our opinions of Jody from Janie, and they have been positive. The two men, however, watch Janie and Jody depart, and in a comic variant of stichomythia, provide a "reading" of the pair:

> "Dat man talks like a section foreman. . . . He's might compellment."
>   "Shucks! . . . Mah britches is just as long as his. But dat wife uh hisn! Ah'm uh son of uh Combunction if Ah don't go tuh Georgy and git me one just like her."

"Whut wid?"

"Wid mah talk, man."

"It takes money tuh feed pretty women. Dey Bits uh lavish uh talk."

"Not lak mine. Dey loves to hear me talk because dey can't understand it. Mah co-talkin' is too deep. Too much co to it." (58–59)

This exchange deepens the narrative considerably, for it provides the first manifestation in the story proper of the "choral" function the townspeople play, a role virtually always adorned, as here, with humor. It provides a kind of frame within the frame as well, both verbally and visually, for we "see" as well as hear: "Already the town had found the strangers. Joe was on the porch talking to a small group of men. Janie could be seen through the bedroom window getting settled," icons for the gendered roles associated with jocular speech and silent domesticity (59).

Finally, the humorous speculations of these two townsmen "flip" our understanding of Jody, a process Janie will painfully and gradually experience over the years. This narrative process of shaking things up, over, or inside out becomes a repeated motif in the book, one frequently associated with humor, as disjunction often is. In her final exchanges with Logan, Janie feels she's "turned wrongside out just standing there and feeling" (53). Her final decision to leave comes with a laugh, when she flips over a hoe-cake. Years later, this scene finds its darker double when disenchantment with Jody causes Janie to discover she has an "inside" and an "outside."

The visual images of Janie and Jody soon find verbal comic expression. Indeed, as Houston Baker has astutely noted, Joe Starks, rather than being the "careless," pollinating "love bee" Janie desires, actually represents a worker bee, busily engaged in a parody (as Logan was on a lower level) of white entrepreneurial economics (*Blues* 58). But Jody can use humor too, especially to transact business. He does so in making his first public point—that the town needs to buy more land from "Cap'n Eaton": "'Y'all ain't got enough here to cuss a cat on without gittin' yo' mouf full of hair,'" but the men's disbelieving laughter comes from the idea of buying more land, period, rather than the expression: "The idea was funny to them and they wanted to laugh. They tried hard to hold it in, but enough incredulous laughter burst out of their eyes and leaked from the corners of their mouths." Joe notices and senses a test, and indeed, several go with him to show him the way to Maitland and "to be there when his bluff was called" (61). This male testing of Joe has a parallel with Janie, for Hicks significantly "mounts" the porch to try to make time with her. Janie doesn't respond to his loaded offer: "'Anything Ah kin do tuh help out, why you kin call on me,'" prompting his

"'Folks must be mighty close-mouthed where you come from,'" enabling her to "cap" him with "'Dat's right. But it must be different at yo' home'" (61).

In a key passage, Hicks learns Jody actually bought twenty acres and plans to set up a store and post office. "He wasn't ready to think of colored people in post offices yet. He laughed boisterously. 'Y'all let dat stray darky tell y'all any ole lie! Uh colored man sittin' up in uh post office!' He made an obscene sound" (63). Hurston clearly wants to show how white culture has made the idea of black men in authority ridiculous for so long that the victims themselves have come to believe in the ludicrous images that were popular in the press, such as the exaggerated cartoons of black ape-like congressmen lolling in legislative halls during Reconstruction. Coker, however, has learned the lie of this from Jody's actions and reproves Hicks's self-defeating laughter: "'Us colored folks is too envious of one 'nother. Dat's how come us don't git no further than us do. Us talks about de white man keepin' us down!'" (63). This scene clearly echoes Hambo's basket of crabs in *Jonah*.

In a brilliantly managed scene, Joe emerges as town leader at the purposely ceremonial dedication of his store, which he intends to be the heart of the town. Cleverly, he has Tony Taylor act as chairman, for the latter's lack of verbal ability underlines Jody's mastery. Tony's bumbling speech gets interrupted repeatedly by raucous, mocking laughter. When he wants to know why, he's told, "'Cause you jump up tuh make speeches and don't know how. . . . You can't welcome uh man and his wife 'thout you make comparison about Issac and Rebecca at de well,'" and others "titter" at "his ignorance" (68). Hurston thus signals the importance of verbal ability to the reader as well, significantly through the community's cruel but nevertheless corrective laughter. We also notice the people's expectation of biblical knowledge, which sets the "text" of even secular "sermons."[9] Jody recognizes and carefully orchestrates a ritualistic occasion, dressing Janie totemically in wine-colored silk. He seizes the opportunity to preach his secular gospel, ending with "Amen." His anointment as mayor unsurprisingly follows immediately, but in his first act he silences Janie; she's called on to make a speech, but Jody intervenes: "'Thank yuh fuh yo' compliments, but mah wife don't know nothin' 'bout no speech makin'. Ah never married her for nothin' lak dat. She's uh woman and her place is in de home'" (69). A disturbed Janie forces herself to laugh in response—apparently this is what a decorative woman does, giggle and be still—and thus dons a mask she will wear for years.

Joe's identification of Janie with his "high class" position dictates this pose. But later in the narrative Hurston demonstrates that the other women of Eatonville have considerably more verbal freedom. Joe forbids Janie to attend the mock-funeral of Bonner's mule, but other women go. They get "mock-happy," shout, and require the men to hold them up, mimicking their weekly behavior in church, a demonstration of healthy self-parody and creativity on their part and yet a welcome reminder to readers (especially those who haven't read *Mules and Men*) that Janie's exclusion from the realm of comic creativity should not be read as representative of all black women.[10] Thus there are women in the community with the creative and emotional energy to compete with the men verbally, but Janie's orders are to "class off" from such behavior.

Laughter aplenty, however, gushes out in the years that follow from the salty, humor-drenched "lyin'" sessions on the porch of his store. Hurston obviously relishes the opportunity to reprise material first used in *Mules* and "The Eatonville Anthology." Although Joe forbids Janie to take part, she obviously listens well: "When the people sat around on the porch and passed around the pictures of her thoughts for the others to look at and see, it was nice. The fact that the thought pictures were always crayon enlargements of life made it even nicer to listen to" (81). As this passage shows, Janie's silences are pregnant with creativity and explode later in her great tirade against Jody. Furthermore, since crayons are associated with a rainbow-like array of vibrant colors and crayon-colored photographs would be "adorned" representations, we may view the store-porch tales and signifying Janie describes as "crayon enlargements of life" as equivalent to the colorful "verbal hieroglyphics" Hurston discusses in "Characteristics"; obviously, much of the "coloring" involves the bright hues of humor.

Meanwhile, the introduction of Matt Bonner's skinny yellow mule into the narrative provides great fun, initially through a whole series of jokes played on Bonner. The town has a genuine animus toward Bonner because of his stinginess. Victor Raskin has demonstrated that ethnic jokes usually take one of two routes; jokers view their victims as stupid, lazy, and dirty or cunning and stingy (Raskin 194). The jokes against Bonner thus have an edge of malice in them, for he is certainly cunning and stingy, which makes him all too like slaveowners and contemporary white bosses. In a sense, then, the comic assaults directed at him are really aggressive ethnic jokes against negative "white" qualities. The humor, however, masks a veritable palimpsest of serious meditations on the mule's symbolism in black culture. Earlier, of course, Nanny bemoans the black woman's fate as the "mule of the world" (29), and here the beast becomes a general symbol for all black people under white oppression, but also for silenced black women like Janie, also "yaller," like the mule. Bonner has obviously mistreated the animal, but in a comic exchange with the townsmen, assigns the blame to the victim, just as slaveowners did: "'Ah does feed 'im. He's jus' too mean tuh git fat. He stay poor and rawbony jus' fuh spite. Skeered he'll hafta work some.' 'Yeah, you feeds 'im. Feeds 'im offa 'come up' and seasons it wid raw-hide'" (83). As with Tony Taylor earlier, Bonner suffers doubly as a butt because of his inability to answer in kind, a verbal failure exacerbated by Hurston's exploitation of his stutter, a rather cruel but effective comic technique used by many writers as a mode of caricature.

Other barbs, however, are more playful: "'De womenfolks got yo' mule. When Ah come round de lake 'bout noontime mah wife and some others had 'im flat on de ground usin' his sides fuh uh wash board.' ... Janie loved the conversation and sometimes she thought up good stories on the mule, but Joe had forbidden her to indulge. He didn't want her talking after such trashy people. 'You'se Mrs. Mayor Starks Janie'" (85). This dictum against joking adds to Janie's estrangement from the people: "She slept with authority and so she was part of it in the town mind. She couldn't get but so close to most of them in spirit" (74); much of this distance comes from her forced sobriety, for humor often offers the quickest bridge to intimacy.

Jody's orchestration of Janie's role may make her the "bell-cow," but the details of his other actions make it plain that he unconsciously has parodied the white culture he saw when working in a bank in Atlanta. His props—white man's desk, spittoons, the "gloaty white" paint on what the townspeople call his "big house," surrounded by the "quarters" of the rest of the town—are all drawn from the white world. Janie, his centerpiece, seems intended as a replica of "Big Missy." The most significant material prop may consequently be her stand-in, the dainty, floral-painted "lady-size spittin' pot" he buys for her, and it truly alienates the town. "It was like seeing your sister turn into a 'gator. A familiar strangeness. You keep seeing your sister in the 'gator and the 'gator in your sister, and you'd rather not" (76). The humor here proves revealing, for it indicates the folk feel Janie has been "conjured" into a spittoon by white materialism. This comic but deeply disturbing fetishization of Janie has another ironic dimension, for Nanny states earlier that she wants to prevent Janie being turned into a "spit-cup" for black or white men. Nanny, as she so often does, employs a sexual metaphor; ironically, Janie is turned into a spit-cup, but an asexual one, a commodity that functions as a somber and alienating sign of Joe's "white" success. His increasing verbal abuse of her fits here too, for she silently accepts and accumulates them, the way the pot does spit.[11]

Joe does, however, notice Janie's outrage over the cruel physical torture of the old mule, one of the clearest demonstrations in the book that human humor can sometimes be despicable. He buys the animal and pastures him just outside his store, as a gesture of largesse, but we realize this ironically creates more of a display of power rather than of charity.

This gesture moves Janie, however, and in her "maiden speech" acclaims Jody in front of the town as "'uh mighty big man ... something like George Washington and Lincoln. Abraham Lincoln, he had de whole United States tuh rule so he freed de Negroes. You got uh town so you freed uh mule. You have tuh have power tuh free things and dat makes you lak uh king uh something.'" Hambo in turn praises Janie as "'uh born orator.... Us never knowed dat befo'. She put ju's de right words tuh our thoughts'" (92). Readers, though, see the irony; unlike the mule, Janie remains indentured. People never "knowed befo'" because Jody, like Bonner, continues to be stingy with her liberties. Moreover, an underlying comic disjunction underlies her analysis of Jody, certainly no Washington or Lincoln. True, he "frees," but only because he's a tyrant, "uh king," who's trying to be seen as benevolent. And indeed, his generosity seems always before the public as "new lies sprung up about his free-mule doings," making the mule rambunctious, intrusive, and a metaphor for all freed slaves, virtually transforming the traditional signifying monkey into the signifying mule. The animal's liberating humor, really that of the folk, undercuts all modes of authority in the town, including Jody's. In one story, the mule sticks his head in the Pearsons' window while the family is eating; Mrs. Pearson mistakes him for Rev. Pearson and hands him a plate. Obviously, this vignette constitutes Hurston's personal contribution to the comic preacher tale tradition.

When the mule dies, the big voice and sense of humor that Joe used to win Janie are effective with the town as well; at a sham funeral that mocks "everything human in death," he leads off with a great comic eulogy on "our departed citizen, our most distinguished citizen" (95). He makes sure to attend, for as he tells Janie before the event, "'They's liable tuh need me tuh say uh few words over de carcass, dis bein' uh special case'" (94). Significantly, when he rises from the table after saying this, he wipes ham gravy off his lips. Joe, a linguistic performer, a "ham," who never misses a chance for a dramatic performance, especially favors secular occasions that call for a parody of religious ritual, such as his pseudo-religious ritual of lighting the town's first streetlamp.[12]

The mule's funeral offers a perfect example of what Bakhtin calls a carnival pageant, and indeed, in medieval Europe there was a mock "feast of the ass." The animal-inspired mock masses featured braying priests; laughter was the leading motivation, for, as Bakhtin notes, "The ass is one of the most ancient and lasting symbols of the material bodily lower stratum, which at the same time degrades and regenerates" (*Rabelais* 78). Obviously, since the mule has frequently been used as a metaphor for black people, this one's comic funeral represents the people's triumph over their fear of death. As Hurston says, "They mocked everything human in death" (95). Bakhtin would add, "The people play with terror and laugh at it; the awesome becomes a 'comic monster'" (*Rabelais* 91). Moreover, here, as in the festivals he describes, "the basis of laughter which gives form to carnival rituals frees them completely from all religious and ecclesiastic dogmatism" and they are free to parody the church's forms. Another benefit: no distinction exists between actors and spectators in carnival; everyone participates. "Carnival is not a spectacle seen by the people; they live in it, and everyone participates because its very idea embraces all the people" (5–7). Jody understands this, and another reason for his attendance may be that he fears the townspeople will seize the occasion to signify on him if he isn't there. Although his very participation in this "'mess uh commonness,'" as he describes it to Janie, has the potential to "uncrown him," staying away might be worse.

Sam Watson's speculations about "mule heaven" parody the folktales about blacks flying around Heaven, utilizing the absurd image of mule-angels: "'Miles of green corn and cool water, a pasture of pure bran with a river of molasses ... and ... No Matt Bonner.... Mule-angels would have people to ride on'" (95). This particular image recalls folktales about the trickster rabbit conniving the fox to ride him on his back. These comic reversals are ubiquitous in black folktales that offer basic images of social inversion. Once again, we have a parody of a parody, and yet more, for the signification on "mule heaven" maybe Hurston's sly dig at the white folks' love of the play *Green Pastures*, which she hated.

We have talked of silences being eloquent. Jody knows that his mule speech will be received more attentively precisely because he has marshaled his "big voice" carefully: "He bought a desk like Mr. Hill or Mr. Galloway over in Maitland with one of those wing-around chairs to it. What with him biting down on cigars and saving his breath on talk and swinging round in that chair, it weakened people" (75–76). As Klaus Benesch has observed, this "smug reticence" adds to the image we have of Jody's "acting white" and adds substantially to what Benesch sees as "an extremely effective caricature" of this "big man" (632). Although we do not know what Jody says on this occasion, we understand his words must have been funny. We acknowledge here, as Hurston seems to, that humor can deceive as well, for she tells us that Jody's comic speech makes him "more solid than building the school-house had done" (95), a tribute to the role humor plays in creating a long-desired sense of intimacy (on their part) between the people and their mayor. His coming down to their level pleases them, but their elevation of empty rhetoric above a truly useful deed points to the dangerous role humorous discourse can play in the machinations of a demagogue.

Janie also learns how powerful the omission of events, speeches, and commentary can be. Surely the fact that she as narrator omits any detail of Joe's greatest oration, the mule's eulogy, means something (especially since she excerpts Sam's), and indeed it does, for it sets up what follows. In a daring move, Hurston extends the scene into the realm of the surreal by adding a parody of the parody: after the humans leave, a group of vultures headed by their "Parson" descends on the carcass. "'What killed this man?'" cries the "minister" in his first "call." The response: "'Bare, bare fat.' 'Who'll stand his funeral?' 'We!!!!' 'Well, all right.' So he picked out the eyes in the ceremonial way and the feast went on" (97). Since Janie is telling the tale to Pheoby, this becomes *her* added touch, *her* "mule story" voiced at last, and also revenge against Jody, who forbade her to attend the ceremony, much less speak of it.

Moreover, her comic signification contains a moral lesson, one connected with the title. The leader of the buzzards has a white head. He and his kin can do as they will with a "dead" animal. In picking out the eyes, he selects the choicest bits, for as the book repeatedly emphasizes, truly "seeing" provides the key to truly living. White culture first deadens minorities through economic and social oppression and then steals their positive images of themselves. Jody, a prosperous man, nevertheless seems spiritually dead, and the white world has indeed plucked out his eyes for his values are entirely supplied by the white world. The "fat" that killed him? The deadening substitution of material value for the spiritual in his daily diet. Thus Janie not only has revenge for being silenced at the time but also the last word on Joe's entire life.[13]

Jody, who seemed to relish the mock funeral, takes on a smug, "dicty" attitude of disapproval after the fact in a revealing passage: "'Ah had tuh laugh at de people out dere in de woods dis mornin', Janie. You can't help but laugh at de capers they cuts. But all the same, Ah wish mah people would git mo' business in 'em and not spend so much time on foolishness'" (98). Janie's response suggests Hurston has in mind here those Harlem Renaissance critics who accused her of cuttin' the monkey for the white folks. "'Everybody can't be lak you, Jody. Somebody is bound tuh want tuh laugh and play'"—a reflection of Janie's inner yearnings. (99).

Jody "has to laugh," too, at the verbal duels of Sam Watson and Lige Moss, regulars on the store porch. Hurston gives them some choice lines from her Eatonville folklore collections, in tales of sheer hyperbole. Some are saucy comments to the young women passing, but "the girls and everybody else help laugh. . . . They know it's not courtship. It's acting-out courtship and everybody is in the play" (108), an indication of the importance of communal parody in this culture.[14]

Hurston significantly inserts an ugly scene in the midst of these comic ones. Janie, normally a good cook, one day prepares what Hurston comically describes as "a scrochy, soggy, tasteless mess" that some "fiend" has slipped into her pots and pans (112). Joe, enraged, slaps Janie for the first time, but chooses to tell her "about her brains" instead of her cooking. Janie's reaction sets up a paradigm for understanding the rest of the book:

> She stood there until something fell off the shelf inside her.
> Then she went inside there to see what it was. It was her image
> of Jody tumbled down and shattered. But looking at it she saw
> that it never was the flesh and blood figure of her dreams. Just

something she had grabbed up to drape her dreams over. . . . She found that she had a host of thoughts she had never expressed to him, and numerous emotions she had never let Jody know about. Things packed up and put away in parts of her heart where he could never find them. She was saving up feelings for some man she had never seen. She had an inside and an outside now and suddenly she knew how not to mix them. (112–13)

In an earlier version of this scene struck from the original manuscript, Hurston sets the episode in the second rather than seventh year of Janie's marriage, and before the slap scene, Janie lives "with her insides turned outward towards Joe, her Jody." After the slap, however, the manuscript states, "she began to fold in on herself and to take without giving. Saving up feelings for a man she had never seen" (30). In the published version the statement "No matter what Jody did, she said nothing" follows the slap. Although Janie's voice has been said to begin after the slap, with the awareness of an inside and an outside, and thus the separate parts of her identity (B. Johnson 212), one can see the opposite process described here, one of silence, one of flowers closing inward.

At least ten years pass before she finally explodes into "killing" signification. The "unpacking" of the drawers of her heart takes place later, when Tea Cake tells her she has the keys to the kingdom, which are also the keys to those compartments in her heart. The original manuscript makes this clear too: "Everywhere there were little compartments with doors. Doors shut tight and locked. She had key symbols of life but she wasn't living. And she had so meant to live. Here she was inching along with keys" (30).[15]

A fascinating parallelism emerges here in the paired images of the sacred compartments of her heart and the foul repository of the spittoon, her other sign. Jody's ugly, slighting humor builds up, like spit, while her love thoughts and, I would suggest, her comic thoughts build up and are stored away for future use, for in lines such as "Janie loved the conversation and sometimes she thought up good stories on the mule" (85) indicate an active, but silent, comic creativity.

Janie's acquisition of how to handle Jody with silence and "taking without giving" suggest Janie's mastery of "fronting." Thomas Kochman defines this as a mechanism whereby African Americans are "consciously suppressing what they truly feel or believe." As he notes, blacks often have good reason to distrust the seemingly detached mode whites use in all manner of debates. Fronting becomes a daily reality for African Americans from childhood on. As W. E. B. Du Bois claimed, all members of the race are born with a "double-consciousness" (364), which he surely would agree generates fronting ability. Fronting thus represents the prudence of silence when speech would likely involve risk (*Black* 22).

Her acknowledgment of this conscious strategy of silence could be considered one of Janie's acquisitions of "voice"; silence, after all, may paradoxically constitute a voice as well as a lack of one. After the slap she can wield this new weapon more effectively, for she had been using it in her dealings with the white community all along. She surely had an awareness of an inside and an outside long before this scene, but she had just never applied it to her marriage. This implies that henceforth she must relate to Jody as if he were white.

Hurston quickly returns to comic matters, however, enclosing this very serious scene within an envelope of mirth. One of the funniest episodes in the book reprises "Mrs. Tony," the begging woman from "The Eatonville Anthology." Once again, she begs Joe for some meat—for "'Tony don't fee-eed me!'" Hurston adds some delicious details: "The salt pork box was in the back of the store and during the walk Mrs. Tony was so eager she sometimes stepped on Joe's heels, sometimes she was a little before him. Something like a hungry cat when somebody approaches her pan with meat. Running a little, caressing a little and all the time making little urging-on cries." But when Jody cuts off a smaller piece than she wants "Mrs. Tony leaped away from the proffered cut of meat as if it were a rattlesnake. 'Ah wouldn't tetch it! Dat lil eyeful uh bacon for me an all mah chillun!' . . . Starks made as if to throw the meat back in the box. . . . Mrs. Tony swooped like lightning and seized it, and started towards the door. 'Some folks ain't got no heart in dey bosom'. . . . She stepped from the store porch and marched off in high dudgeon!" (113–15).

Some of the men laugh, but another says that if she were his wife, he'd kill her "cemetery dead," and Coker adds, "'Ah could break her if she wuz mine. Ah'd break her or kill her. Makin' uh fool outa me in front of everybody'" (116).

Although Mrs. Tony's caricature amuses, it also has much to do with several levels of the plot, and offers a fine example of the way Hurston uses humor to convey a serious meaning. Mrs. Tony, urging Jody on, calling him a "king," exposes Stark's enjoyment in playing the "great man," the man who can afford to be generous in public, as he was earlier when he paid for the mule's "retirement" fund. Furthermore, the scene brings out Jody's falsity since he charges Tony's account anyway and comically underlines his marital stinginess toward Janie—he doesn't "fee-eed" her spiritually or emotionally. Finally, the men's communal insistence on the propriety of using violence to "break a woman" and the shared assumption that Mr. Tony rather than his wife is the ultimate butt of their humor lends male communal sanction to Jody's slap and prepares the reader for Janie's final public showdown with Jody.

When Jody's youth and good health begin to wane, he tries to draw attention away from himself by publicly ridiculing Janie. "'I god amighty!

A woman stay round uh store till she get old as Methusalem and still can't cut a little thing like a plug of tobacco! Don't stand dere rollin' yo' pop eyes at me wid yo' rump hangin' nearly to yo' knees'" (121). Such a ritual insult, "talkin' under clothes," if directed at a man would possibly initiate a game of the dozens or physical violence, but Jody, assuming Janie will know her place and not engage in a forbidden joking relationship, expects her silence. Instead, she accepts his challenge and powerfully concludes a spirited exchange of charges with him: "'You big-bellies round here and put out a lot of brag, but 'taint nothin' to it but yo big voice. Humph! Talkin' 'bout me lookin' old! When you pull down yo' britches, you look lak de change uh life.' 'Great God from Zion!' Sam Watson gasped. 'Y'all really playin' de dozens tuhnight'" (123).[16]

Not only has Janie dared to play a male game, she has "capped" Joe forever with this ultimate insult, and in fact, in the eyes of the community, has effectively emasculated him. "They'd look with envy at the things and pity the man that owned them . . . and the cruel deceit of Janie! Making all that show of humbleness and scorning him all the time! *Laughing at him!* and now putting the town up to do the same" (124; my emphasis). In fact, Janie's charge immediately inspires rebellion from the male ranks of his followers as well, for Walter taunts, "'You heard her, you ain't blind,'" a joke within a joke, clearly "sounding."

What Jody expresses here is more than a sense of betrayal; he actually casts Janie in the diabolical role of trickster, that omnipresent menace of folktales, who like the Signifying Monkey or Brer Rabbit, two of his avatars, strikes down his physical superiors, as David slew Goliath. Significantly, however, Joe refuses to consciously give her this much credit, and so compares Janie to Saul's scheming daughter, a figure who publicly mocks her husband for drunkenly dancing in the streets and accidentally exposing his genitals. Michal's outcry, however, has the effect of publicizing something few actually saw and thus functions on the level of Janie's public "exposure" or "talkin' under clothes." As a result David spurns Michal's bed and she dies childless, a condition shared by Janie (2 Sam. 6:15–23).

Moreover, in this ultimate explosion of signification against Jody, we see the symbolic "overturning" or inversion of the years of epithets he hurled at her. No longer an "object," mute and decorative like the spittoon, but a speaking, acting, fighting human being, Janie utilizes the linguistic resources of her culture. This surely represents an extreme example of what Hurston refers to as the "baptism of laughter."[17]

We identify spit, as a bodily fluid, with excrement, and the contents of a spittoon would be brown from tobacco. Hurston thus creates one of those cherished confrontations of the intellect and the buttocks that Bakhtin delineates, always a comic occasion. This also fits with another line that describes Janie's eleven years of relative silence: "She received all things with the stolidness of the earth which soaks up urine and perfume with the same indifference" (119). The earth, however, sometimes has volcanic eruptions.

When Janie later tells this story to Pheoby in the framing device and, by extension, the community, she does so from a somewhat privileged position. She is free from many of the restrictions against expressing herself humorously in public in this private situation, but remember, the story is meant to be "passed on." In many cultures older women, especially after menopause, are permitted much more verbal freedom and eventually are allowed to compete with men, if they so choose (Apte 79). In this sense, Janie's story and her earlier challenge of Jody in the male territory of tall tales, verbal dueling, escalating insults, and capping doesn't outrage the community as it might have years earlier, for she is mature, experienced, and widely recognized as a relatively wealthy, independent woman and presumably not vulnerable to sexual manipulation and appropriation.

After Jody's death, part of Janie's gradually revealed exuberance comes from shedding the duty of clerking in the store, something she entrusts to Hezekiah. This seventeen-year-old imitation of Joe practices smoking cigars and rearing back in his swivel chair. His attempt to make a prosperous paunch out of his trim abdomen reminds us of Joe Banks's similar imitation of Slemmons in "The Gilded Six-Bits." Janie openly laughs at Hezekiah's comic parroting of Jody's expressions, as when he tells a customer asking for more credit, "'I god, dis ain't Gimme, Florida'" (142). Janie laughs, partly in joyous acknowledgment that a copy stands before her, not the real thing. We are hearing the laughter of liberation.[18] Some men in the community, however, don't understand this. Another reason Janie learns to laugh again stems from the hypocrisy of her abundant suitors: "Janie found out very soon that her widowhood and property was a great challenge in South Florida.... 'Uh woman by herself is uh pitiful thing,' she was told over and again" (139). But Janie has different plans. Like the woman who thinks she's become a widow in Kate Chopin's "The Story of an Hour," Janie exults because "she would have the rest of her life to do as she pleased" (137).

Her relationship with her next husband, Tea Cake, central to the book's meaning, begins on a note of humor. He walks into the store on a slow day; most of the community is off at a ball game in Winter Park. "'Good evenin', Mis' Starks,' he said with a sly grin, as if they had a good joke together. She was in favor of the story that was making him laugh before she even heard it" (144). Their entire first interchange consists of a series of little jokes, and Janie's thrilled reaction to his invitation to play checkers could just as well apply to his subsequent willingness to privilege her as his comic equal: "She found herself flowing inside. Somebody wanted her to play. Somebody thought it natural for her to play. That was even nice" (146). Tea Cake wants her to play in every sense of the word, ending the long line of nay-sayers that stretches back to Nanny.

It interests us that Janie does not learn his name, Vergible Woods, until the entire afternoon has been spent together in play; but folks call him Tea Cake. Janie laughs and makes a joke: "'Tea Cake! So you sweet as all dat?' She laughed and he gave her a little cut-eyelook to get her meaning. 'Ah may be guilty. You better try me and see. . . . B'lieve Ah done cut uh hawg, so Ah guess Ah better ketch air.' He made an elaborate act of tripping to the door stealthily. Then looked back at her with an irresistible grin on his face. Janie burst out laughing in spite of herself. 'You crazy thing!'" (149). But Tea Cake remains. "They joked and went on till the people began to come in. Then he took a seat and made talk and laughter with the rest until closing time" (150).

It seems important to note here that Tea Cake courts Janie both in private and in public. His second visit again involves a game of checkers, but this time they play in front of an audience. "Everybody was surprised at Janie playing checkers but they liked it. Three or four stood behind her and coached her moves and generally made merry with her in a restrained way" (154).

Janie and the rest of the community come to love Tea Cake for his spontaneity, creativity, and positive attitude toward life. He and Janie are always making "a lot of laughter out of nothing" (154), an obvious parallel to the ubiquitous expression in African America, "making a way out of no way." In a moving scene, Hurston pinpoints his tenderness and his teaching quality. Tea Cake combs Janie's hair for her and says, "'Ah betcha you don't never go tuh de lookin' glass and enjoy yo' eyes yo' self. You'se got de world in uh jug and make out you don't know it. But Ah'm glad tuh be de one tuh tell yuh.'"[19] When Janie objects that he must tell this to all the girls, he replies, "'Ah'm de Apostle Paul tuh de Gentiles. Ah tells 'em and then agin Ah shows 'em'" (157–58). Tea Cake's gospel of laughter here becomes the New Testament revision of the black aesthetic, replacing the tragic "Old Testament" litany of Nanny and others like her who still labor under the stubborn heritage of slavery. Nanny, we remember, believes that "'folks is meant to cry 'bout somethin' or other'" (43), and Tea Cake's creed reverses this. His forward-looking stance thus provides the encouragement Janus/ Janie has always needed for that part of her personality. His doctrine rings out as profoundly American and hopeful, even though he too has been and will be the victim of white racism; indeed, one could argue he dies from it, in his crazed belief that Janie wants to leave him for a lighter-skinned man.

Like Hurston, Tea Cake refuses to let racial oppression blind him to the glories of the world or to define the possibilities of the self. As Emerson and Whitman urged, he believes in living in the now, but his self-love and sheer joy in living come out of a black heritage, and his admonition to Janie echoes a traditional blues lyric: "Baby, Baby, what is the matter with you? / You've got the world in a jug / Ain't a thing that you can't do." His identification with present tense throws him into contrast with Nanny, who operates entirely out of an obsession with the past, and Killicks and Starks, who mimic white culture by constantly building up financial capital for the future at the expense of emotional and spiritual health.

This sense of the present moment and its possibilities functions importantly in the world of play. Huizinga has proven play to be a basic human need, which strongly relates to laughter; play, he flatly states, is an instinctual impulse that must be satisfied. Janie, who said as much to Jody, wants no exception to this rule and relishes her third husband's sense of play and laughter. She learns as much as she can from him on this subject during their brief two years together. The verb "to laugh" crops up again and again in the chapters devoted to their marriage.

Play frequently occurs within social parameters (as with the communal game of checkers, card games, the evenings with the people in the Everglades), but it often takes place on the periphery of convention or even outside it. At one point Janie and Tea Cake go fishing in the middle of the night: "It was so crazy digging worms by lamp light and setting out for Lake Sabelia after midnight that she felt like a child breaking rules. That's what made Janie like it" (155). Tea Cake seems to be a master of breaking rules and conventions, even inverting night into day, but in an "even nice" way. One feels Janie also delights in breaking the "rule" of age in taking up with a man at least twelve years her junior, one of Hurston's lifelong habits. Janie herself refuses to abide by the rules during their first checker game, objecting when Tea Cake legitimately takes her hard-won king (a figuration on "uncrowning"), and eventually she upsets the board. But this may be a momentary urge from a woman still laboring under the legacy of twenty-odd years of silencing by a real-life "king."

The games Janie loves most are those that involve Tea Cake's imagination and creativity. Early in their relationship he pretends to play on an imaginary guitar. Later, arriving in a battered car, he jumps out and makes the gesture of tying it to a post. But he brings the car because he wants to teach Janie how to drive, how to have and relish the power of mobility. As she tells Pheoby, "'Ah always did want tuh git round uh whole heap, but Jody wouldn't 'low me tuh'" (169). He also instructs her on how to plant seeds in her garden and chops down an ugly tree by the window she has always hated that Jody probably liked. All this obviously translates into metaphors for freedom, growth, the cutting down of rigid patriarchal traditions, and the general power of self-assertion. Tea Cake tells her to "'have de nerve tuh say whut you mean'" and shows her how to have the nerve to be creative, prune away dead limbs on her spiritual tree, and make joyful plans for a mobile future, one not tied down to her possessions.

Paradoxically, the town sees all this as "signs of possession" and thinks that "Poor Joe Starks" must be turning over in his grave. They fail to realize that they're still looking at Janie as an extension of Joe, as his spoils, waiting to see if an appropriate claimant will come along, someone like the oft-mentioned undertaker from Sanford. They fail to "see" because their eyes are watching the wrong god: Mammon. The humorless nature of their communal discourse here testifies to a blind adherence to a joyless Puritan ethic. Even the usually astute Sam fails this test; he rightly and wryly detects Janie's growing love for Tea Cake: "'New dresses and her hair combed a different way nearly every day. You got to have something to comb hair over. When you see uh woman doin' so much rakin' in her head, she's combin' at some man or 'nother. . . Tea Cake can't do nothin' but help her spend whut she got. Ah reckon dat's whut he's after. Throwin' away whut Joe Starks worked hard tuh git tuhgether'" (167). Pheoby agrees and favors the undertaker because "'de man's wife died and he got uh lovely place tuh take her to—already furnished. Better'n her house Joe left her'" (167). Both speakers discount the idea of choice and creativity, preferring a life "already furnished," one defined by possessions. Neither see the creativity Tea Cake awakens in Janie, which the varying attire and hair styles suggest. Their sense of Janie "throwin' away Joe" shows that even her best friend and the relatively sensitive Sam still define her through a dead man. The fact that they favor a new suitor known only by his extremely unplayful trade fits in well.

Eventually Pheoby "picks" her way to Janie's, comically "like a hen to a neighbor's garden," talking with people on the way, "going straight by walking crooked" (169) so as to appear to be dropping advice on Janie by accident, a charming bit of folk custom that relates to the indirection of humor.[20] The case she makes to Janie on behalf of the community's outrage over Tea Cake's dragging her down from her class begins censoriously, with "everybody's talkin'," but humor punctuates their conversation, especially when it drifts to intimate matters. Letting Pheoby know she's been sleeping with Tea Cake ("'We'se just as good as married already'") Janie adds, "'Ah ain't puttin' it in de street. Ah'm tellin' you,'" to which Pheoby replies, "'Ah jus lak uh chicken,'" fitting with her "picking" her way to Janie's "like a hen"; "'Chicken drink water, but he don't pee-pee,'" and Janie concludes, "'We ain't shame faced. We jus' ain't ready tuh make no big kerflommuck as yet'" (173).

In still another comic inversion, Janie has flipped the town's expectations; instead of mourning atop the pedestal Jody created for her, she has lost her "class" by gambling on Tea Cake and love. They want her back as an icon of respectability, but that isn't what they say. Pheoby, their emissary, warns Janie, "'You'se taken' uh awful chance,'" to which Janie, twice-married already, replies, "'No mo' than Ah took befo' and no mo' than anybody else takes when dey gits married. . . . Dis ain't no business proposition, and no race after property and titles. Dis is uh love game'" (171), thereby setting the play element of their relationship out for the community.

This statement needs to be taken more seriously than it has been. Tea Cake is a teacher, as the first part of his name and all of his relations to Janie suggest, and teachers give tests. Janie's faith, and ours as readers, gets sorely tested in Jacksonville, for during their honeymoon there, Tea Cake vanishes with her hidden two hundred dollars. Many students and some critics have been upset by this, and the scene has increasingly been brought into service for the growing attack on Tea Cake in Hurston criticism. Michael Awkward has said that Tea Cake "steals" from Janie (17). Writing Tea Cake off as a bum, a thief, and a "wife-beater," which some presentist readers seem to be doing, makes seeing his real role in the novel impossible. We need to remember that he has insisted, prior to this, that he finance their expeditions, that he buy groceries for their church picnic even though Janie owns a store, and that he is often absent because he is working for this courtship money. Hurston never suggests a scheme to appropriate Janie's real hoard, which still awaits her in the bank when she returns to town after burying Tea Cake. He terrifies Janie when he comes back from his gaming wounded, but as she tends to him he gives her the $322 he has won, Hurston's metaphorical comment on the exponential rewards of trusting the "love game" and her folk illustration of the biblical injunction to cast your bread upon the waters.

Tea Cake tells her to put the original $200 back in the bank, but that is beside the point. He simply does not value money the way most of us do. He sees more in life than the building up of capital. Although we may prefer to believe we are offended here by a violation of Janie's trust, we must face the fact that we may be led to that position because Tea Cake has actually offended our capitalist values. If so, we have failed a test Hurston has provided for readers by identifying Janie through her possessions. As Janie said, "'Dis ain't no business proposition. . . . Dis is uh love game,'" and love games put your faith and trust on the line. Hurston as narrator thus uses a practical joke to teach. Janie learns here to trust herself as well as others, but also to take chances. She bears up under the strain and is still there, waiting, when Tea Cake comes home.

His humorous assurance nevertheless glistens with sincerity: "'You doubted me 'bout de money. . . . De girl baby ain't born and her mama is dead, dat can git me tuh spend our *money* on her. Ah told yo' before dat you got de keys tuh de kingdom'" (181; my emphasis). His roistering narrative of the party he has given for his friends constitutes a comic masterpiece, replete with revelry, feasting, fighting, and jokes. When Janie asks him why he didn't invite her (our question as well), we find she isn't the only one who has had doubts. If she has questioned whether he could really love an older woman, he has doubted she could accept his friends: "'Dem wuzn't no high muckty mucks. . . . Ah wuz skeered you might git all mad and quit me fo takin' you 'mongst 'em. . . . Tain't mah notion tuh drag you down wid me,'" a telling illustration of the way white class patterns can disrupt even the most loving relationships. Janie's instructive response proves she can teach with jokes too and will be heeded during the rest of the book: "'If you ever go off from me and have a good time lak dat and then come back heah tellin' me how nice Ah is, Ah specks tuh kill yuh dead. You heah me?'" (186). Ironically, this has much to do with why she has to kill him, for in his rabid state he thinks she's too nice to really love a black black man.

Tea Cake subsequently isn't afraid to suggest their removal to the Everglades "muck" community. The learning experience among the common folk there seems just as important to Janie as Tea Cake's love in making her complete and whole, which is instigated by him as teacher. In this folk "classroom," folks "'don't do nothin' . . . but make money and fun and foolishness,'" and Janie grows there, like everything else: "'Ground so rich that everything went wild. . . . People wild too'" (193).

Janie's "education" proceeds a bit before the bean harvest begins, when Tea Cake insists, via a joke, on teaching her how to fire a weapon and hunt: "'Even if you didn't never find no game, it's always some trashy rascal dat needs uh good killin''" (195). In a terrible irony, rabies later turns him into a murderous "rascal," forcing Janie to shoot him when he attacks her. The joke doubles yet again, and terribly, by the idea that in killing him she kills the "love game" he represents.

Here on the muck, Tea Cake, with his guitar, his songs, his infectious laughter, plays Orpheus for the folk. This extends a pattern established earlier, for back in Eatonville we saw him simultaneously joking and playing a mean blues piano, twining together the folk traditions of humor and music.

Janie's growing ability to joke and laugh soon makes her a favorite with the people too, especially after she starts working alongside Tea Cake in the fields. We note here that she does so because he misses her so much during the day, quite opposite to Logan Killicks's desire to have her plowing. When she and Tea Cake carry on behind the boss's back, "It got the whole field to playing off and on," recalling the role humor played in relieving the drudgery of field work during slave times (199). Soon, Janie joins Tea Cake in storytelling for the appreciative audience that gathers each night at their shack: "The house was full of people every night. . . . Some were there to hear Tea Cake pick the box; some came to talk and tell stories, but most of them came to get into whatever game was going on or might go on. . . . Outside of the two jooks, everything on that job went on around those two" (200–201). Janie learns to "woof," to "boogerboo," to play all the games, and through it all, "no matter how rough it was, people seldom got mad, because everything was done for a laugh" (200). In this school and laboratory, Janie "marks" (imitates) the other storytellers and becomes an accomplished comedian/ "liar" herself.[21]

In particular, life on the muck acquaints us with all sorts of card games and their comic lingo, as expertly played and "sayed" by folk comedians whose very names, such as Sop-de-Bottom, Bootyny, Stew Beef, and Motor Boat, cause a smile. Their lingo, emerging directly from black folk culture, is equally tinged with violent menace and outrageous, creative play, as when they raise stakes: "'Ah'm gointuh shoot in de hearse, don't keer how sad de funeral be'"; "'You gointuh git caught in uh bullet storm if you don't watch out.'" Black-on-black-jokes play a role as well: "'Move from over me, Gabe! You too black. You draw heat'" (201).

The happy times don't last, however, and after the hurricane, when they are safe in Palm Beach, Tea Cake asks Janie if she had expected all this when she took up with him. Her answer says much: "'Once upon uh time, Ah never 'spected nothin' Tea Cake but bein' dead from the standin' still and tryin' tuh laugh. But you come 'long and made somethin' outa me'" (247). Life and laughter are the equation for fulfillment.

More so here than in any other place in Hurston's oeuvre, Janie and Tea Cake in their scenes on the muck, surrounded by their people and enjoying and creating black folk culture, best express what Alice Walker has called "racial health; a sense of black people as complete, complex *undiminished* human beings" (*In Search* 85).

An extremely important passage regarding Hurston's feeling about black laughter comes in this section, when Janie meets the near-white Mrs. Turner. This color-struck troublemaker hates her own race and tells jokes a klansman could love, as when she repeats her son's crack that some people are so black they draw lightning. As always, context is all. Black Gabe's friend earlier made the same kind of joke, but affectionately, and within the group. Here, Mrs. Turner, making the same remark, but to an equally light-skinned (and presumably "dicty") audience really intends to project contempt. Her ordinary conversation is no better. Damning color again, she asks, "'Who want any lil ole black baby layin' up in de baby buggy lookin' lak uh fly in buttermilk? Who wants to be mixed up wid uh rusty black man, and uh black woman goin' down de street in all dem loud colors, and whoopin' and hollerin' and laughin' over nothin'?'" (210–11).[22] Mrs. Turner, who has her own brother in mind, urges Janie to marry a whiter man than Tea Cake. When Janie asks her, point-blank, "'How come you so aginst black?'" she immediately replies, sounding much like Jody: "'Dey makes me tired. Always laughin'! Dey laughs too much and dey laughs too loud. Always singin' of nigger songs! Always cuttin' de monkey for white folks. If it wuzn't for so many black folks it wouldn't be no race problem. De white folks would take us in wid dem. De black ones is holdin' us back'" (210). She brags about her almost white brother, who tore Booker T. Washington to pieces in a speech. "'All he ever done was cut de monkey for white folks. So dey pomped him up. But you know whut de ole folks say, 'de higher de monkey climbs de mo' he show his behind' so dat's de way it wuz wid Booker T'" (212). Mrs. Turner thus becomes Hurston's surrogate for all those critics who accused her of cuttin' the monkey for white folks, and it reminds us that though Janie functions as Hurston's alter ego in the novel, so does Tea Cake, for here he becomes the polar and positive opposite of Mrs. Turner, as an agent of the laughter she hates, and he plots her banishment after overhearing her diatribe against blacks in general and him in particular from the adjoining room. Mrs. Turner's speech provides reader-author irony at her expense as well, for she rails against black culture by using its resources in her pungent citation of the "ole folks."

Hurston does not stop with Mrs. Turner, either; she exposes the similarly color-struck and sexist views among black men, whose repository of "black black women" jokes she despised. When Tea Cake slaps Janie for supposedly flirting with Mrs. Turner's brother, Sop-de-Bottom compliments him for having a light-colored woman:

> "Uh person can see every place you hit her. Ah bet she never raised her hand tuh hit yuh back, neither. Take some uh dese of rusty black women and dey would fight yuh all night long and next day nobody couldn't tell you ever hit 'em. Dat's de reason Ah done quit beatin' mah woman. You can't make no mark on 'em at all....
>
> Mah woman would spread her lungs all over Palm Beach County, let alone knock out mah jaw teeth.... She got ninety-nine rows uh jaw teeth and git her good and mad, she'll wade through solid rock up to her hip pockets." (218–19)

Yet after this Sop-de-Bottom agrees that Mrs. Turner is "color-struck" and helps to run her off the muck. Hurston's clever juxtaposition of these sentiments could hardly be more ironic or more damning.

Still, here as elsewhere, Hurston refuses to stop the action for a righteous lecture on the errors of Sop's ways. She obviously appreciated humor, even when it expressed views she didn't share, a quality that any anthropologist would have to cultivate. As Mary Douglas has demonstrated, a joke is primarily a play upon form; but to appreciate it properly, you must have the context of the joke. If the play on form is missing, what you have, in most cases, is ordinary insult ("Social" 365). Black-on-black jokes, while unfortunate, are almost always examples of the former. Should anyone doubt Hurston's abhorrence of these attitudes toward her darker sisters, they should consult *Dust Tracks* (225–26), where she expresses devastating contempt for the tradition. She also discussed this syndrome's other aspect, its grudging admiration for the strength of very dark women, in "Characteristics" (45).

Although Hurston would probably be surprised, the scene where Tea Cake slaps Janie inevitably causes a great deal of discussion in the classroom. Some students regard it as a sign that Tea Cake is an abusive husband. While this violence against Janie should disturb us, and it is gratifying to see students object to such behavior, we need to avoid reading the scene out of context, with contemporary values. We must recognize that Hurston's narrative takes place in a relatively violent southern society of the 1930s, where many people, men, women, and children of both races, frequently experienced physical abuse from their loved ones, beginning with whippings as children, and *offered* the same in return. A biblically inspired people takes seriously the various biblical dictums sanctioning punishment, and in fact, frequently equates corrective violence with love.

Moreover, Janie and Zora do the same. We should remember that Janie reacts to Nunkie's attempts to seduce Tea Cake by physically striking him, and that in her role as author she specifically tells us Tea Cake's slapping of her was just that: "No brutal beating at all . . . two or three face slaps" (218). I would also point to Hurston's own physical fights with her stepmother, which she apparently remembered with relish and the portions of *Dust Tracks* that detail her violence against men in her life.

Most importantly, Tea Cake only does this to signal to Mrs. Turner and the community that he refuses to give up his woman to a light-skinned man without a struggle. Critics who complain about his sense of male possessiveness miss Hurston's frequent demonstration that love, if genuine, is possessive by definition, no matter which sex is involved. Here he seems to be in danger of losing what matters most to him because of the color of his skin: "'Ah didn't whup Janie 'cause *she* done nothin'. Ah beat her tuh show dem Turners who is boss. Ah set in de kitchen one day and hear dat woman tell mah wife Ah'm too black fuh her. She don't see how Janie can stand me'" (220). Critics who cite this section as one of Janie's "silences" because she doesn't tell us how she felt usually ignore this comment and also the possibility that Janie in retrospect sees nothing wrong with what Tea Cake did, after realizing, as the text clearly indicates she did, what motivated such behavior.

This is not to condone Tea Cake's actions; violence against women (and men, for that matter) is always deplorable. But readings that insist on applying contemporary standards to texts written in and about a different culture almost sixty years in the past are simply ahistorical presentist interpretations of both literature and culture. It is worth noting that until this line of argument was raised, many critics quite rightly praised this novel as one of the great love stories in our literature; unfortunately, that reading seems to be receding as an important but not definitive detail of the narrative has been interpreted out of context.

In any case, Tea Cake soon finds a better way to deal with the troublemaker Mrs. Turner, significantly involving humor. The wild melee he and the other men stage in Turner's restaurant provides an excuse to wreck the place; while the destruction goes on, they pay elaborate compliments to their distressed hostess. Tea Cake yells out, "If you don't want tuh respect nice people lak Mrs. Turner, God knows you gointuh respect me!" (224). The scene releases the chaotic energy of the Marx brothers films, but we see the serious purpose; clearly the real message is for Mrs. Turner and gets summed up in the last two words of Tea Cake's dictum. Mrs. Turner scurries away to Miami, "'where folks is civilized'" (226) and, presumably, less humorously inclined.

When the folk on the muck fear the coming hurricane, they turn to the cheering resources of their culture; they first sit in Janie and Tea Cake's house and tell stories about Big John de Conquer and his feats and tricks.[23] They also listen to Tea Cake's guitar and then sing a song that comes from the dozens:

> Yo' mama don't wear no *Draws*
> Ah seen her when she took 'em *Off*
> She soaked 'em in alco*Hol*
> She sold 'em tuh de Santa *Claus*
> He told her 'twas aginst de *Law*
> To wear dem dirty *Draws*.   (232–33)

The combination of the hilarious John de Conquer stories and snippets of bawdy dozens lines helps the figures gird up their loins against cosmic forces. John, a traditional and daring figure, frequently gambles with both God and the Devil; similarly, the defiance of the dozens humor seems directed against a malevolently approaching storm. A beneficent Culture attempts to ward off a threatening Nature. Eventually they have to leave the shack and face the storm in a struggle to reach higher ground, an effort that ironically fulfills yet another of Nanny's dreams/prophecies of taking "a stand on high ground" (32).[24]

Tea Cake and Janie are amused when they find that Motor Boat, whom they left dozing in a house at the height of the storm, slept through it all and survived, even though the raging waters moved the house. They joke about it: "'Heah we nelly kill our fool selves runnin' way from danger and him lay up dere and sleep and float on off!'" (256–57). Weeks later, their amusement pales, for if they had stayed with Motor Boat, Tea Cake would never have been bitten by what they now know was a rabid dog.[25]

In the aftermath of the hurricane, whites impress Tea Cake for a burial squad and several other examples of racial oppression are raised. The situation becomes less oppressive through a terrible kind of levity, also a quality of the hurricane scenes. The grim sequence of events that lead to Tea Cake's infection with rabies is chilling, but looked at with a surrealist's detachment, getting bitten by a mad dog that is riding the back of a cow in a hurricane is wildly funny, a scene only a cosmic joker could write. And in fact, when Janie ponders, "Did He mean to do this thing to Tea Cake and her? . . . Maybe it was some big tease and when He saw it had gone far enough He'd give her a sign" (264), it seems the biggest joker in the book, on whom all eyes are turned, has to be God.[26]

Humanity has its own absurdities, however; making the impressed men determine whether the bodies are white or black so as to bury them in segregated graves creates gallows humor with a vengeance. Only the whites get cheap pine coffins, causing Tea Cake to say, "'They's mighty particular how dese dead folks goes tuh judgement. Look lak dey think God don't know nothin''bout de Jim Crow law'" (254).

Interracial humor permeates the penultimate scenes. Tea Cake bitterly remarks, "'Every white man think he know all de GOOD darkies already. . . . All dem he don't know oughta be tried and sentenced tuh six months behind de United States privy house at hard smellin'. . . . Old Uncle Sam always do have de biggest and de best uh everything. So de white man figger dat anything less than de Uncle Sam's consolidated water closet would be too easy'" (255). The bitter pun implicit in United States privy/United States privileges appropriately bristles. When Tea Cake comments further on the dangers of being "'strange niggers wid white folks'" Janie adds, "'Dat sho is de truth. De ones de white man know is nice colored folks. De ones he don't know is bad niggers,'" which causes Tea Cake to laugh too, helping both of them to bear an unbearable situation (255). Those who think Hurston glibly accepts American racism should reread these scenes, alongside her bitterly comic diatribe, "Crazy for this Democracy," where the "Arsenal of Democracy" receives refiguration/conjuration as the "Ass-and-all of Democracy" ("Crazy" 45).

More of this ugly humor occurs when Tea Cake lies dying of rabies, and Janie summons a white doctor to make a diagnosis. We remember Mrs. Turner's earlier statement: "'Don't bring me no nigger doctor tuh hang over mah sick-bed'" (211), and here we see her preference tested. This physician initially greets his patient with some racist jocularity: "''Tain't a thing wrong that a quart of coon-dick wouldn't cure. You haven't been gettin' yo' right likker lately, eh?' He slapped Tea Cake lustily across his back and Tea Cake tried to smile as he was expected to do but it was hard" (261). To be fair, however, we should remember that this same man testifies on Janie's behalf during her murder trial.

The grim absurdity of the courtroom scene seems oddly "funny too. Twelve strange [white] men who didn't know a thing about people like Tea Cake and her were going to sit on the thing" (274), a not-so-subtle comment on the gross injustices of southern juror selection in the 1930s.

As narrator of the book, Janie chooses to be silent about her exact testimony in court, which has troubled several critics, notably Michael Awkward and Mary Helen Washington. Perhaps one of the reasons Janie omits her speech to the jury may be found in a short story Hurston published in the *Saturday Evening Post* in 1950, "The Conscience of the Court." The tale describes the trial of a domestic servant, Laura Lee, for beating up a black loan shark, Beasley. The villain takes advantage of the absence of Mrs. Celestine Clairborne, Laura Lee's lifelong employer, to demand her valuable antiques as payment for a note he holds. The impoverished white woman took out the loan to bury Laura Lee's husband "like a big mogul of a king" (21). Beasley attacks Laura Lee after she defends the property; she subsequently beats him to a pulp, prompting the lawsuit. Miss Clairborne, away on vacation, can't be reached. After hearing damning but false evidence against her, Laura Lee cleverly makes capital out of her status: "I am a unlearnt woman and common-clad. . . . I ain't never rubbed the hair of my head against no college walls'" (20); she tells the moving but maudlin story of her childhood with Miss Celestine, the death of the latter's young husband, and the mutual devotion of maid and mistress. As Laura Lee speaks, Hurston notes the shift in sentiment in the crowded white courtroom. Hurston establishes interracial communitas through a narrative that creates intimacy and understanding, partly by humor, but mostly through pathos. A touch of the "noble savage" crops up: "With the proud, erect way she held herself, she might be some savage queen. The shabby house-dress she had on detracted nothing from this impression" (17). The judge dramatically produces the loan note and reveals the months-away due date, adding that the plaintiff intercepted Laura Lee's letter to Mrs. Clairborne. Laura Lee, acquitted, goes home realizing she wrongfully thought her mistress had deserted her.

I present this story at length to show what we miss through Janie's silence. Like Laura Lee, if she *truly* has the personal and verbal resources we think she has at this point in the book, Janie would have to employ them in a demeaning way before a white jury, something John Pearson refuses to do in the courtroom scene in *Jonah*. This late short story reprises Janie's courtroom, treats a recent widow whose husband received a regal burial, dresses her shabbily, reduces the supportive white women to one, recreates the "hushed" response to a pathetic story, and demonstrates the special need for eloquence and silence the black community has when placed in the jaws of an unjust legal system. Perhaps because she had recently been a victim of the legal system herself, the Hurston of the 1950s wanted to ironically remind white America of this. She has her "good" judge intone that "'the protection of women and children . . . was inherent, implicit in Anglo-Saxon civilization, and here in these United States it had become a sacred trust.'" We note that he doesn't allocate this trust only for Anglo-Saxons.[27]

Most importantly, however, the defendant's real enemies (indeed, in Laura Lee's case, the plaintiff) are from the black community. In *Their Eyes*, the courtroom "tongue storm" of black voices, tongues "cocked and loaded," provides a threatening communal symbolic replication of the natural disaster of the hurricane and the individual threat, which gets met in kind, of Tea Cake's gun. This "killing" humor seems to be less directed at Janie per se than at the black spectators' bitter perception of the injustices of white law and their knowledge that their "tongues cocked and loaded" are "the only real weapon left to weak folk. The only killing tool they are allowed to use in the presence of white folks" (275). Thus the bitter acknowledgment "'you know whut dey say "uh white man and uh nigger woman is de freest thing on earth." Dey do as dey please'" (280). So Janie must talk, not walk, her way through a gauntlet of hostile auditors. The potentially killing tongues also look forward in the chronological narrative to the gauntlet of killing laughs and tongues Janie will face in Eatonville.

Janie buries what she actually said in the courtroom in two brief paragraphs of vague prose. This suggests she wants to hide something, namely that her performance in court was in some ways a pose, a careful manipulation of her now-developed vocal power to literally save her life by creating the image the jury wants of a "broken woman." Her equally manipulative but honestly felt and expressed version of the same story in the black community signals not only the truth of what happened, minus her exact testimony, but offers eloquent proof of her confident identity as a black woman, signaled by her mastery of humorous, inventive, and captivating narrative; something that would not have worked in the white courtroom.[28] Thus her manipulation of narrative, in white society, in the larger version told to Pheoby, the community, and us, demonstrates the accuracy of Glynis Carr's perception that Hurston "offers storytelling as the sine qua non of black life. In fact, storytelling for Hurston is synonymous with the mastery of life" (190).

Simultaneously, Janie's performance in court offers another example of that skill she acquired during her marriage with Jody, fronting. This extends to narration of the book as well; Janie has already learned how to edit things from her story, for earlier she had decided to omit Jody's oration over the mule. During her narration of the trial, Janie's silence keeps us from reading her story the way the white jury apparently does, for they are charged to choose whether she is a "wanton killer" or "a poor broken creature" (279), melodramatic or pathetic terms. Surely one of the most vital uses of the syndrome of fronting for African Americans has been in life-or-death situations like these, legal minefields, where the letter of the law can mean anything if you're black. The detached modes of discourse we examined in connection with this concept earlier surely find their most salient example here. Silence, or stories that mask hidden facts, become life-saving devices. Another reason for fronting would be the loss of dignity, a scenario John faces in the similar courtroom scene in *Jonah*, where he refuses to reveal Hattie's evil ways, particularly her negative use of hoodoo, before the mocking white judge and jurors.

One further aspect of Janie's various narrative voices seems pertinent. The power of *Their Eyes*, as John Callahan has demonstrated, comes from the scaffolding of call-and-response patterns that supports virtually every scene, but particularly in the frame, where Pheoby and Janie personify this format. The white courtroom, with its de jure mode of oral argument, erases any possibility of this call-and-response narrative. Further, it obviously functions within the narrative as a representative of white/black discourse in general, which similarly breaks down when racial scenarios produce monologism rather than dialogism.

As readers, we also object to this scene because the rest of the novel succeeds so well in indoctrinating us in the modalities of black linguistic activity, which always proceeds with the assumption that ideas must be tested and validated verbally, with all involved parties participating in the process. Janie's performance here no doubt works in tandem with the white doctor's testimony; he acquaints the court with the seriousness of Tea Cake's illness, Janie's tender care, and the threat rabies presents to the whole town. The perceptive reader will see that the latter fact probably sways the white jury more than anything else he says and that whatever Janie offers the court must be subservient to the doctor's testimony as a white man, one respected as a "diagnostician"/reader of humanity.

Hurston would later exploit this technique of omission extensively in *Dust Tracks*, which has repeatedly been attacked (unjustly, in my view) for its many silences on issues such as Hurston's love life, particulars of her religious beliefs, details of controversial relationships, and the like. We would do well to remember that such expectations come from a tradition of white autobiography, and although unconscious, a lack of understanding of black discursive practice. Hurston was astute enough to realize that by writing an autobiography, she was placing herself in the dock (as all autobiographers do) before a largely white audience, and her mode of narration followed accordingly. She skillfully masks many of these silences through humorous diversions, a sign that she was well aware of the judgmental expectations of her readers.

These expectations apply to Hurston's fiction too. Rachel Blau DuPlessis has demonstrated that the whole of *Their Eyes* centers on the notion of trials, "one by white people's rules, another by black men's rules, a third by the rules of 'Mouth-Almighty'—her black working-class rural community." Pheoby, as auditor, represents a "proper jury" (a peer) *and* judge (106). I would add that the book tests the reader's preconceptions about a number of issues and attitudes as well. Obviously, Janie's exuberant story of liberation, as told to Pheoby, forces us to radically different conclusions from the white jury's; to us, she seems neither a "wanton killer" nor a poor "broken creature," and we arrive at our decision largely on the evidence of her convincing comic creativity.

The anger of Tea Cake's male friends, led by Sop-de-Bottom, over Janie's acquittal becomes more understandable if one figures in the mocking "justice-for-blacks-is-a-game" attitude of the white courtroom, led by the judge himself. If Janie had killed a white man, the tone and outcome would have been very different, and everyone knows it. Hurston knew a woman, Babe, from Polk County, who had shot her husband to death, fled to Tampa, bobbed her hair, and eluded capture, but was finally arrested. Eventually the authorities released Babe, and the case was forgotten. "Negro women *are* punished in these parts for killing men, but only if they exceed the quota. I don't remember what the quota is. Perhaps I did hear but I forgot. One woman had killed five when I left that turpentine still where she lived. The sheriff was thinking of calling on her and scolding her severely" (*Mules and Men* 65). Hurston inserts a very serious issue here under the garb of a comic presentation, but in *Their Eyes* the perspective becomes quite different. Reading racist humor correctly reveals multiple modes of judgment at work during Janie's trial.

Janie obviously understands and sympathizes with the men and thus finds her way to reconciliation with them. Presumably, she has seen to it that the actual facts have filtered out, at least to the people who were with them on the muck, for Sop-de-Bottom testifies to a new understanding of what happened. In a prefiguration of Pheoby's role in Eatonville, he explains and reverses his earlier reading of Tea Cake's death and simultaneously "testifies" for Janie: "'Naw, Ah ain't mad wid Janie,' Sop went around explaining. 'Tea Cake had done gone crazy. You can't blame her for puhtectin' herself. She wuz crazy 'bout 'im. Look at de way she put him away. Ah ain't got anything in mah heart aginst her. And Ah never woulda thought uh thing, but de very first day dat lap-legged nigger [Mrs. Turner's brother] come back heah makin' out he was lookin' fuh work, he come astin' me 'bout how wuz Mr. and

Mrs. Woods makin' out'" (282). The men run the brother, now their comic scapegoat, off the muck yet again, thereby purging any animus left toward Janie, demonstrating that even the "killing" humor can be productive.

But just how do readers assess the circumstances of Tea Cake's death? An ominous prefiguration occurs in a seemingly innocuous scene early in the novel, when Jody asks Janie her name. She tells him it used to be Janie Mae Crawford, but now it's Janie Mae Killicks. We notice the way marriage repeatedly stifles Janie, sometimes even with Tea Cake, the "bee" for her "blossom," as the scenes on the muck so abundantly prove. It does change her from a Janie Mae Crawford who "may" "crawl forth" from her tragic origins into selfhood into a frustrated woman, Janie-may-kill, as the wife of both Logan and Jody. Of course, Janie has innocently but ironically stated, much earlier in the narrative, that she loved Tea Cake "fit tuh kill" (168).

Paradoxically, both these identities come into play simultaneously, as the various sides of Janie merge after Tea Cake's death. Janie Woods comes back to the community bearing seeds, completed and generative with her story, yet she has killed the one husband who belied the prophecy of her first change of name. On the other hand, setting Tea Cake's actual identity and undeniable worth aside, only after she "kills" oppressed versions of herself (married/man-defined woman) can her individual self clearly "crawl forth" as a separate entity. This final crawling forth and, presumably, standing represents a further development of being drawn out of the ordinary by love. Just before going on the muck with Tea Cake she looks down on him as he sleeps and feels "a self-crushing love. So her soul crawled out from its hiding place" (192).

Her use of the term "Mouth Almighty" in the first chapter to describe the communal critics judging her return to Eatonville constitutes more than an epithet: it has a double meaning, like many other terms in the novel. While it labels the smug appropriation of Godlike powers of judgment, it simultaneously offers tribute to the justice of communal debate and deliberation, which her tale-telling tacitly acknowledges by being given to them through their agent, Pheoby. For Janie had known what to expect from the town; "'sitters-and-talkers gointuh worry they guts into fiddle strings till dey find out'" (284), and Janie intends her tale, told to Pheoby, to function like Tea Cake's bundle of seeds, which Janie has brought with her. Their story is meant for planting in the community, which needs the laughing, loving example this pair of lovers offers. This intention finds results in Pheoby's reaction: "'Lawd! . . . Ah done growed ten feet higher from jus' listenin' tuh you, Janie. Ah ain't satisfied wid mahself no mo'. Ah mean tuh make Sam take me fishin' wid him after this. Nobody better not criticize yuh in my hearin'"" (284).

There are three interesting aspects to this seemingly simple utterance. First, it precludes closure to the narrative. Second, it earmarks Sam as the next candidate to be reformed by Janie's story. Finally, it introduces the completion of a pattern of imagery that has been somewhat submerged, the linkage of Janie and Tea Cake to a mythic mode of representation that centers on the figures of Isis, Osiris, and St. Peter.

Pheoby's announcement precludes closure to the story, for its continual telling means that the "seeds" (words) planted here will sprout. Sam Watson will be the next to benefit from Janie's story. He and Pheoby thus become Janie's ambassadors to the worlds of male and female discourse within the community. Sam would appear to be the perfect figure to intercede for Janie in another sense too, for Janie herself says of this comic King of the Porch early in the novel, "'Sam is too crazy! You can't stop laughin' when youse round him'" (16). His comic approach to life makes Pheoby's affinity to Janie stronger in this ongoing marriage's parallelism with Janie and Tea Cake's and makes the sense of continuity and regeneration at the end of the book even stronger too.

Tea Cake's seeds and their link with the sprouting of the story itself are part of the network of Egyptian symbolism that pervades the novel. Tea Cake is buried "like a Pharaoh" with a guitar in his hands; he is repeatedly described as the sun of the Evening Sun; and the circumstances of his death associate him with flood, thus figuring him as an avatar of Osiris. Further, he resembles the Egyptian black god of fertility, ruler of the lower world, whose symbol was an eye opened wide as a sign of his restoration to light by Isis (Seyffert, Nettleship, and Sandys 439). The novel begins with Janie described as "a woman . . . come back from burying the dead . . . eyes flung wide open in judgment" (9). In the novel's final scene, Janie climbs the stairs with a lamp; soon after, Tea Cake appears to her, "prancing around her," reborn like Osiris, who was also king of the upper air and of light.[29]

Osiris was brother, lover, and equal to Isis. Hurston, we remember, chose to name her fictional equivalent Isis in "Drenched in Light" and *Jonah*. The goddess, like Osiris, was associated with the flood, and her symbol was the cow, which may well account for the awkwardness of the mad dog scene in *Their Eyes*. She was also the goddess of ships and navigation (Seyffert, Nettleship, and Sandys 324–25) with obvious ties to the sea.[30]

Sam and Pheoby will really go fishing; Janie with her "net" symbolically does so at the end of the novel, and this brings us to Hurston's daring overlay of the Osiris/Isis imagery with that associated with St. Peter. Tea Cake asserts repeatedly that Janie has "the keys to the kingdom." We have seen that the woman with keys comes from a black folktale about woman's power, but keys play an important role in the Bible as well. Peter, formerly a fisherman, and then a "fisher of men," is awarded the keys to the kingdom by Christ, who says he will build his church on this rock (Matt. 16:18–19). In the gospel of John, the risen Jesus (like Tea Cake here) appears again to his disciples and bids them cast their nets on the right side of the boat: "Simon Peter went up, and drew the net to land full of great fishes, an hundred and fifty and three, and for all there were so many, yet was not the net broker)" (John 21:11). Janie, taking her light up the stairs (echoing the spiritual, "this little light of mine / I'm gonna let it shine") has already demonstrated her fitness to carry forth Tea Cake's "religion" of fully lived life and in fact has made her first convert in Pheoby.

Recognizing this pattern suggests a future for Janie beyond sitting in her room and living off memories. Peter, after all, was a great preacher, so perhaps Janie will become one too. We should remember that all of Nanny's fears/prophecies for Janie have come true. Janie is transformed into a mule, first of work, by Logan, then of decorative leisure, like Bonner's mule, by Jody. She does become a spit cup, as we have seen. Janie has already preached one sermon "from on high," as Nanny wished, and it may be that the novel's conclusion predicts many more.

On the other hand, a curious scene in the novel might be read as a caution against making too much of this Christian mythic patterning. One of the men on Jody's porch tells a comic Big John de Conquer story, claiming ole John was gone for centuries because he was in Egypt, hanging around, eating up "'dem Pharaoh's tombstones. Dey got de picture of him doin' it. Nature is high in uh varmint lak dat'" (104). African American mythology ultimately and joyously gobbles up all others in this narrative.

We know this story has to be told for another reason. Earlier, Mrs. Annie Tyler brought out the cruel side of the community's humor. Seduced, abandoned, and robbed by a series of young men, this older woman goes off laughing on her final fling with yet another younger man named, appropriately, Who Flung. Two weeks later a pitying Eatonville man finds her abandoned and penniless in Tampa; she becomes the laughingstock of the community upon her return. Similarly, at the beginning of the frame story, when Janie returns alone, the neighbors' "burning statements" and killing laughter once again create mass cruelty (10). Janie's transformation, however, gives her words to soothe these sentiments and to turn them to her favor since her story, which cheers and illuminates, points the way toward personhood. The opposition here is not just between Janie and the community, but between modes of comic creativity. Like the Hindu godhead, humor has both a healing, preserving, uniting aspect (Vishnu) and a destructive, revenge-seeking, purging one (Shiva), once again pointing to the Janus imagery. Janie magically transforms this communal energy into something constructive and uniting—her story.

This has importance beyond the pertinent details of the scene. Black literature, especially that written in dialect, has often been accused of locating itself in a narrow orbit between "humor and pathos," as James Weldon

Johnson once put it (Poetry), which could translate as "between minstrelsy and melodrama. "Janie wants to avoid both extremes—being cast as the butt in a comic script like Mrs. Taylor or being seen as a pathetic "broken woman," the way the white judge and jury choose to read her.

Back in Eatonville, Janie has to "make her case" among her people, with their involvement. Individual achievement finds its ultimate fulfillment in conjunction with others, and as Mary Helen Washington wisely observes, "the deepest and most lasting relationships occur among those black people who are most closely allied with and influenced by their own community" (*Black-Eyed* xxx). Janie instinctively knows that she can find peace only when the story untold at the trial becomes lodged in the figurative bosom and collective memory of her home community. The telling of her story, in the people's own loving, laughing voice, confirms its communal, cultural relevance, assures its immortality, and embalms her love for Tea Cake.

Throughout *Their Eyes Were Watching God* Hurston indicates that in refusing one's heritage, a person commits cultural suicide, and the loss of laughter represents an early symptom of that internal death. In a unique way, both Janie Crawford Killicks Starks Woods and Zora Neale Hurston recognized and harnessed humor's powerful resources; using its magical ability to bring people together, they established the intimacy of democratic communion.

On the other hand, Washington has also warned us against reading this novel too positively, for Janie indeed is silenced at any number of places, and we have no assurance that her voice will reverberate in the community again beyond the telling of her story through Pheoby. Janie herself issues a qualification as she summarizes the buzzing curiosity and gossiping of the townspeople to Pheoby: "'Dem meatskins is got tuh rattle tuh make out they's alive. Let 'em consolate theyselves wid talk. 'Course, talkin' don't amount tuh uh hill uh beans when yuh can't do nothin' else. And listenin' tuh dat kind uh talk is jus' lak openin' yo' mouth and lettin' de moon shine down yo' throat. It's uh known fact, Pheoby, you got tuh go there tuh *know* there. . . . Two things everybody's got tuh do fuh theyselves. They got tuh go tuh God, and they got tuh find out about livin' fuh theyselves'" (285). Ultimately, as this passage suggests, language itself becomes limited, unable to reach what Hurston calls that "gulf of formless feelings untouched by thought" (43). People thus need the other arts and any other feeble tool they can create to assault the voids of silence that divide us.[31]

Humor, I would suggest, springs from the failures of ordinary, standard language to adequately communicate human needs, emotions, and expressions. It offers an expansion of language that goes even beyond metaphor. Indeed, as Hurston indicates in "Characteristics of Negro Expression," humorous gestures can function as communication, displacing and frequently transcending the limitations of spoken or written discourse. Comic creation of all types, however, paints, as Hurston might say, a "hieroglyphics" of mirth, speaking to us in a way that unadorned speech never can, moving us as close as language can ever get to what Janie instinctively understands as "the inaudible voice of it all." (24).

NOTES

1. Hurston knew Swift's work as a child; some white women sent her a set of books that included *Gulliver's Travels* (*Dust Tracks*, 53). I thank my friend Asun Elizagierre for drawing my attention to this line in Swift.

2. Several early and appreciative critics nevertheless read the novel reductively. See, for example, George Stevens, who finds the book "simple and nonpretentious" (3). More damningly, Hurston's friend/enemy/sibling rival Alain Locke declared the novel "folklore fiction at its best," but added "when will the Negro novelist of maturity who knows how to tell a story convincingly—which is Miss Hurston's cradle-gift, come to grips with motive fiction and social document fiction? Progressive southern fiction has already banished the legend of these entertaining pseudo-primitives whom the reading public still loves to laugh with, weep over, and envy. Having gotten rid of condescension, let us now get over oversimplification!" ("Jingo" 10).

3. Joseph Campbell's formulation of narrative pattern in heroic quest is enumerated in his *The Hero with a Thousand Faces*.

4. See especially Missy Dehn Kubitschek's reading. Other articles on this topic are listed in *Awkward*.

5. *Columbia Encyclopedia*, 3d ed. Cyrena Pondrom has made a strong case for Frazer's multivolume *Golden Bough* as the source for much of Hurston's detailed knowledge of classical myth. There Janus/Jana (the male/female pair) is interchangeable with Diana. I would add that Jana/Diana was embraced in the sacred grove of Nemi by the King of the Woods, Virbius, whom Frazer claims was merely a local form of Jupiter in his aspect as god of the Greenwood. Virbius's union with Jana/Diana constituted a regal couple, the King and Queen of the Woods, and he was charged with the protection, "*at the peril of his life*," of the sacred oak (376–87; my emphasis). The royal union was deemed essential for the fertility of the earth. Clearly, Virbius would be an obvious source for Vergible Woods, whose last name suggests the sacred grove. Tea Cake does indeed die as a result of trying to protect Janie, who identifies with the pear tree. Hurston intrigues us by her decision to identify Janie with a male god rather than with his female counterpart, saving that maternal, moon-associated aspect for Pheoby.

6. Zora Neale Hurston to Charlotte Mason, Sept. 28, 1932, Moorland-Spingarn Research Center, Howard University Library, Washington, D.C.

7. As Lawrence Levine reminds us, Hurston's great contemporary, the stand-up comedienne Moms Mabley, frequently used down-home food and humor together to create intimacy between herself and her audience. Appearing in Washington, D.C., she told an audience, "I'm telling you I'm glad to be at *home*. And I had my first real meal in months. My niece cooked me some hog *mawwws*, and some cracklin' corn *b-r-e-a-d*, and a few greens on the side. *Thank* the Lord I'm talking to people that know what I'm talking *about*" (363).

8. Wright wrote a scathing review of *Their Eyes* ("Between Laughter and Tears"), dismissing it as a form of minstrelsy; he found its humor inappropriate for a novel about black life, a collective history he could only read as overwhelmingly tragic. A passage that Wright must have found more to his liking, Nanny's moving and eloquent personal history, which comprises most of chapter 2, is appropriately sober and heartbreaking.

9. This scene is further proof that Hurston's entire career may be understood as a kind of preaching. Her novels have biblically inspired titles, which "set the texts"; within them, one finds symbolic references to biblical themes, which are then illustrated by ensuing narrative events, all of which have both surface and deep messages. Furthermore, in virtually every case, the biblically inspired scene has a comic and a serious interpretation. For example, the motif of a stranger receiving water at a well from a woman is employed in all her novels and sets the text for ensuing narrative events that are both comic and serious, as when John first meets Lucy in *Jonah*.

10. More evidence is provided by "The Bone of Contention," which served as the basis for *Mule Bone*. As in the play, Joe (named Clarke rather than Starks) presides over a trial that pits a Baptist against a Methodist, and therefore their congregations exchange verbal blows as well. A hilarious exchange between Sister Lewis, a Baptist, and Sister Taylor, a Methodist, offers a good example of what Jody refuses to let Janie do, signify in public: "'Some folks,' she said with a meaning look, 'is a whole lot mo' puhtic'lar bout a louse in they church than they is in they house.' A very personal look at Sister Lewis. 'Well' said that lady, 'mah house mought not be exactly clean, but nobody caint say *dat*—indicating an infinitesimal amount on the end of her finger—'about my chaRACter! They didnt hafta git de sheriff to make Ike marry ME!' Mrs. Taylor leaped to her feet and struggled to cross the aisle to her traducer but was restrained by three or four *men* [my emphasis]. 'Yas, they did git de sheriff tuh make Sam marry me!' She shouted as she panted and struggled, 'And Gawd knows you sho oughter git him agin and make *some* of these men marry yo' Ada'" (8–9). Joe Clarke/Starks orders these "moufy wimmen" to "'Shet up,'" but both he and Lum Boger, the marshal, are cowed by the women's fiery frowns.

11. Rachel Blau DuPlessis has also written about the spittoon as the fulfillment of Nanny's feared projection and as one of the signs (the other, of course, is the mule) "under which Janie's marriage to Joe Starks unfolds" (112). Although DuPlessis sees the humor associated with the mule, she doesn't extend this argument to the spittoon.

12. In these scenes, Hurston once again makes use of "The Bone of Contention." In that sketch Lindsay agrees with Rev. Simms's demand that Mayor Joe Clarke build a jail and tells the latter, "Jus' cause you stahted the town, dat dont make yo' mouf no prayer book nor neither yo' lips no Bible. They dont flap lak none tuh *me*" (4).

13. The scene also bears a remarkable resemblance to one of Thomas Nast's most famous cartoons, which depicted Boss Tweed and his gang around a public's carcass. The leader asks, "Shall we pray?" The cartoon was recycled by Herblock during the Watergate crisis, substituting Nixon and his henchmen for the Tweed gang.

14. Several passages devoted to the humor directed at and fielded by Daisy Taylor are taken from *Mule Bone*. There and here, Jim and Dave are rivals for Daisy's attention and engage in yet another comic verbal duel, reprising and foreshadowing much of the humor of courtship so central in both *Jonah* and Seraph, with comically exaggerated declarations of love, such as "'A'll take uh job cleanin' out de Atlantic Ocean fuh you any time you say you so desire'" (108). Hurston the anthropologist thereby signals to us the ritualized nature of Eatonville humor and the value it has in courtship and for the community, but once again underlines Joe's exclusion of his wife, as he orders her into the store.

15. This conceit reminds us of Emily Dickinson's poem:

The Bustle in a House
The Morning after Death
is solemnest of industries
Enacted upon Earth—

The Sweeping up the Heart
And putting Love away
We shall not want to use again
Until Eternity. (242)

16. As Michael G. Cooke notes, however, Janie and Jody are not technically playing the dozens. She categorizes him ("big-bellies"); as Cooke states, she "seems to crash through signifying and into denunciation" (77).

17. The scene also has important comic and structural parallels with Ralph Ellison's hilarious episode in *Invisible Man* where the narrator, significantly dressed in overalls, passes through the Men's House in New York. He thinks he sees President Bledsoe, who betrayed him with false letters to northern entrepreneurs. Outraged, he empties a nearby spittoon on his head, but flees when it turns out the man is a Baptist preacher; the parallels between secular and sacral language and duplicity are obvious. The narrator is later told by an amused porter that he's been banned from the Men's House, and "'after what you did, I swear, they never will stop talking about you. You really baptized ole Rev!'" (258). The porter delights in one of his fellows on the lower end of the social totem pole inverting the social order, just as we do with Janie's signifying on Joe. Paradoxically, although both Ellison's narrator and Janie have violated the sanctum sanctorum of the "Men's House" of male discourse, they have both proved they are more than eligible for inclusion.

18. Hezekiah's portrait may operate on yet another satirical level. Hurston's oldest brother was named Hezekiah Robert. This satirical portrait is akin to the one Hurston painted of her sister Sarah in the character of Larraine in *Seraph*. There has been some confusion as to the names and ages of Hurston's siblings. Hemenway doesn't provide a list and mentions only a few of them in his biography. Hurston listed them, however, presumably in chronological order, in a letter to Godmother: "H. [Hezekiah] R. [Robert] Hurston, Physician and surgeon, Memphis, Tenn.; John Cornelius Hurston, Meat market and Florist shop, Jacksonville, Fla.; Richard William Hurston, mechanic, Newark, N.J.; Sarah Emmeline Hurston Mack, housewife, Asbury Park, N.J.; Joel Clifford Hurston, rural education, Montgomery, Ala.; Ben Franklin Hurston, PhC., Drugstore proprietor, Memphis, Tenn.; Zora Neale Hurston, bum and Godmother's pickaninny, New York City; Edward Everett Hale Hurston, P.O. clerk, Brooklyn N.Y. (Dec. 20, 1930, Moorland-Spingarn Research Center, Howard University Library, Washington, D.C.). However, the family Bible lists nine children, in this order: Hezekiah Robert, Isaac, John Cornelius, Richard William, Sarah, Zora Neal Lee (note the spelling), Clifford Joel, Benjamin Franklin, and Everett Edward. All but the last three are listed as being born in Notasulga (for details see Bordelon). In the letter the characteristic self-effacement before Godmother surfaces in the "bum/pickaninny" soubriquet, but also serves to contrast with and underline Hurston's justifiable pride in her siblings' accomplishments.

19. See 1 Cor. 13:12. Paradoxically, Tea Cake's mode as a teacher may doom him as a character, for as Claire Crabtree claims, Hurston seems to be determined to privilege folktale over novel in her narrative structure. In the folktale, Crabtree reminds us, "the magical teacher is dispensed with as the hero triumphs, and so is Tea Cake left behind on Janie's journey" (65). Additionally, this scene is likely the basis for Alice Walker's similar one in *The Color Purple*, where Shug gives Celie a mirror and urges her to examine and get to love every part of her body. Mary Helen Washington, however, has told me that consciousness-raising groups began urging women to do this in the early days of the contemporary women's movement, so this could be Walker's source as well. This latter phenomenon was satirized with a vengeance in the novel and film *Fried Green Tomatoes*.

20. Pheoby's mode of navigation is also a reflection of one of Hurston's favorite expressions, "hitting a straight lick with a crooked stick," and an illustration of a concept she discusses in "Characteristics" under the topics of angularity and asymmetry. She finds this in black dancing, furniture arrangement, and other aspects of black life and attributes it to African aesthetics, seen in African sculpture and doctrine. African Americans are pictured as intent on avoiding "the simple straight line." Paradoxically, however, as Hurston remarks, the asymmetry of the dancing is simultaneous with the regularity of musical rhythm. Although she doesn't say so, the angular placement of furniture depends on the geometric regularity of the interior space (41). We may go further and suggest that the dialectical and grammatical rupturing of standard English, which is very important in the role speech plays in black humor, operates similarly, causing the "liberation" Freud speaks of in *Jokes*. The "angularity" of approach also stems from the need for linguistic caution (and thus indirection and coded allusion) in a dangerous racist society. Curiously, although Hurston has a "dialect" section in "Characteristics," she doesn't make this connection.

21. Mary Helen Washington has argued that Janie's quest for identity is also a quest for blackness, a frame of reference that is achieved through authentic mastery of folk language, black culture ("Zora" 68ff.). Surely the acquisition of comedic styles, repertoires, and attitudes plays a key role in both activities and educates the reader simultaneously. Melvin Dixon, in a fine essay on Hurston's use of geography and geographical imagery in *Their Eyes*, notes that Janie walks back into town with black mud on her overalls, "proof of her new baptism" (94). Although he doesn't say so, he (and Hurston) surely suggest an immersion/baptism in blackness, the kind Washington has in mind, and this returns us to this chapter's epigraph, for Janie indeed is baptized with humor, one of the things the "black mud" symbolizes. Baptism also fits with Robert Stepto's claim that *Their Eyes* is "quite likely the only truly coherent narrative of both ascent and immersion" in black literature (164), an assertion he subsequently undercuts by discounting the novel's mode of narration. Nevertheless, his initial observation stands.

22. These passages remind us of the dicty blacks' color prejudices satirized by Nella Larsen in *Quicksand* (1928), especially in the scenes set at Naxos College, and of the treatment the very dark heroine receives from her family and college classmates in Wallace Thurman's *The Blacker the Berry* (1928), books Hurston surely had read.

23. Hurston's juxtaposition of humor with an encroaching natural disaster, the hurricane, is stunning, and was based on actual events. The legendary Florida hurricane of September 1928 devastated the state, killing thousands and causing tremendous damage to property. Another storm killed 425 in 1935, just before Hurston wrote *Their Eyes* (Federal Writers' Project 61–62). Furthermore, Hurston was in the Bahamas in October 1929, where she survived a terrible hurricane (Hemenway 127). Several novels featuring hurricanes had been written, including one Hurston may have known. Theodore Pratt's *Big Blow* (1936) is set in the very same area near Lake Okeechobee and came out just a year before *Their Eyes*. Interestingly, Pratt, who had come to Florida from New York in 1934 and would write about the state in many novels and nonfiction works during the rest of his career, would get to know Zora quite well, attend her funeral, and write a number of essays about her. Most of the hurricane-genre books routinely use the storm as Hurston does, placing it at the end of the book to bring the narrative to an exciting conclusion. Pratt's, however, combines the threat of a double lynching (of a white and a black man, both in trouble with local "trash") with the storm tradition. Nature, there, however, is a somewhat melodramatic agent of justice, for the "trash" are killed violently by the storm before accomplishing their goals, and long-yearning lovers finally embrace as the storm's last winds roar past. Pratt's description

of the storm and its effects is powerful and detailed. Hurston possibly borrowed the idea of using a piece of roofing from him.

24. The theme of higher ground has set many a text for the black pulpit and is also the subject of the popular Baptist hymn "Higher Ground":

> I'm pressing on the upward way,
> New heights I'm gaining ev'ry day;
> Still praying as I onward bound,
> Lord, plant my feet on higher ground.
> Lord, lift me up and let me stand,
> By faith, on heaven's tableland,
> A higher plane than I have found;
> Lord, plant my feet on higher ground. (Sims 319)

25. Hurston here uses graveyard irony and thus echoes a classic story of a Baghdad merchant, the epigraph of John O'Hara's brilliant novel *Appointment in Samarra* (1934), a book she could have read. The merchant's servant runs into Death in the marketplace, who makes a threatening gesture. The servant tells his master he's fleeing to Samarra. Momentarily, the master sees Death in the marketplace and asks him why he threatened the servant. Death's reply is: "That was not a threatening gesture . . . it was only a start of surprise. I was astonished to see him in Baghdad, for I had an appointment with him tonight in Samarra."

26. In these indirect speculations about God, also found in *Moses*, Hurston sounds similar to Jung, who specifically stated: "If we consider, for example, the daemonic features exhibited by Yahweh in the Old Testament, we shall find in them not a few reminders of the unpredictable behaviour of the trickster, of his pointless orgies of destruction and his self-appointed sufferings, together with the same gradual development into a saviour and his simultaneous humanization" (196).

27. Hurston was clearly working out some of the bitterness she still felt in 1950 about the most devastating event of her life, her unjust accusation in 1948 by a black woman of sexually molesting a young black boy. Although the charges were dismissed, the black press across the nation had picked up the story; Hurston felt her race had betrayed her, as an October 30, 1948, letter to Carl Van Vechten reveals (James Weldon Johnson Memorial Collection, Yale Collection of American Literature, Beinecke Rare Book and Manuscript Library, Yale University, New Haven, Conn.).

28. Richard Wright, in the title of his *New Masses* review of the book, might have seemed to be signaling Hurston/Janie's success at navigating between these two modes of presentation. However, a humorless Wright finds her guilty of a new kind of minstrelsy.

29. As Cyrena N. Pondrom has shown us, both Tea Cake and Osiris are twenty-eight. She has also noted a few of the other similarities I have pointed out here. She leans much more heavily toward Tea Cake as Tammuz, however, and brings in other gods as well. She takes the same approach with Janie. Hurston was much more attracted to Egyptian myth than to those of other cultures, such as the Babylonian and Greek myths Pondrom highlights, because she believed that as Africans the Egyptians were black.

30. Hurston, ever the mythic synthesist, had no doubt considered the obvious parallels with Christ. Tea (red, like blood) Cake (the body), like Christ, is sacrificed so that others (first Janie, then the community who hears his story), might "live."

31. Pheoby's name may be important here as well, since the appellation "Phoebe" was associated with the goddess Artemis in terms of her role as moon goddess (Seyffert,

Nettleship, and Sandys 486, 573). Hurston's reference to gossiping talk as moonshine underlines Pheoby's doubled role, both as someone who has heard gossip and then sped to solace its object only to find that she will be able to silence the original tales by narrating Janie's canceling narrative. The moon, of course, relays light to earth it reflects from the sun, the orb constantly associated with Janie. Lucy Hurston's advice to her children to jump at the sun, and maybe you'll at least get the moon (which becomes Lucy's advice to John in *Jonah*), has ironic relevance here, since Janie-the-Sun's neighbors do indeed "jump" her in the novel's opening, but they have to be content with getting her story/reflection second-hand from Pheoby-the-moon. Rachel Blau DuPlessis has similarly noticed the classical derivation of Pheoby's name and linked her with the moon as a reflector of the sun.

SUSAN EDWARDS MEISENHELDER

"Mink Skin or Coon Hide": The Janus-faced Narrative of Their Eyes Were Watching God

As in *Jonah's Gourd Vine*, Hurston also focused on "family matters" in *Their Eyes Were Watching God*, examining in greater detail models of black male and female identity and the larger social worlds they both reflect and shape. Echoing John Pearson, Bentley, and Muttsy in her depiction of Janie's husbands, she critiques a false model of masculinity drawn from a white world and the notion of black female identity it assumes. As suggested in the allusions to the two-faced Janus figure Hurston exploits in her delineation of Janie, Janie struggles between two identities in the novel, one like Pinkie's drawn from the white world and foisted upon her and a more vigorous model of black womanhood she tries to forge for herself.[1] The discursive difficulties Hurston faced in telling this story were perhaps even greater than those she faced in writing *Jonah's Gourd Vine*, for the powerful black woman Janie becomes resists oppression not merely by haunting her husband after her death as Lucy does, but much more directly, "killing" one man with words and another with a gun. In *Their Eyes Were Watching God* Hurston cloaks this more daring expose of female resistance in lush naturalistic imagery and rich folk idiom to create a novel in which racial and sexual conflict was so carefully masked that it was read by most of her contemporaries (as she fully expected) as one merely celebrating the spontaneous primitivism of black life.[2]

From Hitting a Straight Lick with a Crooked Stick: Race and Gender in the Work of Zora Neale Hurston, pp. 62–91, 209–213. © 1999 by the University of Alabama Press.

The novel's rich metaphors, many of which Hurston developed in revision of the novel's manuscript, emphasize both race and gender in Janie's struggle for self-fulfillment. Certainly the most explicit reference in the novel to their interaction in the lives of black women is Nanny's speech to Janie before her first marriage:

> Honey, de white man is de ruler of everything as fur as Ah been able tuh find out. Maybe it's some place way off in de ocean where de black man is in power, but we don't know nothin' but what we see. So de white man throw down de load and tell de nigger man tuh pick it up. He pick it up because he have to, but he don't tote it. He hand it to his womenfolks. De nigger woman is de mule uh de world so fur as Ah can see. (29)[3]

Drawing her model of black female identity from her own experience with the harshest forms of racial and sexual oppression (slavery and rape), Nanny is both accurate in her assessment of the world "where the white man is the ruler" (as many incidents in *Mules and Men* suggest) and limited in her conception of alternatives. Accepting the hierarchies and inequalities of her world as universal and immutable, she hopes to save Janie from becoming either a mule or a "spit-cup" (37) by placing her under the "big protection" (41) of an economically secure husband. Unable to imagine a world where black woman and mule are not synonymous, she embraces an ideal that from her experience seems the only alternative, one drawn from a romanticized conception of the lives of white women. Although Janie's first two marriages show the limitations of Nanny's understanding, detailing both the enervating effects of "settin' on porches lak de white madam" (172) as well as the many ways women can be spit-cups and mules with male protection, Nanny's mule metaphor is, nevertheless, a very complicated piece of social commentary, more accurate in its analysis of race and gender in a world where "de white man is de ruler" than the young Janie realizes. As the rest of the novel will reveal, in a community ruled by whites or their black surrogates, race and gender interact in complicated ways, creating artificial status and power differences between black men and women.[4]

Although Nanny cannot imagine a world free of hierarchy and domination, such a vision is expressed in Janie's metaphor of the pear tree, itself a densely complex social metaphor:

> She was stretched on her back beneath the pear tree soaking in the alto chant of the visiting bees, the gold of the sun and the panting breath of the breeze when the inaudible voice of it all came to her. She saw a dust-bearing bee sink into the sanctum

of a bloom; the thousand sister-calyxes arch to meet the love embrace and the ecstatic shiver of the tree from root to tiniest branch creaming in every blossom and frothing with delight. So this was a marriage! She had been summoned to behold a revelation. Then Janie felt a pain remorseless sweet that left her limp and languid. (24–25)

On one level, an obvious metaphor for sexual relationships, the passage is a powerful contrast to Nanny's spit-cup and mule metaphors with their suggestions of rape and female dehumanization. Echoing the male/female equality extolled in the "Behold the Rib!" sermon of *Mules and Men*, this metaphor for sexuality is one free of domination and active/passive polarities: there is no suggestion of rapacious violence on the part of the (male) bees who "sink into the sanctum of a bloom" or of passive victimization on the part of the "sister-calyxes [who] arch to meet the love embrace." The sexual relationship imaged here, one between active equals, is not only one of sexual fulfillment and "delight" but, as the metaphor of pollination implies, one of creativity and fecundity.[5]

Casting this metaphor in naturalistic and mythic terms seemingly unrelated to race, Hurston further masks its import by assigning it a domestic referent, marriage. Although she does not identify her metaphor as in any way racially specific, it forms a part of a larger pattern of tree imagery developed in the novel to describe black identity. In contrast to those characters whose lives have been largely shaped in a white-dominated world and who are described as mutilated trees (Nanny [26], her daughter, and Killicks [39], for instance), only Tea Cake—with Woods for a last name—and Janie, who at the chronological end of the novel sees her life "like a great tree in leaf" (20), experience the kind of relationship imaged in the pear tree and appear as the racially and sexually vibrant, "undiminished human beings" (85) described by Alice Walker. As their relationship and experience on the Muck suggests, the kind of relationship imaged here—sexual or more broadly social—cannot flourish in a world of hierarchy and domination. Only possible where the white man is not the ruler of black people's lives, the pear tree images the model of relationships necessary for black vitality—male *and* female. The novel, in large measure, chronicles the struggle between the racial and sexual identities packed into Janie's and Nanny's metaphors. Although the novel will reveal complications in both, the options facing Janie are clear early in the novel: to live as the mule or imitation white woman implied in Nanny's vision or as the vigorous black one imaged in her own.

The difficulties Janie will experience trying to become such a woman married to Joe Starks are clear from the very beginning of their relationship, for Hurston is careful in almost every detail of his character to paint him as a false model of black manhood, one like John's drawn from white world. As deeply influenced as Nanny by the experience of "workin' for white folks all his life" (47) and as committed to the underlying dynamics of her social metaphor and the multilayered hierarchy on which it rests, he strives simply to usurp the white man's place at the top of the social ladder. Aware from his own experience that "de white folks had all de sayso where he come from and everywhere else" (48), he moves to the all-black community of Eatonville, where, as "a big voice" (48), he can play the white man's role, tossing his load to the black men beneath him and the black women beneath them. As Hurston shows, Starks's attempt to emulate whites—even Janie immediately notices that he looks (56) and acts (49) like white men—ultimately shapes his relationship with his community and with his wife.[6] Forfeiting the possibility of healthy black relationships imaged in the pear tree, he becomes sexually dead and socially isolated, elevated above but alienated from other black people, an observer rather than a participant in the porch-front banter and cultural life of his community. No representative of "sun-up and pollen and blooming trees" (50), his big voice takes the "bloom off things" (69), leaving him a tree as starkly denuded as Killicks' stump.

Starks's desire to imitate white men and its effect on his relationship with the people in Eatonville is evident in the objects with which he surrounds himself. To go with his desk (one "like Mr. Hill or Mr. Galloway over in Maitland" [75] owns), he buys a fancy gold spittoon "just like his used-to-be bossman used to have" (75) that symbolizes for him his sophistication and status above the common people. In addition to humorously spoofing white pretensions here (this is, after all, a spit-cup despite its price tag), Hurston emphasizes the damaging effects of Starks's finery on the black people around him. Just as Starks behind his desk "weakened people" (76), his spittoon makes them question their own identity: "how could they know up-to-date folks was spitting in flowery little things like that? It sort of made the rest of them feel that they had been taken advantage of. Like things had been kept from them. Maybe more things in the world besides spitting pots had been hid from them, when they wasn't told no better than to spit in tomato cans" (76). Whereas the community members are awed and intimidated by Starks, they sense something unnatural in his actions: "It was bad enough for white people [to act like he did], but when one of your own color could be so different it put you on a wonder. It was like seeing your sister turn into a 'gator. A familiar strangeness. You keep seeing your sister in the 'gator and the 'gator in your sister, and you'd rather not" (76). Paradoxically, both Starks's and the community's sense of identity are damaged with the purchase of this spittoon, for he (as the people recognize) becomes a freakish hybrid, neither black nor white.

When he comes to town, Starks also brings with him white definitions of leadership and power. He inadvertently reveals his plans when he arrives, responding in telling astonishment to an announcement that the town has no mayor: "'Ain't got no Mayor! Well, who tells ya'll what to do?'" (57). Whereas Starks sees himself as a "leader" who brings order and progress to the community, Hurston suggests a more sinister motive: he plans to control the town like his former "boss-men," a fact evident when he immediately puts the men to work cutting trees. Talking like a "section foreman" (58) with "bow-down command" (75) in his face, Starks recreates power dynamics of the most oppressive sort, a fact recognized by the residents themselves, who, when forced by Starks to dig ditches, "murmured hotly about slavery being over" (75). Significantly, he builds for himself a slave owner's mansion to symbolize his power over the community and installs the light post in imitation of the white god he worships.[7]

Just as Starks draws his model for social relationships from the white world, his view of the ideal relationship between a man and a woman is similarly imported. Vowing to place Janie on "de front porch" so she can "rock and fan [herself] and eat p'taters dat other folks plant just special for [her]" (49), Starks promises only a modification rather than an abolition of Nanny's hierarchy. While Janie will be above "the gang," she will be subjugated and objectified in her relationship with Joe: her pedestal will place her above other black women, but decidedly beneath him. Nanny, thus, fails to recognize the complexity of her own "mule" metaphor, for merely replacing a white man's face with a black one does not free Janie. Ironically, she lives a life Nanny worked so hard to avoid for her, enduring what Nanny feared despite having attained the economic circumstances she desired. Although in more complex ways than the literal rape Nanny feared, Janie becomes a spit-cup for Joe, her passive status exemplified in the spittoon he gives her. "A little lady-size spitting pot" (smaller, of course, than Joe's) with "little sprigs of flowers painted all around the sides" (76) in seeming contrast to its earthy function, the fancy spitting pot symbolizes the deceptive appearance of Janie's relationship with Starks. Although Janie, like white women, ostensibly lives on "a flowery-bed-of-ease" (*Mules and Men* 85) with Joe, this veneer of economic affluence and elevated class status relative to other blacks only thinly covers the degradation she experiences.[8]

As other critics have pointed out, Janie also becomes a mule in her relationship with Starks, a parallel Hurston buries in the anomalous, "comic" story of Matt Bonner's mule.[9] Underneath what appears merely a playful depiction of folk life and the richness of storefront banter, Hurston reveals that Jody's "noble" (91) behavior toward the mule is very much like his "solicitous" treatment of Janie; his motivation in pampering both mules is simply to elevate himself in the community, and in both cases, his "kindness" is deadly. Just as Joe's "solicitation" spiritually strangles Janie, Hurston also ironically suggests that Starks's munificence kills the mule, for the mule dies in a way that "wasn't natural and . . . didn't look right" (93) after Jody begins the practice of piling up fodder for it (92). The suggestion that the mule dies from over-feeding is reinforced in the later anomalous section depicting the buzzards coming to feed on the mule's carcass. In their declaration that "Bare, bare fat" (97) has killed the mule, we see the double paradox in Starks's behavior: the mule dies from his cruel kindness just as surely as Janie is spiritually starved by his poor, poor wealth.

The broader treatment of the black woman as mule is further reinforced in this chapter through the story of Mrs. Tony Robbins, the woman who comes to beg food from Joe Starks. Like the yellow mule episode and many episodes in *Mules and Men*, this scene (judging from the male characters' reactions) seems also simply a lighthearted interlude with Mrs. Robbins as easy a target for scorn as Matt Bonner. Just as Jody and the town men enjoy "mule-baiting" and teasing Matt Bonner (89), Joe relishes "baiting" (113) and "jok[ing] roughly" (113) with the woman when she comes to the store. Significantly, Joe Stark' responds to her hunger with the same penury Matt Bonner did to his mule's. Like Bonner who only fed his mule with a teacup (83) and "was known to buy side-meat by the slice" (88), Jody stingily cuts off a tiny slab of meat for Mrs. Robbins (115), not forgetting, of course, to charge it to her husband's account. In fact, the yellow mule is finally treated more generously than Mrs. Robbins. In a telling comment on the fate of women who do not passively accept their status as mules, the men on the porch-front respond to Mrs. Robbins's complaint that her husband does not feed her with violent wrath, one vowing "Ah'd kill her cemetery dead" (115–16) and another saying "Ah'd kill uh baby just born dis mawnin' fuh uh thing lak dat."[10]

In ways that would undoubtedly have surprised Nanny, Janie thus finds herself in a world of "mules and men" married to Joe; and for much of their relationship, she accepts her status. Like the "fractious" mules celebrated in *Mules and Men*, however, she increasingly resists his control, speaking out in Big Sweet fashion first for the yellow mule, then for Mrs. Turner, and finally for herself. In her famous rejoinder to Starks's public humiliation of her, she breaks out of Nanny's hierarchy, refusing to be the mule and deflating the pretensions of the man who has made her one: "'You big-bellies round here and put out a lot of brag, but 'tain't nothin' to it but yo' big voice. Humph! Talkin''bout *me* lookin' old! When you pull down yo' britches, you look lak de change uh life'" (123).[11]

Janie's equations here are significant ones reminding us how completely Jody's identity—his big belly, which makes him "Kind of portly like rich white folks" (56), and his "big voice"—is drawn from the white world. As Janie's final allusion to sexual impotence suggests, it is an empty model of male identity, for Joe's illusions of masculinity and power are immediately destroyed when Janie refuses to play her supporting role. Hurston's description of Starks's lingering illness further suggests the emptiness of white models of manhood, for Jody is almost literally deflated by Janie's comments, gradually losing weight until even his big belly is only a saggy remnant of his former grandeur, "A sack of flabby something [that] hung from his loins and rested on his thighs when he sat down" (126).

In every respect, Tea Cake Vergible Woods is portrayed as Starks's antithesis, his feminized nickname promising a "sweeter," gentler kind of masculinity and his surname a healthy black identity compared to the sterility implied in Joe's. Hurston stresses this contrast by painting Tea Cake as emphatically black and by detailing his defiance of the hierarchical values Starks imports from the dominant white culture. He also repeatedly rejects the definition of male/female relationships that Joe had internalized and forced on Janie. In teaching Janie to play checkers, to shoot, to drive, and in inviting her to work alongside of him, Tea Cake breaks down the rigid gender definitions Joe sought to impose, bringing Janie into the cultural life of the black community and building a relationship with her grounded in reciprocity rather than hierarchy. Unlike Starks, who uses language to intimidate, dominate, and silence Janie, Tea Cake encourages her to voice her own feelings honestly, to "'Have de nerve tuh say whut you mean'" (165). His belief in the legitimacy of black women's self-expression is evident in his courting behavior, which contrasts sharply with the other male courting rituals and "mule talk" described in Chapter Six. When Jim and Dave engage in their love talk, Daisy is merely a silent and passive vehicle for them "to act out their rivalry" (107). As they vie with one another for the most hyperbolic sign of their devotion, promising to give her passenger trains and steamships, the male audience for their performance explodes in "A big burst of laughter at Daisy's discomfiture" (107).[12] Tea Cake, on the other hand, brings Janie into his game as an active participant. When Janie gases him for his generous purchase of two Coca-Colas with the comment, "'We got a rich man round here, then. Buyin' passenger trains uh battleships this week?'" (153), Tea Cake addresses his love talk to Janie rather than the other male in the store: "'Which one do *you* want? It all depends on you'" (153). That invitation initiates the first instance in the novel of a man and woman engaged in the kind of playful discourse normally reserved for males:

> "Oh, if you'se treatin' me tuh it, Ah b'lieve Ah'll take de passenger train. If it blow up Ah'll still be on land."
> "Choose de battleship if dat's whut you really want. Ah know where one is right now. Seen one round Key West de other day."
> "How you gointuh git it?"

"Ah shucks, dem Admirals is always ole folks. Can't no ole
man stop me from gittin' no ship for yuh if dat's what you want.
Ah'd git dat ship out from under him so slick till he'd be walkin'
de water lak ole Peter befo' he knowed it." (153–54)

As this evidence of Tea Cake's belief in linguistic reciprocity suggests, Janie is
right that Tea Cake teaches her "the maiden language," for he is the first man
who has not wanted to make her a spit-cup for his words.

Tea Cake's fundamental defiance of the dominant culture's notions
concerning both race *and* sex and his rejection of the oppressive hierarchies
that typify a world of mules and men make him "a bee to [Janie's] blossom"
(161). In every aspect of their early relationship, he represents the model
of masculinity imaged in the bee, encouraging Janie to express the equality
and activity expressed in the blossom. Tea Cake's brand of masculinity and
the kind of reciprocal relationship it makes possible are imaged early when
Janie falls asleep and wakens to find Tea Cake combing her hair. Unlike
Starks who asserts his oppressive masculinity, controlling Janie's sexuality
by forcing her to bind up her hair, Tea Cake here not only engages in
a traditional female activity but also luxuriates in the freedom her hair
represents. Whereas Starks sees Janie's hair as a symbol of his control of her,
Tea Cake combs Janie's hair in the spirit of reciprocity that characterizes
their early relationship, experiencing pleasure in giving it (157). Ready to
accept Janie as the person she is rather than attempting to remold her
to his desires, he not only combs her beautiful hair but also "scratch[es]
the dandruff from her scalp" (156). With such a "bee-man," Janie becomes
"petal-open," and the union of bee and blossom that results is, as Janie
realizes, the real "beginning of things" (163), a profoundly creative moment
contrasting sharply with Starks's parody of Creation.

As Cynthia Pondrom and John Lowe have suggested (195–96),
Hurston draws heavily on the myth of Isis and Osiris in her creation of Janie
and Tea Cake to suggest their equal stature and power and to create a mythic
analogue for her pear tree vision. The same age as Osiris, associated with trees
and enjoyment as the Egyptian god was and called by his title, "Son of the
Evening Sun" (264), Tea Cake represents an ideal of masculinity in pointed
contrast to Starks's oppressive, white male god and is the fitting mythic
consort for the powerful black woman that Janie becomes. In drawing on the
Isis and Osiris myth, Hurston grounds this relationship, one characterized
by reciprocity and self-affirmation rather than oppression and hierarchy, in
African rather than in European culture. Significantly, Janie and Tea Cake's
relationship flourishes not in Nanny's or Joe Starks's world but on the Muck,
a setting Hurston depicts as a black Eden free of outside cultural influence
and the deadly insipidity of the dominant white world. Stressing both the

blackness of the soil and the rich plant life it supports in her first description of the Muck, Hurston images (as she had in the supernatural tales of *Mules and Men*) the flowering of black people possible outside white influence:

> everything in the Everglades was big and new. Big Lake Okechobee, big beans, big cane, big weeds, big everything. Weeds that did well to grow waist high up the state were eight and often ten feet tall down there. Ground so rich that everything went wild. Volunteer cane just taking the place. Dirt roads so rich and black that a half mile of it would have fertilized a Kansas wheat field. Wild cane on either side of the road hiding the rest of the world. People wild too. (193)

The interpersonal relationship that Tea Cake's racial and gender identity makes possible with Janie is here translated to a larger societal level. In the soil of this black milieu grow vigorous black people, plants contrasting sharply with the ones stunted and mutilated in a white world. With the status differences and white values that Starks sought to reinforce absent on the Muck, artificial hierarchical divisions evaporate: Janie is just another person rather than Mrs. Mayor, and the Saws, instead of being ostracized, are accepted as equals. The gender hierarchies of Nanny's metaphor are also foreign to this community. With no white man tossing his load to the black man, black men do not toss it on to black women; and in the absence of oppressive sex roles that restrict women to serving men, Janie and Tea Cake "partake with everything," sharing in both paid labor and domestic work (199). On their porch, everyone takes part in the rich cultural life of the community, including Janie, who is no longer merely an outside observer or a spit-cup for men's words, but an active participant who "could tell big stories herself" (200).

The exception to the vigorous racial and sexual identities in the community (in fact, the serpent in this Eden) is Mrs. Turner, a female version of Joe Starks, who also rejects her own blackness and the cultural vitality around her. Hurston stresses the spiritual insipidity and deformed identity that result from her worship of white gods in her description of her as "a milky sort of a woman that belonged to child-bed. Her shoulders rounded a little, and she must have been conscious of her pelvis because she kept it stuck out in front of her so she could always see it" (208). Like Starks whose body looks "like bags hanging from an ironing board" (125), Mrs. Turner's "was an ironing board with things throwed at it" (208). Just as Starks's definition of maleness finally makes him impotent, Mrs. Turner is sexually insipid and symbolically uncreative. Even though she has given birth to six children, only one has lived (211), and he is, as Mr. Turner tells Tea Cake, "de last stroke of exhausted nature" (214). Her husband, an ideal mate for her, is another emphatically diminished human being: "He was a vanish-looking kind of man as if there used to be parts about him that stuck out individually but now he hadn't a thing about him that wasn't dwindled and blurred. Just like he had been sandpapered down to a long oval mass" (214).

Largely a ludicrous and pathetic figure (merely a source of gossip "when things were dull on the Muck" [217]), Mrs. Turner poses no threat to the community as long as she is met with the kind of unruffled indifference Janie displays.[13] Tea Cake's response is quite different, however. His statement that he "hates dat woman lak poison" (213), as later events will show, signals not a rejection of her cultural whiteness, but his own insecurity in the face of it. Jealousy of another man as vigorous as himself would have been understandable and benign (as Janie's of Nunkie is), but his fear that Janie will respond to Mrs. Turner's match-making attempts arises not from lover's passion but from his own submerged racial and sexual insecurity. The first evidence that Tea Cake has been infected with Mrs. Turner's poison and the effect this will have on his pear tree relationship with Janie arises when he beats Janie. It is not the violence of the act that Hurston pinpoints as problematic, but Tea Cake's motives for it, a fact emphasized in the contrasts between Tea Cake's beating of Janie and their earlier fight over Nunkie. When Janie feels jealous of Nunkie, she tackles both her and Tea Cake in the heat of passion, "Never th[inking] at all . . . just act[ing] on feelings" (204). That the honest expression of feelings among equals—even when acted out violently—poses no threat to the balance of their relationship is depicted in Hurston's description of their reconciliation. Their reunion, described in language that echoes the pear tree metaphor, reflects the reciprocity of their fight: "They wrestled on until they were doped with their own fumes and emanations; till their clothes had been torn away; till he hurled her to the floor and held her there melting her resistance with the heat of his body, doing things with their bodies to express the inexpressible; kissed her until she arched her body to meet him and they fell asleep in sweet exhaustion" (205). Like the bee that "sink[s] into the sanctum of a bloom" and "the thousand sister calyxes [that] arch to meet the love embrace" (24), Tea Cake and Janie here reenact the pear tree scene, fighting and loving as equals.

Tea Cake's violence toward Janie—no spontaneous expression of feeling but a premeditated "brainstorm" (218) hatched after Mrs. Turner's brother returns to the Muck—has both a very different motivation and a very different effect.[14] Fundamentally manipulative and coercive, the beating is calculated to assert his domination of Janie: Tea Cake whips her "Not because her behavior justified his jealousy, but [because] it relieved that awful fear inside him. Being able to whip her reassured him in possession. No brutal beating at all. He just slapped her around to show he was boss" (218).

His target (as he admits) is not Janie, but Mrs. Turner: "'Ah didn't whup Janie 'cause *she* done nothin'. Ah beat her tuh show dem Turners who is boss'" (220), to "'let her see dat Ah got control'" (220).

Equating light skin with passive female victimization and blackness with defiance, the men on the Muck express admiration not only for Tea Cake's assertion of dominance but also for what they fantasize as Janie's acquiescence:

> "Uh person can see every place you hit her. Ah bet she never raised her hand tuh hit you back, neither. Take some uh dese of rusty black women and dey would fight yuh all night long and next day nobody couldn't tell you ever hit em. Dat's de reason Ah done quit beatin' mah woman. You can't make no mark on 'em at all. Lawd! wouldn't Ah love tuh whip uh tender woman lak Janie! Ah bet she don't even holler. She jus' cries, eh Tea Cake." (218–19)

Although it is hard to imagine the Janie who has fought on equal footing with Tea Cake over Nunkie just a few pages earlier as this simpering victim, Tea Cake's satisfied response, "'Dat's right'" (219), ominously suggests his rejection of Janie's equality and his acceptance of an identity she has fought to reject. Tea Cake's changed view of Janie is further emphasized in this interchange among the men. When Sop-de-Bottom bemoans his fate of being equally matched with his woman, Tea Cake's bragging rejoinder, bespeaking an ominous value on Janie's social status and wealth, could well have been spoken by Joe Starks: "'Mah Janie is uh high time woman and useter things. Ah didn't git her outa de middle uh de road. Ah got her outa uh big fine house. Right now she got money enough in de bank tuh buy up dese ziggaboos and give 'em away'" (219). His final remark violates their reciprocal agreement to "partake wid everything" and makes explicit the oppression developing in his attitude toward Janie: "'Janie is wherever Ah wants tuh be'" (219). As these comments foreshadow, Tea Cake's behavior changes from this point on, echoing the falsely solicitous actions of Starks who oppresses Janie at the same time that he places her on a pedestal. To assert the power of his masculinity by assuring himself of Janie's passive femininity, he "would not let her go with him to the field. He wanted her to get her rest" (228).

With this set of values introduced and the "pear tree" paradise of the Muck spiritually destroyed, it is little surprise that Janie and Tea Cake are driven out by the hurricane that strikes in the next chapter. That this banishment is punishment for Tea Cake's "sin" is strongly hinted at in Tea Cake's reaction to signs of the approaching storm. When a friend, Lias, stops by and urges them to leave because "De crow gahn up" (230), Tea Cake ignores this natural warning, arguing in a way that indicates both acceptance of white superiority and an uncharacteristic concern for money: "'Dat ain't nothin'. You ain't seen de bossman go up, is yuh? Well all right now. Man, de money's too good on the Muck'" (230).[15] His acceptance of Mrs. Turner's social "pecking-order" is further revealed when Lias tries to persuade Tea Cake to evacuate by pointing to the Indians leaving. Tea Cake responds with a racist comment on the Indians he clearly sees as his inferiors: "'Dey don't always know, Indians don't know much uh nothin', tuh tell de truth. Else dey'd own dis country still. De white folks ain't gone nowhere. Dey oughta know if it's dangerous'" (231). With the new set of values Tea Cake embraces, it is fitting that, when he finally does try to leave, he takes his insurance papers with him (237) and abandons his guitar (238).[16]

Hurston embellishes her racial theme in the storm episode of the novel. Beneath the surface of what seems simply dramatic action and vivid language, she carefully develops the storm as a symbolic ritual of purification, a rejection of those characters who have betrayed the sexually egalitarian and culturally autonomous values of black life on the Muck. Hurston suggests this idea in the contrasts between those who are saved and those who perish. Characters such as Lias, Stew Beef, and Motor Boat, whom Hurston paints as ethnically secure and immune to Mrs. Turner's influence, survive. The casualties are those who look to the white world for answers, placing their trust in its power and failing to appreciate the storm's:

> The folks in the quarters and the people in the big houses further around the shore heard the big lake and wondered. The people felt uncomfortable but safe because there were the seawalls to chain the senseless monster in his bed. The folks let the people do the thinking. If the castles thought themselves secure, the cabins needn't worry. Their decision was already made as always. Chink up your cracks, shiver in your wet beds and wait on the mercy of the Lord. The bossman might have the thing stopped by morning anyway. (234)

The function of the storm as the symbolic destroyer of white power is also revealed in the language Hurston uses to depict the storm's aftermath. The apparent chaos it brings is actually described as the breakdown of artificial hierarchies; for instance, the storm dissolves boundaries between the human and the natural as the lake's waters enter the houses and a terror-stricken baby rabbit seeks refuge in the house with Janie, Tea Cake, and Motor Boat (235). Even the lines between water and land become blurred when stray fish are found "swimming in the yard" (236) and the "water full of things living and dead. Things that didn't belong in water" (244). Significantly, when these boundaries are erased, so are racial distinctions. Unable to distinguish white corpses from black, white officials are stymied in their ludicrous attempt to ensure that white corpses get coffins and black ones quick-lime (253).

The destruction wreaked by the storm is also described as an act of liberation. Destroying the dike, a futile human attempt to control Nature's power, the storm loosens the lake's "chains" (239) and turns it into "a road crusher on a cosmic scale" (239), rushing "after his supposed-to-be conquerors, rolling the people in the houses along with other timbers" (239). Tea Cake and Janie sense a new order in the bizarre scenes they encounter while trying to escape: "They passed a dead man in a sitting position on a hummock, entirely surrounded by wild animals and snakes. Common danger made common friends. Nothing sought conquest over the other" (243). Even the rattlesnakes do not bite during the storm (244) in this world momentarily purged of violence and oppression.[17]

In addition to depicting the storm as the cultural equivalent of the biblical flood, Hurston also buries in the novel an implicit definition of its identity. Its fury compared to the sound of African drums (233–34), it is subtly identified as a black power, striking at night and bringing darkness in its wake. A "God" (235, 236) at war with and finally more powerful than the false white god, it literally "put[s] out the light" (236), symbolically the white principles of hierarchy and oppression embraced by Starks and rekindled by Tea Cake. Hurston also implies a gendered identity for this power. Whereas the lake is repeatedly identified as "he" (234, 235, 239), the storm—"Havoc there with her mouth wide open" (246)—is, through Hurston's symbolic use of folk saying, labeled "she." Hurston repeats this gender identification and a reminder of the storm's power to destroy white men's creations; as Janie and Tea Cake survey the ravaged city of Palm Beach, they see "the hand of horror on everything. Houses without roofs, and roofs without houses. Steel and stone all crushed and crumbled like wood. The mother of malice had trifled with men (250–51). This black, female power cleanses the world through its flood, freeing even its male counterpart in Hurston's ironic and subversive revision of the biblical myth.

Given the changes that have occurred in Tea Cake's sense of racial and gender identity, it is not surprising that he, too, is killed as a result of events surrounding the storm. Numerous details woven into this episode suggest that his death is not merely a tragic ending to a love story but rather the symbolic expurgation of the false values he has come to represent. Hurston dramatizes these changes in Tea Cake in her description of his illness. Although he seems selfless and noble, sacrificing himself to save Janie, Hurston very subtly but carefully suggests his symbolic identity with the mad dog that bites him. Walking with a "queer loping gait, swinging his head from side to side and his jaws clenched in a funny way" (271), "snarl[ing]" and giving Janie a "look of ferocity" (269), he is no longer the bee-man Osiris but the oppressive male dog of black folk culture alluded to by Big Sweet in *Mules and Men* and critiqued in Hurston's short story, "Muttsy."[18] As these details and the fact that Janie survives even though bitten by Tea Cake suggest, the illness that kills Tea Cake is a spiritual one—symbolically, he is the mad dog and not its noble victim.

Tea Cake now presents a mortal threat to Janie, as his increasing similarity to Starks suggests. For instance, Tea Cake's first thoughts about why he might feel sick echo Starks's criticism of Janie in the store: "He was not accusing Janie of malice and design. He was accusing her of carelessness. She ought to realize that water buckets needed washing like everything else. He'd tell her about it good and proper when she got back. What was she thinking about nohow? He found himself very angry about it" (259). Whereas Janie desperately tries to "partake wid everything," pleading with Tea Cake to let her share his pain (258), the reciprocity characterizing their early relationship is glaringly absent. Like Killicks and Starks, who both hid from Janie any signs of vulnerability, Tea Cake tries to hide his illness from Janie (264), hoping his symptoms "would stop before Janie noticed anything. He wanted to try to drink water again but he didn't want her to see him fail" (264). Although Tea Cake wants to let Janie comfort him as they have done for one another repeatedly, his obsession with making her realize "'it's uh man heah'" (248) makes him fearful of appearing weak and keeps him silent (266). As he moves to control her voice (271) and her movements (268, 270), his attempt to kill Janie merely images the mortal spiritual danger he poses to her. No passive victim of an uncontrollable physical disease, "even in his delirium he took good aim" (272), his three misfired shots signaling the gravity of his betrayal.[19] The events leading up to his death, thus, demonstrate the partial truth in Nanny's comments on love. In a world of "mules and men," in which relationships between men and women are not reciprocal ones, love can be—and in Janie's relationship with Tea Cake nearly is—"de very prong . . . black women gits hung on" (41).

Although Hurston's critique is necessarily veiled, Janie's character at the end of the novel is, in some ways, even more elusive and has led to vast disagreement among critics concerning her. Whereas most have argued that she emerges from the Muck as an independent female, some have concluded at the other extreme that the novel is far from feminist, one that finally paints Janie as a devoted wife who adores a husband who beats and finally tries to kill her. Jennifer Jordan provides a strong critique of the novel that highlights some of its ambiguities. Tea Cake's death, she argues is "a typical resolution of the tale of courtly love in which the young troubadour or knight engages in an all-consuming passion with a lady of high rank. Tea Cake, the young bluesman and Janie's social inferior, falls in love with a lady, dedicates himself to making her happy, and sacrifices his life fighting a dragon, a kind of mad cow/dog/monster. Hurston creates an alliance of pure romance, a life of adventure and sexual union in a kind of Eden" (110).[20] Key to such readings of Janie as no autonomous woman is the fact that we see no reaction from Janie to Tea Cake's beating (in contrast to her realization about Joe when he slaps her [112]) and hear no comments but loving ones expressed to him as his behavior becomes more threatening. Even after his death, Janie never verbalizes any defiance of Tea Cake or understanding of the changes in him that she had expressed after Joe's death. Focusing on these silences, some critics have concluded that Janie emerges from *Their Eyes Were Watching God* not as a liberated woman but as a dependent one blinded by love.

Whereas these critics point to an important issue in our evaluation of Janie, it is not adequate to see her as simply self-deluded or her silence as Hurston's own ideological blindness. She does actually kill Tea Cake when his threat to her is a mortal one—no insignificant symbolic act—as a number of readers since Alice Walker have pointed out. With a focus on this action and the less explosive narrative possibilities open to Hurston for ending the book, Hurston's novel could just as easily be read as an inversion of the canonical story Jordan finds. To have "the lady" save herself at the novel's end stretches the seams of the genre; to have "the monster" she slays be her lover and the traditional story's hero rips them apart.

The frames at the beginning and end of the novel further suggest neither a broken nor a deluded woman. Physically powerful, "her firm buttocks like ... grape fruits in her hip pocket; the great rope of black hair swinging to her waist and unraveling in the wind like a plume; [and] her pugnacious breasts trying to bore holes in her shirt" (11), she strides into Eatonville, Hurston suggests, a strong and vigorous woman committed to life and experience despite the death of her lover. She looks over her past, not with wistful nostalgia but with a sober, philosophical eye, seeing "her life like a great tree in leaf with things suffered, things enjoyed, things done and undone" with "dawn and doom ... in the branches" (20). No stump or mere leaf, hers is not the mutilated identity of other characters in the novel who have sold themselves to dreams that destroyed them. Rather, the beginning and ending frame for the novel suggest, she has become the kind of active female imaged in her pear tree vision, one who has experienced much in her relationship with a "bee-man" but who is not defined by that relationship. In fact, when she first talks with Pheoby, she speaks not of romance and adoration of Tea Cake but of experiences much wider than love or even Tea Cake as an individual: "'Ah been a delegate to de big 'ssociation of life,'" she tells her; "'Yessuh! De Grand Lodge, de big convention of livin' is just where Ah been dis year and a half y'all ain't seen me'" (18). In contrast to some readers' focus on romance and Janie's relationship with Tea Cake, living—not just loving—is what Janie stresses in reviewing her own experience. Such a focus is also the omniscient narrator's. When in the book's final images, Janie pulls in her horizon "like a great fish-net," it is "life" (286)—including, but certainly not limited to love—that she finds in its meshes. When Janie does speak to Pheoby about love, it is not to depict her relationship with Tea Cake as perfect or necessarily even the sole love of her life but to describe love as many-faceted and ever-changing. Love, for a woman who is supremely confident and self-affirming, "'ain't somethin' lak uh grindstone dat's de same thing everywhere and do de same thing tuh everything it touch. Love is lak de sea. It's uh movin' thing, but still and all, it takes its shape from de shore it meets, and it's different with every shore'" (284). As Janie here suggests, she emerges from the novel as no conventional romantic heroine searching to duplicate her relationship with Tea Cake or turning away from life because of the futility of doing so but as an autonomous black woman who faces the future in a spirit of engagement and openness to the flux of experience, "the dawn and doom" she has learned make up love and life.

The frames at the beginning and end of the novel presenting Janie back in Eatonville are thus critical in any evaluation of her character, for they show a woman who has gained the self-affirmation and self-expression she had sought before ever meeting Tea Cake. Having found years earlier "a jewel down inside herself" that she yearned to "gleam ... around" (138) and having first done so in her relationship with him, the Janie of these frames is not a woman who "glow[s]" (146), "beam[s]" (153), and "lights up" only in the presence of her lover. At the novel's end, she walks with her own lamp, its light "like a spark of sun-stuff washing her face in fire" (285), fully able, even with her lover now dead, "to show her shine" (139).

Janie's wisdom and strength—even her regal, almost haughty indifference toward the gossip of the porch-talkers—indicate a woman, like Isis, not destroyed by the tragedy of her life but able to transform it. Just as Isis collected the parts of Osiris's body after his death and reanimated him, Janie remembers Tea Cake, not as the mad dog or even the "man" who needed assurance that he was one, but as a "bee-man," an Osirian figure her spiritual equal and appropriate counterpart. Burying him with his guitar and imagining him "prancing" through her room, she embraces the ideal of full reciprocity that characterized the best of their relationship. She brings home the symbol of that equality imaged in the pear blossom and bee— some seeds from the Muck, evidence not only of the creativity resulting from such healthy relationships between black women and men but also of her own unfinished life and future growth. The reconstituted masculinity and femininity that Hurston imagines are beautifully depicted in our final images of Tea Cake and Janie. Using the kind of androgynous images she had used earlier in the novel to suggest Janie and Tea Cake's healthy versions of male and female identity—Janie shooting a gun and Tea Cake combing her hair, for instance—Hurston closes the novel by cloaking Tea Cake with a feminine image, "with the sun for a shawl" (286), and Janie with a masculine one, her horizon draped over her shoulder "like a great fish-net" (286). As Janie's final thoughts, they show her embracing a conception of male and female identity that, transcending polarities of active/passive, strong/weak, replaces the gender hierarchies of Jim and Arvey Meserve's world.

As the fish-net image suggests, Janie's memory of Tea Cake is avowedly selective, not the self-deluded inability to distinguish among Tea Cake's different selves, as some critics have argued, but an active remembering. In collecting the "bee-man" parts of Tea Cake, she displays Isis's power to refashion a vibrant black man, one not dwarfed, mutilated, or dehumanized (as so many characters in the novel are) by submission to the dominant white world or its values. Just as Isis's act is responsible for the rebirth of spring, Janie's is not merely that of an adoring lover who saves and serves her love but one with much broader social significance. In imagining the possibility of black manhood different from Joe Starks or the "mad dog," Janie plants the seeds of a world purged of oppressive hierarchies, a world neither sexually nor racially one of mules and men.

Although the beginning and ending frames for the novel are an unequivocal tribute to Janie's stature and power—in a profound sense, the townspeople whose eyes are glued on Janie as she walks through her gate are also "watching God"—the narrative of Janie's relationship with Tea Cake is more ambiguous in its treatment of her experience and awareness. Whereas most critics who disagree about Janie tend to be selective, focusing either on Janie's silence and Tea Cake's beating or on the image of Janie at the beginning of the book, the complex relationship between both must be addressed. To smooth out the narrative wrinkles in the novel is both to simplify the tale of race and sex Hurston tells and to miss an important element of the strategy she fashioned to tell such a story.

That Janie's story should be subject to so many divergent interpretations among critics should not be surprising, for (as Hurston is careful to illustrate) the same is true for reactions to her story within the novel itself. The porch-talkers of Eatonville, for instance, who as Pheoby points out, "'done "heard" 'bout [Janie] just what they hope done happened'" (16), see in Janie's solitary return evidence of an older woman used and spurned by a young rake while the black men at her trial tell a story of a loving Tea Cake betrayed by her. The white jury and audience at Janie's trial have yet another interpretation of Janie's experience, one that Hurston carefully but quite subtly suggests is equally suspect.[21]

Even though they find her innocent of murder, Hurston emphasizes their lack of real knowledge about Janie or Tea Cake (274–75) and the limited version of Janie and Tea Cake's experience that they hear. We do not know exactly what Janie tells them (details Hurston quite strategically omits), but Dr. Simmons, who sets the stage and the tone for white reaction to Janie, focuses understandably on what he knows—Tea Cake's illness and death: Dr Simmons "told about Tea Cake's sickness and how dangerous it was to Janie and the whole town, and how he was scared for her and thought to have Tea Cake locked up in the jail, but seeing Janie's care he neglected to do it. And how he found Janie all bit in the arm, sitting on the floor and petting Tea Cake's head when he got there. And the pistol right by his hand on the floor" (276–77). This scene, as powerful for the judge and jury as it is for Dr. Simmons, is nevertheless limited and partial as "the whole truth and nothing but the truth" (278) about Janie and Tea Cake, for it erases both the vigorous equality of their relationship and the threats to it the changes in Tea Cake constitute.

The terms in which the judge presents the case to the jury, indebted to Simmons's testimony, similarly obscure the complexities of Janie and Tea Cake's relationship. He tells them to decide "'whether the defendant has committed a cold blooded murder or whether she is a poor broken creature, a devoted wife trapped by unfortunate circumstance who really in firing a rifle bullet into the heart of her late husband did a great act of mercy'" (279). With the first speakers setting the tone, it is no surprise that the jury sees in Janie's story not "a wanton killer" (279) but an adoring wife who took her loving husband out of his misery. It is an interpretation that wins her her freedom and the goodwill of the white women in the room who "cried and stood around her like a protecting wall" (280), but in its view of "Janie Woods the relic of Tea Cake's Janie" (275), it falsifies Janie's experience, diminishes her stature, and transforms the self-preservation in her shooting of Tea Cake into selfless female devotion. Like the porch-talkers, the members of the white audience at the trial have heard the tale "they hoped to hear"—in this case, a story of traditional romance with characters more nearly resembling Arvey and Jim Meserve than Janie and Tea Cake.

Constantly expressing worry about being misunderstood, Janie too seems to recognize the ambiguity of her own story. As she informs Pheoby, she wants not only to tell her her story but also to help her see its significance— "'ain't no use in me telling you somethin' unless Ah give you de understanding to go 'long wid it. Unless you see de fur, a mink skin ain't no different from a coon hide'" (19). Janie's comment indicates not only her view of Pheoby as ideal listener for her tale but also the vast difference of interpretation to which it can be subject. Without having "see[n] the fur," the white people, the porch-talkers, and the black men at the end of the novel hear what they want to hear in Janie's experience, reaching interpretations that say more about their racial and sexual identities than about Janie's.

In each of these cases, Hurston is careful to suggest that race and gender play a central role in the interpretation of Janie's story. The townspeople, the narrator explicitly announces, are not simply mean spirited gossipers but black people who "had been tongueless, earless, eyeless conveniences all day long. Mules and other brutes had occupied their skins. But now, the sun and the bossman were gone, so the skins felt powerful and human. They became lords of sounds and lesser things. They passed nations through their mouths. They sat in judgment" (9–10). Their animosity toward a black woman grows out of a context of racial oppression as does that of Sop and his friends during Janie's trial, "there with their tongues cocked and loaded, the only real weapon left to weak folks. The only killing tool they are allowed to use in the presence of white folks" (275). Echoing the reaction of Jim Allen, Joe Starks, Mrs. Turner, and others, these "mules" have made themselves feel human by dominating and dehumanizing other victims. In the hierarchical world of race and gender described by Nanny, the black woman is "the mule of the world," the bottom where not only work but also frustrated anger and misdirected aggression ultimately land.

Although the white people's reaction is very different, Hurston emphasizes that their apparent empathy and concern for Janie is as grounded in the politics of race and gender as the black men's antipathy. Hearing a different story from the one Janie tells Pheoby (before speaking, she recognizes that she "was not at home" [278]), the white audience at the trial, Hurston suggests, supports Janie for reasons having as much to do with the context in which Janie tells her story as with whatever details she provided. Undoubtedly influenced by the support of the two powerful white men, the doctor and the sheriff, the white audience is insulated from the threat the killing of a black man by a black woman poses. As the rhetorical question in the narrative—"What need had *they* to leave their richness to come look on Janie in her overalls" (274–75)—suggests, they are untouched by the intragroup struggles between black women and men that have led to Janie's trial or that are evident at it. Rather, like Joe Starks, who owned an entire town and could thus afford to pamper a yellow mule, they too have and in acquitting Janie exercise "the power to free things." Janie's action in no way a threat to their position at the top of Nanny's hierarchy, their support for her costs and risks nothing; in fact, support for a black woman in a conflict with black men buttresses their position. Because the challenge to their dominance comes from the black men at the trial, the judge is quick to protect Janie against their wrath, silencing Sop and his friends with a pointed reminder of their subordination: "'We are handling this case. Another word out of you, out of any of you niggers back there, and I'll bind you over to the big court'" (277). Eager to demonstrate their racial dominance, the white judge silences them and invites Janie to speak. His reaction, the white women's applause, and the jury's acquittal thus demonstrate not their understanding but rather their misinterpretation and appropriation of a black woman's story for their own purposes.

As Hurston suggests in detailing and evaluating the reactions of the white people and the black men (none of these people "understand" [279, 281]), a black woman's story narrated in Nanny's hierarchical world of race and gender is subject to vast differences in interpretation. The pressures of a white context, which exacerbate internal divisions, result not only in the black men's rejection of Janie but also in their more serious misreading of the power relations inherent in her story. Focusing on the white jury's exoneration of Janie, the black men astutely recognize that race has played a role in her trial (it would certainly have been a different affair, as they argue, had she shot a white man), but in missing the gendered component of the racial conflict there (the fact that the judge privileges Janie's story and silences theirs to exercise power over them), Sop and his friends erroneously conclude that "'uh white man and uh black woman is the freest thing on earth. Dey do as dey please'" (280).

Hurston earmarks Pheoby's response to Janie's story as the privileged interpretation among the wide variety it is given. Having received "the understanding" from Janie, she responds in a manner quite different from any other character in the novel. Her brief response, "'Ah done growed ten feet higher from jus' listenin' tuh you, Janie. Ah ain't satisfied wid mahself no mo'. Ah means tuh make Sam take me fishin' wid him after this'" (284), suggests that she has heard a story not of female perfidy, conventional romance, or wifely devotion but of female growth and possibility. Unlike the white women at the trial, she responds not with tears but with demands on the man in her life, evidence that she has been moved by a story of the struggles for female equality rather than one extolling the perfections of Janie's husband.

In addition to demonstrating the interaction of race and gender critical in interpretations of Janie's story, Hurston's detailed account of reactions at her trial also underscore the problems of *telling* such a story of intragroup conflict to a heterogenous audience. Like Janie at the trial, Hurston is enmeshed in a web of racial and sexual factors that make simply telling "the truth, the whole truth, and nothing but the truth" about Janie and Tea Cake the goal only of a naif. A direct presentation of conflicts between women and men would subject her to the same hostility aimed at women in the novel like Janie and Mrs. Robbins whose actions are seen to be challenges to black men and to the kind of racial exploitation evident in the white people's reactions. In telling the story of Janie and Tea Cake, Hurston threads her way through this minefield, camouflaging her story both through the careful weaving of symbols already discussed and through careful narration.

Whereas many critics have commented on Hurston's narrative technique in *Their Eyes Were Watching God*, often ultimately evaluating it quite differently, most have focused on the relationship between narrative voice and Janie's character. Several critics, assuming that the novel is the record of what Janie tells to Pheoby, argue that Janie's finding of a voice at the novel's end meshes with her achievement of autonomous selfhood. Emphasizing the fact that the novel is not narrated in first person, others have argued that Janie's failure to tell her own story is evidence that she finds neither her voice nor her independence in the novel.[22] Still other critics, including Gates, Awkward, and Callahan have discussed the multivocal quality of the narrative as, itself, an affirmation of Janie's stature.[23]

Shifting the focus from what the novel's narrative technique tells us about Janie's character to what it says about Hurston's own position in telling her story, I want to suggest that Janie does find her voice—the woman whose words kill Joe Starks and inspire Pheoby, who speaks so directly in the opening and closing frames certainly has—but that Hurston very self-consciously does not allow the reader to hear the story in Janie's own words. This aspect of the novel is not a failing—either Janie's or Hurston's—but a strategic maneuver by Hurston in telling a very incendiary tale, a strategy she uses to protect Janie and her complex tale of race and gender from the kind of exploitation and appropriation evident at her trial.

Hurston actually goes to some lengths to emphasize that the narrative is much more complicated than a simple record of what Janie told her "bosom friend" as they sat on her back porch in the darkness. In addition to the movements between first and third persons, which signal voices other than Janie's, Janie expressly refuses to tell her own story. Her comment to Pheoby, "'You can tell 'em what Ah say if you wants to. Dat's just de same as me 'cause mah tongue is in mah friend's mouf'" (17), confirms that we hear Janie's story in someone else's words, someone like Pheoby, on whom Janie can depend "'for a good thought'" (19). The character of Pheoby is thus central to discerning both the "understanding" Hurston attaches to Janie's story as well as the narrative technique she devises to convey it; for through the delineation of Pheoby's character, Hurston cleverly hints at the motives of the novel's narrator and the ways that the narrator selects details to shape the intimate version of her story for a more public heterogenous audience.

A devoted friend to Janie, Pheoby at every appearance both supports and defends her friend from the "killing tools" of the community, trying at the very beginning of the novel, for instance, to fend off malicious gossip about her and vowing at the end that "'Nobody better not criticize yuh in mah hearin'" (284). As supportive of Janie as Big Sweet and Hurston's mother were of her, Pheoby is, indeed, someone Janie can count on "for a good thought," both in real life and in her public rendering of Janie's story. Like other of

Hurston's strong black women, Pheoby is also depicted as a very savvy person who knows her community and how to negotiate power within it. When she goes to warn Janie about the community gossip, she does not go by the direct route that would draw attention to her mission and elicit inquiries about Janie's business; instead, she "picked her way over to Janie's house like a hen to a neighbor's garden. Stopped and talked a little with everyone she met, turned aside momentarily to pause at a porch or two—going straight by walking crooked. So her firm intention looked like an accident and she didn't have to give her opinion to folks along the way" (168–69). Adopting the familiar posture of Hurston's other trickster figures, Pheoby's behavior exhibits the indirection and conscious use of ambiguity that characterize the novel's narration. She also demonstrates her astute awareness of audience in the counsel she gives Janie, repeatedly advising her to be silent, not to speak about her feelings to an unsympathetic audience who could not possibly understand (127, 143, 173). Practicing what she preaches, she is careful (as Janie knows [173]) about what she reveals about Janie to others and proud to acknowledge this sign of their intimacy. As she assures Janie, "'Ah jus lak uh chicken. Chicken drink water, but he don't pee-pee'" (173).

The picture that emerges of the narrator Janie chooses to have relate her story is, thus, a surprisingly full one of someone who has heard the story in Janie's own words and whose response suggests that she represents Janie's ideal listener. Supportive of Janie and astute enough to see problems in uncritically telling her story, such a narrator can hit a straight lick with a crooked stick, narrating Janie's story to be true to its volatile themes but sensitive to the context in which they will be relayed. The novel itself is told by such a circumspect narrator. The story given to the reader is in "a friend's mouth," a "kissing friend" who tells a veiled version of her story, who keeps the full "understanding" implicit in the images and symbols to protect Janie from yet more killing tools and loaded guns.

One strategy Hurston employs is Pheoby's use of silence, keeping Janie silent at the most revealing and incendiary moments in her struggle with Tea Cake. Like Pheoby, who knows when Janie's words would be misunderstood or used against her, Hurston also frequently omits Janie's reactions to and assessments of Tea Cake's abusive behavior not necessarily because she had none but because to present them would subject her story to the same dynamics of audience seen in John's and Janie's trials. For instance, whereas many critics have assumed that Janie passively accepted Tea Cake's beating of her, the narrative itself provides no such certainty. Having shown Janie's willingness to confront Tea Cake both verbally and physically in the fight over Nunkie, such a reaction seems unlikely; but for Hurston to present it directly in the narrative would be quite problematic. Hurston's narrative solution is not only to omit whatever words and actions constitute Janie's response but also to keep her off-stage for the description of it.[24] We learn about this fight after the fact through the biased version Tea Cake braggingly conveys to an envious Sop. Significantly, we also never hear in direct address what Janie thought about Tea Cake's illness and death. The rhetorical power of Hurston's narrative strategy, her decision to put Janie's story not in first person but in her friend's mouth, is clear when one imagines what the Janie of the opening and closing frames, a woman who minces no words and who is utterly indifferent to public reaction, might say. For a black woman to say she had to kill a black man because, as Lucy had advised Isis, she loved herself more, because he had become a mortal threat to her, or because he had begun to act like a white man are words that would alienate some segments of her audience and be used by others. To circumvent those problems, Hurston uses her own "fish-net" in narrating the conflict between Janie and Tea Cake, intentionally telling a story with "holes" in it, strategic gaps and silences— how Janie responded to Tea Cake's beating, what exactly she says in court, what she did and thought on the Muck during the weeks after Tea Cake's death—that mask the conflict in their relationship.

The narrative handling of Tea Cake is equally masterful. Again, what would have been lost in a first-person narration by Janie is critical. She would not be able to provide, for instance, either Tea Cake's radically changed thoughts about Janie or his conversation (208) with Sop and his friends, both of which are important and unbiased signals of the changes that have taken place within him. The narrative approach Hurston takes allows her to convey "the understanding" of what has happened to him; but to avoid having this critique become a weapon in the hands of her own jurors, Hurston is careful to veil his violence toward Janie, to treat his "mad dog" qualities, which could so easily evoke the vengeance directed at Mrs. Robbins and feed the kind of stereotypes John Pearson fears, symbolically. As careful in picking her words to describe Tea Cake's illness as Pheoby is in picking her way to Janie's door, Hurston exploits ambiguity in her description of him, using careful phrasings that seem to exonerate Tea Cake by making him a noble victim at the same time that they pinpoint the reality of what is destroying him.

Perhaps the best example of this strategy is found in Hurston's sole reference to Janie's assessment of Tea Cake's illness and death. In narrating Janie's testimony at her trial before the divided audience that mirrors Hurston's own, the narrator conveys only a summary (and even then in indirect address) that is fraught with ambiguity: "She tried to make them see how terrible it was that things were fixed so that Tea Cake couldn't come back to himself until he had got rid of that mad dog that was in him and he couldn't get rid of the dog and live. He had to die to get rid of the dog. But she hadn't wanted to kill him. A man is up against a hard game when he must die to beat it. She made them see how she couldn't ever want to be rid of him" (278). An excellent example of how Hurston works to convey "the understanding" but mask the intragroup conflict, this passage is accurate in its implied reference to the death of Tea Cake the "bee-man" and Janie's love for "him," the malignity of the "mad dog" and the reason Janie had to kill "it," but it is also ambiguous enough to mesh with the scenario described by Dr. Simmons and the sheriff. By exploiting gaps, ambiguities, and silences in this way, Hurston intentionally tells a tale that can be read as "mink skin" or "coon hide," a story of a black woman's resistance to male oppression that sometimes looks surprisingly similar to the jury's version of Janie's relationship with Tea Cake. To protect the story of a black woman killing her husband from misuse by black men or white people, Hurston uses elements of traditional romance ultimately to subvert the genre. Buried beneath the romantic surface is the story of a woman tempted to succumb to the passive female role assigned her in the prototypical white woman's story but who does not, a woman who does finally love herself more, who neither dies at her lover's hands nor withers away after his death.

Hurston's need to camouflage female resistance is perhaps strongest in the scene in which Janie actually shoots Tea Cake. Just as she had used elements of the supernatural to mask female resistance of "Black Death" and *Jonah's Gourd Vine*, Hurston camouflages female aggression against sexual oppression in this scene through the use of romantic elements, carefully describing Janie's shooting of Tea Cake both to imply the import of her act and to veil its volatile implications. To do so, she depicts the internal struggle in Janie's mind between one woman tempted to protect her lover whatever the cost and another who protects herself from aggressive threat even in the person of her beloved. The entire passage battles between two different selves and two different narrative voices. When Janie first notices the gun under Tea Cake's pillow she responds with surprisingly rational thought, sizing up the situation, weighing alternatives, and taking action. Rushing to see if it is loaded, she checks the ammunition, starts to load the gun, but thinks with foresight, "he might break it and find out she knew. That might urge his disordered mind to action" (270). Neither immobilized by devotion nor content to be sacrificed, she whirls the cylinder to make sure his first three shots will be blanks. Her actions methodical, knowledgeable, and deliberate, she then finds the rifle and strategically moves it to the kitchen "almost behind the stove where it was hard to see" (270). Similarly, immediately before shooting Tea Cake, Janie is in control of her actions, moving "deftly" (272) as she raises her gun, assessing Tea Cake's aim with enough calm to recognize its accuracy. No actions of an acquiescent woman like Arvey, who is paralyzed by her husband's violence, they are, in fact, those of a traditional male hero who skillfully and calmly slays the monster.

Attempting to protect her story from white appropriation and "the killing tools" of black men, Hurston is careful to temper this portion of the narrative with elements of traditional romance. As the narrative reveals Janie unhesitatingly moving to save herself, a different voice (articulating the battle within Janie) utters reassuring words in sharp contrast to her actions: "Tea Cake wouldn't hurt *her*. He was jealous and wanted to scare her. She'd just be in the kitchen as usual and never let on. They would laugh over it when he got well" (270). This passage and others in this section—"Of course she was too fussy, but it did no harm to play safe. She ought not to let sick Tea Cake do something that would drive him crazy when he found out what he had done" (270–71)—both convey the inner conflict in Janie and camouflage the self-possession and undeniable violence of her action. With the real dramatic tension in this scene arising from uncertainty not about what Tea Cake will do so much as about what Janie will, Hurston's narrative vacillation mirrors Janie's struggle: will she play this scene as the love-struck and passive "tender woman" described by Sop or as one of his "ol rusty black women" (218–19) who defends herself.

Although the narrative excuses Janie's actions and the momentous answer to this question that her behavior finally bespeaks as the mere instinct (272) of a scared human being fighting for her life, Hurston shows Janie exhibiting the power imaged in the storm, in Big Sweet, and in her own earlier defiance of Joe when she shoots Tea Cake, acting (as other strong black women in her fiction sometimes must) to purge from her life the racial, spiritual, and sexual threat that Tea Cake has come to represent.[25] At that moment, the woman whom nearly everyone in her life—Nanny, Joe, Sop, and finally even Tea Cake—has tried to make live as a white woman, rejects that role. Only because she resists her greatest temptation to play it and breaks out of the narrow margins of traditional romance is she able to emerge as the autonomous black woman we see in the opening and closing frames of the novel.

This moment, a critical one for Janie in her quest, is also the most volatile one for Hurston in her narration. Hurston thus rounds out the scene with a picture of Janie coddling a dead Tea Cake in her arms:

> It was the meanest moment of eternity. A minute before she was just a scared human being fighting for its life. Now she was her sacrificing self with Tea Cake's head in her lap. She had wanted him to live so much and he was dead. No hour is ever eternity, but it has its right to weep. Janie held his head tightly to her breast and wept and thanked him wordlessly for giving her the chance for loving service. She had to hug him tight for soon he would be gone, and she had to tell him for the last time. (273–74)

Whereas Hurston here uses the tableau that so affects the white jurors and underpins their interpretation of Janie's experience, it is important to recall how tangential it is to Pheoby's. As the fact that she does not respond to Janie's story with vows to take her "sacrificing self" home to give Sam some "loving service" suggests (in fact, "sacrifice" and "service" are hardly the words any of Hurston's readers would use to epitomize Janie and Tea Cake's relationship), Hurston works here to allow a story of female resistance to "pass" as romance, to create an ending that would make possible Janie's "acquittal" with Hurston's own divided audience. That this was Hurston's struggle in the passage is supported by a look at earlier versions of it. Defining "loving service" in the manuscript as "cooking and washing his clothes and such intimacies as patching overalls" (103, JWJ), Hurston deletes that phrase (almost as if she realized it strained credulity, however well it masked the import of Janie's actions) and substitutes the second and third sentences to create a more plausible but still traditional romantic ending for an explosive, conflict-ridden narrative sequence.

The narrator of *Their Eyes Were Watching God* thus tells a Janus-faced story, a tale not only of a woman torn between two identities but one that exploits the resulting ambiguities in relating it to a heterogenous audience. As in the John tales, which succeed because the divided audience finally hears two very different stories in them, Hurston uses elements of romance in narrating Janie's temptation to succumb to it ultimately to mask her treatment of contentious "family matters." Just as white people could hear John tales but miss the import, hear "some scraps" but "not understand because they had nothing to hear things like that with. They were not looking for any hope in those days" ("High John," 70), Hurston counts on and even exploits misunderstanding by some segments of her audience. But the story of a black woman's struggle to define herself as neither mule nor white woman is also there for the Pheobys in Hurston's audience who are looking for hope and models of female resistance. Drawing on traditions of black expressivity in this way, Hurston—even though writing in Nanny's world and, like her, unable to "preach a great sermon about colored women sittin' on high" (32)—is able to "save the text" (32), to tell for those listeners a story not of traditional romance but of quest, not of selfless female devotion but of survival and self-affirming autonomy.

NOTES

    1. John Lowe has discussed the numerous parallels between Janie and the Roman god, Janus.
    2. Significantly, these nonthreatening and apparently apolitical features of the novel were responsible for its popularity with most reviewers in mainstream publications, who often praised Hurston's language, "its raciness, its rich invention, and its music" (Stevens, 3) and the "refreshingly pagan undercurrent·of the joy of life" in the novel (Brickell). (For

similar comments, see also reviews written by Tompkins and Thompson.) Often lapsing into racially stereotypical language to express their enthusiasm, white reviewers sometimes linked their enthusiasm for Hurston's primitivism with approval for her apparent avoidance of The Race Problem. One reviewer, for instance, breathed a sigh of relief that Hurston had written "a simple and unpretentious story" that "never comes to the verge of conscious, sentimental sympathy" (Stevens, 3). Another admired Hurston's picture of black life "in its naturally creative and unselfconscious grace" and found the book (thankfully) "unlimbered of the clumsy formality, defiance and apology of a Minority Cause" (Ferguson).

For a number of her black contemporaries, those features of the novel were precisely the source of criticism. Disillusioned with white voyeuristic response to primitivism during the Harlem Renaissance both Alain Locke and Richard Wright felt that *Their Eyes Were Watching God* reinforced white stereotypes of blacks. Locke found the novel's poetic dazzle superficial and its primitive joyousness simple-minded:

> But as always thus far with this talented writer, setting and surprising flashes of contemporary folk lore are the main point. Her gift for poetic phrase, for rare dialect and folk humor keep her flashing on the surface of her community and her characters and from diving down deep either to the inner psychology of characterization or to sharp analysis of the social background. It is folklore fiction at its best, which we gratefully accept as an overdue replacement for so much faulty local color fiction about Negroes. But when will the Negro novelist of maturity who knows how to tell a story convincingly,—which is Miss Hurston's cradle-gift, come to grips with motive fiction and social document fiction? Progressive southern fiction has already banished the legend of these entertaining pseudo-primitives whom the reading public still loves to laugh with, weep over and envy. Having gotten rid of condescension, let us now get rid of over-simplification! ("Review of Negro Books," 10)

Definitely the most damning review was that published by Richard Wright in *New Masses*. Like Locke, he found Hurston's mastery of language and the story's apparent primitive simplicity most problematic. Her language, "cloaked in ... facile sensuality," "manages to catch the psychological movements of the Negro folk-mind in their pure simplicity, but that's as far as it goes." The book is all surface dazzle; its "sensory sweep ... carries no theme, no message, no thought." Wright's most scathing remarks were directed at what he saw as Hurston's capitulation to white demands for harmless images of blacks: "Miss Hurston *voluntarily* continues in her novel the tradition which was *forced* upon the Negro in the theater, that is, the minstrel technique that makes the 'white folks' laugh. Her characters eat and laugh and cry and work and kill; they swing like a pendulum eternally in that safe and narrow orbit in which America likes to see the Negro live: between laughter and tears."

Of reviews written by her black male contemporaries, the most sympathetic was an unenthusiastic one by Sterling Brown. In less vitriolic language than Wright, he too notes the apparent lack of social commentary in *Their Eyes Were Watching God*: "Living in an all-colored town, these people escape the worst pressures of class and caste. There is little harshness; there is enough money and work to go around. The author does not dwell upon the 'people ugly from ignorance and broken from being poor' who swarm upon the 'muck' for short-time jobs" ("Luck is Fortune"). In a final, undeveloped thought, he points to an aspect of the novel overlooked by other—black or white—reviewers, what he called a "bitterness," sometimes explicit, but often "oblique, in the enforced folk manner" (Brown 110). Although Hurston would have disliked Brown's term, "bitterness," he accurately points to the novel's underlying attack on the white world and to her strategy for making it.

Hurston's oblique method in the novel has also been commented on by Wilentz, who argues that *Their Eyes Were Watching God* is "a novel of resistance" in which Hurston "tricks the white readership by her own positive resistance her ability to negate the values of the dominant culture ... without once saying it outright" (291). Crabtree's discussion of the ways Hurston uses folk material self-consciously and symbolically to develop her themes is also an important one for my own. Echoing the sentiments of Hurston's contemporary reviewers, various critics, including Ford, Gloster, and Byrd, have argued that Hurston ignored race in *Their Eyes Were Watching God*. Those focusing on her treatment of race include Wilentz, Benesch, Washington, and Giles.

3. The manuscript provides evidence that Hurston gradually developed the mule metaphor in writing the novel. This speech by Nanny is inserted in the manuscript, and the story of Matt Bonner's mule (81–85, 86–99) is not in the handwritten manuscript.

4. The limitations of Nanny's vision have been noticed by numerous critics, including Giles (52), Awkward ("'The Inaudible Voice,'" 68) and Crabtree (62). One of the few who stresses the value in her remarks is Lillie Howard, who argues that "Nanny's vision is clearer than Janie's" ("Nanny and Janie: Will the Twain Ever Meet?" 407).

5. The contrast between this metaphor for male/female sexual relationships and that described in *Seraph on the Suwanee* is striking. When Arvey is raped by her future husband under the mulberry tree, Hurston images this phallic rapaciousness in her description of the tree, its "new green leaves, punctuated by tiny fuzzy things that looked like green stubby worms" (34).

6. Critics who have discussed Starks's symbolic whiteness include Washington, Crabtree, Wilentz, Awkward ("'The Inaudible Voice,'" 75), Wall (385), Benesch, and Giles.

7. That Jody sees his act in this way is evident in his comparison of the lamp to the power of "de Sun-Maker" (72). That at least some members of the community accept this interpretation is revealed in the hymn Mrs. Bogle sings at the celebration, "Jesus, the light of the world" (73). The story of Starks's installation of the light post was not part of Hurston's original conception of the novel, for it is absent in the manuscript version of the novel.

8. This complex symbol is also absent in the handwritten manuscript.

9. Darwin Turner has criticized this chapter of the novel: "Digressive and unnecessary, the chapter merely suggests that Miss Hurston did not know how to integrate the folk material which she considered essential for local color" (107).

10. Hurston made Mrs. Robbins's character more ambiguous in the published version of the novel, leaving us with only the men's comments about her. In the manuscript version, her bizarre habit of begging is explained in a sympathetic way that makes the men's response seem even more cruel: "Somehow she had felt like telling Janie about her half-starved childhood and the fear that it might happen to her own children. A little 'off' on the subject of food." See "Eatonville Anthology" for another version of this woman's behavior (*I Love Myself When I Am Laughing*, 177–78).

11. In contrast to Turner's argument that Janie's act is unnecessarily cruel (108), McCredie, Lupton, and Ferguson have discussed its role in freeing Janie.

12. The emptiness of this love talk is obvious when they actually scrape together enough money to buy Daisy a pickled pig's foot (109).

13. The ease with which she can be banished from the community is clear when she flees after the men stage a mock fight that destroys her restaurant. Dealing with her as black tricksters do whites, Tea Cake orchestrates the destruction while appearing to be

Mrs. Turner's ally (233). Thoroughly duped by Tea Cake's smiling mask, "Mrs. Turner beamed on Tea Cake" (223) before returning to Miami.

14. Critical opinion is divided on the ultimate evaluation Hurston makes of Tea Cake's character in the novel. Those who see him as an ideal include Bone, Wilentz, Carr, Thornton, Naylor, McCredie, and S. Jay Walker. Especially revealing of the way an emphasis on race alone slights Tea Cake's faults is the argument put forth by Benesch. Acknowledging the traditional sex roles Tea Cake's beating reinstitutes, he dismisses its significance: "However, according to my argument, Janie's development is above all a function of her meaningful participation in black folk traditions, and only secondarily depends on the opposition of a woman to gender-related expectations" (634). Critics who do emphasize shortcomings in Tea Cake toward the end of the novel include Hooks ("A Subversive Reading"), Pondrom, Ferguson, Lloyd Brown, Saunders, Lupton, Curren, Kathleen Davies, and Awkward ("'The Inaudible Voice'").

15. Tea Cake's respect for money is repeated after the storm. The danger of his false values is evident in his comment to Janie reassuring her that it is safe for him to venture out into Palm Beach: "Ah got money on men, Janie. Dey can't bother me" (250). While he seems to think money erases his blackness, his capture and forced labor by white men reveals how misguided Tea Cake is. This comment, not present in the handwritten manuscript, represents another instance of Hurston strengthening the depiction of Tea Cake's whiteness.

16. Hurston added many of these details that suggest Tea Cake's acceptance of white values in the process of writing the novel. Neither of the comments about the superior judgment of white people appear in the handwritten version. Tea Cake's abandonment of his guitar is inserted in that version.

17. For other discussions of the storm's significance, see Curren, Hubbard, Kathleen Davies, and Gordon Thompson.

18. See Chapter 15, "Risque Tales," in Dance's *Shuckin' and Jivin'* (262–305) for numerous examples of the male as dog in black folk culture.

19. Hurston's description of her own relationship with A. W. P., which was, she asserts, the basis for *Their Eyes Were Watching God*, underscores the seduction and the hazards of such a conception of masculinity. Her lover's desire to "be a *man!*" (*Dust Tracks on a Road*, 253) strong and independent, easily slipped over into something more deadly: "That very manliness, sweet as it was, made us both suffer" (253), she discovered, for it involved a concomitant notion of womanliness in conflict with Hurston's independence. As he becomes more and more "the master kind" (257) and she "his slave" (258), she finally had to "fight [her]self free from [her] obsession" (260) by escaping to Jamaica and work.

20. Most critics, including Carr, Kubitschek, Naylor, Wolff, Wilentz, and Ferguson, have argued that Janie achieves liberation in the novel. Those painting a more qualified portrait of Janie include Reich, Awkward ("'The Inaudible Voice'"), Jordan, duCille, Krasner, Levecq, and Lloyd Brown.

21. For other discussions of Janie's trial, see DuPlessis (102–6), Callahan (140–41), Brigham (416–17), Lowe (190–94), Kaplan (127–31), and Henderson (21–22).

22. Stepto (166), Bell (123), Turner (109), and Hemenway (*Zora Neale Hurston*, 233) have all found the third-person narrative in the novel problematic.

23. Gates, for instance, has argued that Hurston's multivocal narrative voice "echoes and aspires to the status of the impersonality, anonymity, and authority of the black vernacular tradition, a nameless, selfless tradition, at once collective and compelling, true somehow to the unwritten text of a common blackness" (*The Signifying Monkey*, 183). In a similar vein, Awkward, rather than viewing third-person narrative as a flaw, sees it as confirmation

of Janie's status "as a communally oriented, culturally informed Afro-American woman" ("'The Inaudible Voice,'" 100). Callahan has emphasized the narrative's relation to the "rhetoric of intimacy," a relationship between Hurston's voice and Janie's characterized by cooperation and support (119). Critics who have also examined the narrative's multivocal quality include Brigham, Racine, and Kalb. For an excellent review of criticism on the novel's narration, see Awkward's discussion.

24. Awkward ("'The Inaudible Voice'") suggests a very different view of Janie's silence in response to Tea Cake's beating, which he sees as "an application of the strategic self-division that she had employed in her second marriage. She withdraws, when Tea Cake beats her, into voiceless absence. She no more accepts his abuse 'without flinching' than she accepts Starks's mistreatment. Rather, her silence indicates that she employs what has been her only means of protest throughout the entire text of the novel" (85).

25. Critics who see Janie's shooting of Tea Cake as a blow for freedom include Saunders, Ferguson, Lupton, Lloyd Brown, Sadoff, and Willis, who describes it as "the books strongest statement" (71). Alice Walker has argued that Tea Cake's beating of Janie is "the reason Hurston *permits* Janie to kill Tea Cake" (305). Thomas Cassidy has also argued that "events of the hurricane leading to Tea Cake's death after being bit by a mad dog can be read as an eruption of Janie's unconscious turmoil and rage" (261).

DEBORAH CLARKE

"The porch couldn't talk for looking": Voice and Vision in Their Eyes Were Watching God

"So 'taint no use in me telling you somethin unless Ah give you de understandin to go 'long wid it. Unless you see de fur, a mink skin ain't no different from a coon hide." (Hurston, *Their Eyes* 7)

W hen Janie explains to her friend Pheoby the reason that simply telling her story will not suffice, why she needs to provide the "'understandin' to go 'long wid it'," she employs a metaphor of vision: Unless you see the fur, you can't tell a mink from a coon. Stripped of their defining visual characteristics, the hides collapse into sameness. Recognizing visual difference, Hurston suggests, is crucial to understanding how identity is constructed: by skin and color. With this claim, she invokes new avenues into an African American tradition that has privileged voice as its empowering trope. From Phillis Wheatley's demonstration that an African can have a poetic voice, to Frederick Douglass's realization that freedom is measured by words and the ability to address a white audience, to Charles Chesnutt's presentation of the triumph of black storytelling in *The Conjure Woman*, voice has prevailed as the primary medium through which African American writers have asserted identity and humanity. Voice announced that visual difference was only skin deep, that black bodies housed souls that were, in essence, no different from those residing in white bodies. *Their Eyes Were Watching God*

From *African American Review,* vol. 35, no. 4, pp. 599–613, © 2001 by Deborah Clarke.

is very much a part of this tradition, and has inspired many fine studies on the ways that its protagonist finds a voice and a self.[1] Yet, as others have pointed out, Janie's voice is by no means unequivocally established by the end of the book. Robert Stepto was among the first to express dissatisfaction with the narrative structure and its third-person narrator; for him, the use of the narrator implies that "Janie has not really won her voice and self after all" (166). More recently, Michael Awkward has pointed out that Janie is not interested in telling the community her story upon her return (6), and Mary Helen Washington argues that Janie is silenced at crucial spots in the narrative. Carla Kaplan, reviewing the discussions of voice that the novel has inspired, examines the ways that voice is both celebrated and undermined, noting that "Hurston privileges dialogue and storytelling at the same time as she represents and applauds Janie's refusal to speak" (121). Clearly, Janie's achievement of a voice is critical to her journey to self-awareness, but the highly ambivalent presentation of voice in the novel indicates that voice alone is not enough. As Maria Tai Wolff notes, "For telling to be successful, it must become a presentation of sights with words. The best talkers are 'big picture talkers'" (226). For Hurston, then, the construction of African American identity requires a voice that can make you see, a voice that celebrates the visible presence of black bodies.

I would suggest that, with its privileging of "mind pictures" over words, *Their Eyes Were Watching God* goes beyond a narrative authority based solely on voice, for, as Janie tells Pheoby, "'Talkin' don't amount tuh uh hill uh beans when yuh can't do nothin' else'" (183). In contrast to Joe Starks, who seeks to be a "big voice" only to have his wish become humiliatingly true when Janie informs him that he "'big-bellies round here and put out a lot of brag, but 'tain't nothin' to it but yo' big voice'" (75), Janie seeks for a voice which can picture, which can make you see. The ability to use voice visually provides a literary space for African American women to relate their experiences in a world where, as Nanny says, "'We don't know nothin' but what we see'" (14). Thus, to expand "what we see" increases what we know. Throughout the novel, Hurston's use of visual imagery challenges dominant theories about the power hierarchies embedded in sight, long associated with white control, with Plato's rationality and logic, and, from a Freudian perspective, with male sexual dominance. She recasts the visual to affirm the beauty and power of color and to provide a vehicle for female agency.

In so doing, Hurston opens up different ways of conceptualizing the African American experience. Responding to the long history of blacks as spectacle—from slavery to minstrelsy to colonized object—she offers the possibility of reclaiming the visual as a means of black expression and black power. Controlling vision means controlling what we see, how we define the world. Visual power, then, brings political power, since those who determine what is seen determine what exists.[2]

In recent times, the Rodney King beating trial highlighted the significance of this power, when white interpretation sought to reverse the apparent vision presented by the video of the assault. Commenting on the trial, Judith Butler writes that the "visual field is not neutral to the question of race; it is itself a racial formation, an episteme, hegemonic and forceful" (17). Zora Neale Hurston recognized this, anticipating what Houston Baker terms the "'scening' of the African presence" as a means of silencing that presence (42). As opposed to the King jurors, who learned not to see what was presented, Hurston's Janie makes readers "see" her story, and thus takes control of both the visual field and its interpretation. Visual control is not, obviously, the answer to racist oppression: Had the jurors "seen" what happened to Rodney King, it would not have undone his beating, and Hurston fully realized that black bodies bear the material evidence of racial violence (indeed, Janie's perceived beauty—her long hair and light skin—results from an interracial rape). But by taking visual control, Hurston looks back, challenges white dominance, and documents its material abuse of African Americans.

She thus manages to present a material self that can withstand the power of the gaze, transforming it into a source of strength. In establishing a rhetoric of sight, Hurston ensures that black bodies remain powerfully visible throughout the novel, particularly the bodies of black women.[3] As Audre Lorde has noted, visibility is the cornerstone of black female identity, "without which we cannot truly live":

> Within this country where racial difference creates a constant, if unspoken, distortion of vision, Black women have on one hand always been highly visible, and so, on the other hand, have been rendered invisible through the depersonalization of racism. Even within the women's movement, we have had to fight, and still do, for that very visibility which also renders us most vulnerable, our Blackness.... And that visibility which makes us most vulnerable is that which also is the source of our greatest strength. (Lorde 42)

In attempting to reclaim visibility, Hurston focuses not just on rendering black bodies visible, but also on redeeming the "distortion of vision" of which Lorde speaks. Neither is an easy task, for Janie's visible beauty makes her vulnerable to both adoration and abuse, and the ability to see does not come readily. As the title of the novel indicates, Hurston is interested in far more than the development of one woman's journey to self-knowledge; she seeks to find a discourse that celebrates both the voices and the bodies of African Americans. By emphasizing "watching God," she foregrounds sight.

The existing theoretical work on vision is both useful and limiting for one seeking to understand Hurston's use of visual language. While various feminist theorists such as Braidotti, Haraway, and Keller have contributed greatly to our understanding of the topic, joining film theorists Mulvey, Doane, and Silverman, their work does not always take race sufficiently into account, though Jane Gaines reminds us of the racial privilege inherent in the gaze: "Some groups," she remarks, "have historically had the license to 'look' openly while other groups have 'looked' illicitly" (25). Some African American theorists such as Fanon, Wallace, and hooks do engage issues of visibility, but it is surprisingly under-examined in African American literary and film theory despite the fact that the visual is critical to black female identity, the source, Lorde insists, of black women's vulnerability and strength. Michelle Wallace has noted that "black women are more often visualized in mainstream American culture ... than they are allowed to speak their own words or speak about their condition as women of color" (*Invisibility* 3). Hurston takes this visualization and turns it into a source of strength and a kind of language, thus redeeming visibility and establishing voice. While vision has long been associated with objectivity, this objective position has been assumed to be raceless (white) and sexless (male). Hurston exposes these dynamics, and in so doing lays the groundwork for a kind of vision that embodies blackness as both body and voice. The visible presence of Janie's material body reflects the complex historical and cultural forces which have created her and offers her a unique, individual identity. The visual, then, allows for a negotiation between the post-structuralist argument that identity is largely a construction and the concerns, particularly by non-whites, that such a position erases individual identity and presence just as non-white peoples are beginning to lay claim to them. Awareness of the visible brings together the "politics of positioning," of who can look, with a recognition of the political and psychological significance of the gaze and with the "real" presence of a material body and individual self (Braidotti 73).

Hurston's insistence on the importance of visual expression, of course, stems largely from racism's disregard for African American individuality. In "What White Publishers Won't Print," Hurston explains the American attitude toward blacks as "THE AMERICAN MUSEUM OF UNNATURAL HISTORY. This is an intangible built on folk belief. It is assumed that all non-Anglo-Saxons are uncomplicated stereotypes. Everybody knows all about them. They are lay figures mounted in the museum where all may take them in at a glance" (170).[4] By characterizing the white American perspective as that of museum-goers, Hurston suggests that the non-white population becomes mere spectacle, "lay figures" to be taken in "at a glance" by white eyes. We generally see this power dynamic in operation when black bodies are displayed. In minstrel shows, as Eric Lott points out, "'Black' figures were there to be looked at, shaped to the demands of desire; they were screens on which audience fantasy could rest, and while this purpose might have had a host of different effects, its fundamental outcome was to secure the position of white spectators as superior, controlling figures" (140–41).

The dynamic still exists. Steven Spielberg's 1997 film *Amistad*, for example, opens with an extended display of naked black bodies and offers its black cast few words, inviting the public to view blackness rather than listen to it.[5] One is defined by how one is seen. For African Americans, this leads to a condition of "hypervisibility," in which "the very publicness of black people as a social fact works to undermine the possibility of actually seeing black specificity" (Lubiano 187). We need only look to Frantz Fanon for confirmation: ". . . already I am being dissected under white eyes, the only real eyes. I am *fixed*. . . . I feel, I see in those white faces that it is not a new man who has come in, but a new kind of man, a new genus. Why, it's a Negro!" (116). The racist power of visibility thus seems daunting, but Hurston not only takes on the challenge of reclaiming the visual as racially affirmative, she does so in response to a masculinist tradition in which visual power so often objectifies women. Her fiction reveals that, even in the context of a black community, the ability to see "black specificity" may be impaired, particularly when the specific individual is a woman. Hurston, a student of Franz Boas, who pioneered the participant-observer model of anthropological study, recognized the need for looking closely and carefully.[6]

Their Eyes opens with almost an anthropological tone, presenting us with a group of people who have been "tongueless, earless, eyeless conveniences all day long" (1). After spending their days erased by white eyes as a specific presence, they become talkers and lookers. In order to regain human identity after "mules and other brutes had occupied their skins," they need to speak, listen, and see. It is important to note that Hurston equates all three sensory apparati; she does not privilege the verbal over the visual. Just as Pheoby's "hungry listening" helps Janie tell her story, so Janie's keen vision provides her with a story to tell. This vision is far different from one which "glances" at objects in a museum; such a way of seeing merely replicates white erasure of everything but skin color. Hurston seeks a uniquely African American vision, a way of seeing that both recognizes color and sees beyond it. But being black does not automatically confer, for Hurston, visual ability. In fact, visual language is predominately associated with women in her work. As Michelle Wallace has observed, "Gender is as important as 'race' to understanding how 'invisibility' has worked historically in all fields of visual production" ("Race" 258). Initially, the "big picture talkers" are male in this novel, and much of the talk centers on impressing and evaluating women. Janie's first appearance in Eatonville causes Hicks to proclaim his plans to get a woman just like her "'Wid mah talk'" (34). Hurston's challenge is to redeploy the language of the visual in ways that do not simply re-evoke the objectification of women of any color by situating them as objects of the male gaze.

In a culture that has so long defined black people as spectacle and black women as sexualized bodies, one needs to transform and redeem the potential of vision. While the visual certainly holds the threat of objectification, it can also serve as action—both personal and political. bell hooks argues that, for blacks, looking can be viewed as an act of resistance. She asserts that "all attempts to repress our/black peoples' right to gaze ... produced in us an overwhelming longing to look, a rebellious desire, an oppositional gaze." With this gaze African Americans declared, "Not only will I stare. I want my look to change reality" (116). Looking becomes an act charged with political resistance, a way to reconfigure the world and its power dynamics.[7] One must look, then, at African American writing as a means of challenging the power of the white gaze. We need to employ what Mae Henderson terms a new "angle of vision" (161), a means of looking back, of seeing without objectifying. To analyze Hurston's "angle of vision," I would argue, necessitates bringing together a wide range of theoretical perspectives, for seeing and being seen are highly complex acts in her fiction, acts which place individuals within an intricate web of personal and historical forces.

In Hurston's work, looking is more than a confrontational challenge. Her fiction is replete with examples of women's need to look, see, understand, and use language visually. In "Drenched in Light," an autobiographical story which recalls Hurston's descriptions of her childhood days, Isis, "a visual minded child," "pictur[es] herself gazing over the edge of the world into the abyss" (942). She escapes punishment for her many mischievous actions by impressing a white lady as being "drenched in light" (946); her strong visual force marks her as a child destined for creative accomplishment. Delia, the protagonist of "Sweat," prefigures Janie in her use of visual metaphors to reevaluate her marriage. "She lay awake, gazing upon the debris that cluttered their matrimonial trail. Not an image left standing along the way" (957). This visual realization grants Delia the strength to defy her abusive husband. "The Gilded Six-Bits" presents the story of Missie May, unable to see through the shining currency to recognize its meager value; this mis-sight leads her to an affair with the man who owns the false coins, nearly ruining her marriage. Interestingly, her husband Joe finally forgives her when her son is born and turns out to be "'de spittin image'" (995) of Joe himself. Only visual proof of paternity can erase his anger.

Jonah's Gourd Vine, in many ways a pre-text for *Their Eyes*, examines many of the same issues of voice and identity with a male protagonist. But though John Pearson, like Janie Crawford, struggles to establish a self, he does not employ her rhetoric of sight. In fact, his white boss specifically associates him with blindness as an explanation for John's lack of foresight:

> "Of course you did not know. Because God has given to all men the gift of blindness. That is to say that He has cursed but few with vision. Ever hear tell of a happy prophet? This old world wouldn't roll on the way He started it if men could see. Ha! In fact, I think God Himself was looking off when you went and got yourself born." (86)

Not only is John a result of God's blindness, but John consistently fails to see his way, particularly in failing to pick up on Hattie's use of conjure tricks to entrap him into a second marriage. The vision in the novel belongs to his first wife, Lucy. She is the one whose "large bright eyes looked thru and beyond him and saw too much" (112). Lucy, far more self-aware and perceptive than John, harnesses the power of vision so successfully that her visions live on after her death. Interestingly, when John finally does attain a degree of vision, it proves highly ambiguous and problematic, leading to his death when he drives his car into a railroad crossing: "He drove on but half-seeing the railroad from looking inward" (167). Lacking Lucy's ability to put her visual power to practical use, John fatally blinds himself to his surroundings and pays the ultimate price for his inability to see. Here Hurston sets up her paradigm: Vision must be embodied, one must see outwardly as well as inwardly.

Hurston establishes the full power of the visual in *Their Eyes Were Watching God*. Initially subjected to the defining and objectifying power of a communal gaze, Janie, unlike John Pearson, learns to employ vision in ways that are self-affirming rather than self-sacrificing. Returning to Eatonville at the novel's start, Janie finds herself in a position very familiar to her. the object that all eyes are upon. When she approaches, the people are full of hostile questions to which they "hoped the answers were cruel and strange" (4). But when she keeps on walking, refusing to stop and acquiesce to their voyeuristic desires, talk becomes specularization: "The porch couldn't talk for looking." The men notice her "firm buttocks like she had grape fruits in her hip pockets; the great rope of black hair swinging to her waist and unraveling in the wind like a plume; then her pugnacious breasts trying to bore holes in her shirt." The women focus on the "faded shirt and muddy overalls." Looking at her body, the men see her as sexed; for the women, gazing on her apparel, she is gendered. In both cases, it seems, Janie vanishes. The men define her as female body parts and the women deny her feminine identity. While the female resentment of her attire may seem less intrusive than the male x-ray vision, both looks constitute "mass cruelty" (2). Yet having set up Janie as spectacle, Hurston then illuminates the positive potential of vision in the ensuing interchange with Pheoby. Here, the visual takes on a different tone. Just as voice, according to Kaplan, becomes a kind of double-edged sword, so can vision—particularly when shared between friends—both specularize and affirm. Pheoby tells Janie, "'Gal you sho looks *good*.... Even wid dem overhalls on, you shows yo' womanhood'" (4). What she sees is presence, not absence. To look like a woman is to look good, a way of visualizing which does not fixate on sexual anatomy but which allows for materiality. She shows her womanhood, a far different sight than that gazed upon by the men, who see not Janie's presence but their own desire, desire which her body is expected to satisfy.

The materiality of Janie's body as an object of desire has, of course, determined much of her history. Her first husband, Logan Killicks, presumably wants to marry her based on what he sees, though her own eyes tell her something very different: "'He look like some old skullhead in de grave yard'" (13). But her vision lacks authority; despite what her eyes tell her, she is married off to him, defeated by Nanny's powerful story of her own oppression which seems to give her the right to impose her will upon Janie. Having "'save[d] de text,'" Nanny uses language to desecrate Janie's vision of the pear tree (16). Joe Starks, Janie's next husband, is likewise attracted to her beauty: "He stopped and looked hard, and then he asked her for a cool drink of water." This time, Janie does not submit passively to this specularization, and tries to look back, to return the gaze, pumping the water "until she got a good look at the man" (26). But her look still lacks the controlling power of the male gaze, what hooks call the ability to "change reality." At this point, Janie has difficulty even seeing reality, as is evidenced by her inability to see through Joe Starks. She takes "a lot of looks at him and she was proud of what she saw. Kind of portly, like rich white folks" (32). What Janie sees is whiteness, and her valuation of this sets her on a path that will take twenty years to reverse. Looking at Joe's silk shirt, she overlooks his language of hierarchy, his desire to be a big voice. She has privileged the wrong kind of sight, a vision that fails to see into blackness and thus fails to see through language.

Still, Janie is not entirely fooled. Joe does "not represent sun-up and pollen and blooming trees, but he spoke for far horizon. He spoke for change and chance" (28). Janie thus gives up a vision she has seen—that of the pear tree—in favor of one she can only imagine: horizons, chance, and change. In allowing herself to be swayed by his language, she fails to notice that his rhetoric is that of speech, not vision. Joe only speaks; he does not see. Consequently, Janie's own vision deteriorates even further. Having initially recognized that Joe does not represent "sun-up and pollen," she later manages to convince herself that he does: "From now on until death she was going to have flower dust and springtime sprinkled over everything. A bee for her bloom" (31). Stubbornly, she tries to force Joe into her vision, possibly to justify running off with him. Convincing herself to see what is not there leads Janie into an unequal marriage in which she is expected to sit on a "high chair" (58), an infantilizing position where she can overlook the world and yet also be subjected to its envious eyes.

But Joe has a problem, for while he wants to put Janie on display in order to reap the benefit of reflected glory as her owner, this is precisely the position which is threatened by the eyes of other men. He wants her to be both present and absent, both visible and invisible, a task he attempts to accomplish by insisting that she keep her hair tied up in a head rag because he sees the other men not just "figuratively wallowing in it" (51) but literally touching it, and she "was there in the store for him to look at, not those others" (52). Joe wants to engage privately in scopophilia within a public forum, without subjecting Janie herself to this public gaze. Once she is fixed by gazes other than his own, he loses his exclusive ownership of her body. As Lorde notes, while visibility entails vulnerability, it can also be a source of great strength, a characteristic Joe certainly does not want to see in Janie. But the situation reflects more than Joe's concern about Janie's gaining cultural power; Janie's visibility also invokes a classic Freudian scenario. Laura Mulvey, in her groundbreaking psychoanalytic study "Visual Pleasure and Narrative Cinema," notes that the female figure, beyond providing pleasure for the looker, also implies a certain threat: "her lack of a penis, implying a threat of castration and hence unpleasure.... Thus the woman as icon, displayed for the gaze and enjoyment of the men, the active controllers of the look, always threatens to evoke the anxiety it originally signified" (21). Indeed, Joe's greatest anxiety is not focused on Janie's body but on his own. He wants to have the dominant position, but without being visually objectified by the viewers. "The more his back ached and his muscle dissolved into fat and the fat melted off his bones the more fractious he became with Janie. Especially in the store. The more people in there the more ridicule he poured over her body to point attention away from his own" (73–74).

But the racial situation problematizes this notion of woman as icon, which presumes looking to be a masculine act. The cultural permutations of the significance of the gaze within the African American community challenge a strictly Freudian reading. If looking is an act of political defiance, it cannot be exclusively associated with black masculinity, particularly given the long history of black female activism and resistance. When Janie challenges Joe, she does so not just to defend her female identity—"'Ah'm uh woman every inch of me'" (75)—but also to protest against Joe's almost constant oppression. Joe, with his prosperity and seemingly white values, fails to realize that his mouth is not all-powerful, that, despite his favorite expression, "I god," he is not divine. His centrality as mayor and store owner renders him even more vulnerable to specularization than Janie, and he falls prey to a kind of reversed Freudian schema of the gaze which entails serious repercussions for his political power.

Having set up the dynamics of the body as visualized object, Joe becomes its victim, as Janie linguistically performs the castration of which she is the visual reminder. As she tells him publicly, "'When you pull down yo' britches, you look lak de change uh life,'" her pictorial language renders it impossible for him to deny the vision she creates. He tries to erase the image by questioning her speech. "'Wha—whut's dat you said?'" It doesn't work, however, for Walter taunts him, "'You heard her, you ain't blind.'" This comment highlights the interconnection between hearing and seeing; to hear is to see. And yet, given the words of her insult, Joe might as well be blind, for Janie has, in fact, revealed his lack of visual difference. By not using a visual metaphor in this case, she emphasizes that there is nothing there to see. She bares his body to the communal gaze, not only denying his masculinity but displaying his lack to other men: "She had cast down his empty armor before men and they had laughed, would keep on laughing" (75). Feminized by the visual dynamics that he has established, Joe dies, unable to withstand the gaze which erases his masculinity and identifies him as empty armor. Not only is it impossible for him to continue as mayor under these circumstances, it is impossible for him to continue. Joe has no life once denied both sexual and political power.

Though Hurston uses the visual to expose the vulnerability of a phallocentrism which abuses women, she also recognizes its empowering potential. In transforming the visual into a tool of female power, Hurston reclaims the power of the visual as a vehicle for examining African American women's experiences. After all, if one erases vision, one erases race, which is culturally visualized by the physical body, the sign of visual difference. As Michelle Wallace notes, "How one is seen (as black) and, therefore, what one sees (in a white world) is always already crucial to one's existence as an Afro-American. The very markers that reveal you to the rest of the world, your dark skin and your kinky/curly hair, are visual" ("Modernism" 40). Racial visibility as a marker of difference allows black women to "show" their womanhood.

Yet, as Joe's experience makes clear, this must be a particular kind of vision, a way of seeing which expands rather than limits understanding. Despite Joe's entrapment in his own gaze, the novel is replete with examples of the affirmative quality of the visual. Janie's attempts to define a self originate with the act of looking. Her "conscious life" begins with her vision of the pear tree, leading to her sexual awakening. Having felt called to "gaze on a mystery" (10), she beholds a "revelation" in the bees and flowers. She seeks her own place in the picture, searching for "confirmation of the voice and vision." Looking down the road, she sees a "glorious being" whom, in her "former blindness," she had known as "shiftless Johnny Taylor." But the "golden dust of pollen" which "beglamored his rags and her eyes" changes her perspective (11). Johnny Taylor's kiss, espied by Nanny, sets Janie's course in motion. Whether or not Johnny Taylor represents a better possibility is both impossible to determine and irrelevant; what matters is Janie's realization that her fate is linked to her vision, though the recognition will lead her astray until she learns effectively to interpret what she sees.

This vision, after her mistake in mis-seeing Joe Starks, is finally fulfilled when she meets Tea Cake, a man who is willing to display himself rather than subject others to his defining gaze. When Janie says, "'Look lak Ah seen you somewhere,'" he replies, "'Ah'm easy tuh see on Church Street most any day or night'" (90–91). By denying any anxiety in thus being viewed, Tea Cake transforms sight from a controlling, defining gaze into a personal introduction, demystifying himself by inviting inspection. In fact, Tea Cake cautions her about the importance of looking closely in the ensuing checkers game, challenging her claim that he has no right to jump her king because "'Ah wuz lookin' off when you went and stuck yo' men right up next tuh mine. No fair!'" Tea Cake answers, "'You ain't supposed tuh look off, Mis' Starks. It's de biggest part uh de game tuh watch out!'" (92). His response underscores the importance of watching, of using one's vision not to fix and specularize but to see and think, to understand. Consequently, Janie realizes that he "could be a bee to a blossom—a pear tree blossom in the spring" (101), a man who can confirm her initial vision. She defines him with visual metaphors: "He was a glance from God." This metaphor highlights Tea Cake's connection to the visual; he recognizes the need to combine voice with understanding, remarking that Janie needs "'tellin' and showin'"" (102) to believe in love.

But Janie does not need simply to find a man capable of assimilating voice and vision, she needs to learn for herself how to formulate a self which is not predicated upon oppression. She finds the task particularly challenging because her racial identity is founded upon invisibility, upon her inability to see herself. The photograph which reveals her color, her difference, divides her from her previous notion of the identity of sameness: "'Before Ah seen de picture Ah thought Ah wuz just like de rest.'" To be black is to be not just different but absent, for Janie looks at the photograph asking, "'Where is me? Ah don't see me'" (9). Both blackness and femininity are culturally predicated upon lack; thus Janie needs to learn to show her womanhood and to find visible presence in blackness. Priscilla Wald has suggested that Janie's problem with seeing herself stems from her "white eyes": "The white eyes with which Janie looks see the black self as absent, that is, do not see the black self at all" (83). This is a particularly important point, for it indicates that Janie needs not just vision, but black vision—black eyes. Vision, which initially divides her from herself, must then provide the means for re-inventing a self, one in which racial identity adds wholeness rather than division. To deny either her blackness or her whiteness is to deny the specificity of her being, for her body is the site of the physical evidence of white oppression and a partially white origin. The answer is not to retreat into colorlessness but to reconstitute the definition of the self into something that acknowledges the conditions of her physical being: the visible evidence of her whiteness and her blackness, the heritage of slavery and sexual abuse.

Janie takes the first step toward acquiring this visual sense of self in response to Joe's oppression. "Then one day she sat and watched the shadow of herself going about tending store and prostrating itself before Jody, while all the time she herself sat under a shady tree with the wind blowing through her hair and clothes" (73). She sees the self that prostrates itself before Jody as her shadow, and this realization acts on her "like a drug," offering an escape from an oppressive life. In order to move from passive spectator to active doer, however, she needs to take that vision further. The act of seeing must become active and affirmative before she can re-integrate the disparate parts of her identity into one unified whole. As Andrew Lakritz has written, "Some of the most powerful moments in Zora Neale Hurston's writings occur when a figure in the narrative is represented as watching events unfold, when such acts of looking become constitutive of the entire question of identity" (17). But looking itself does not automatically constitute identity; one must learn how to do it. Barbara Johnson's much cited analysis of Janie's recognition of her division into inside and outside also can be viewed as an experience in learning to use the visual. Johnson identifies Janie's realization that the spirit of the marriage has left the bedroom and moved into the parlor as an "externalization of the inner, a metaphorically grounded metonymy," while the following paragraph where Janie sees her image of Jody tumble off a shelf "presents an internalization of the outer, or a metonymically grounded metaphor." This moment leads Janie to a voice which "grows not out of her identity but out of her division into inside and outside. Knowing how not to mix them is knowing that articulate language requires the co-presence of two distinct poles, not their collapse into oneness" (Johnson 212). If, indeed, the moment leads her to voice, it does not lead to a voice of self-assertion, as Janie remains silent under Joe's oppressive control for several more years.

I would suggest that the moment does not engender Janie's voice so much as it moves her toward a way of visualizing her experience which will, in time, lead her toward a picturing voice. In imagining her marriage as living in the parlor, she creates, as Johnson notes, a metonymy. But her metaphor of Joe as statue is also a metaphor infused with vision:

> She stood there until something fell off the shelf inside her. Then she went inside there to see what it was. It was her image of Jody tumbled down and shattered. But looking at it she saw that it never was the flesh and blood figure of her dreams. Just something she had grabbed up to drape her dreams over. In a way she turned her back upon the image where it lay and looked further. She had no more blossomy openings dusting pollen over her man, neither any glistening young fruit where the petals used to be. . . . She had an inside and an outside now and suddenly she knew how not to mix them. (67–68)

The significance of this moment lies not just in Janie's recognition of the division between inside and outside but also in the ability to turn her back on the image and "look further." No longer content with surface vision, Janie is learning to "look further," a necessary precondition for finding an expressive voice.

Joe's death offers her further opportunity to use this knowledge as she fixes her gaze upon herself. Janie goes to the mirror and looks "hard at her skin and features. The young girl was gone, but a handsome woman had taken her place" (83). This scene illustrates why vision is so crucial to Hurston's work. Recalling Butler's comment that the "visual field" is a "racial formation," one sees Hurston establishing precisely that. In looking hard at her "skin and features," Janie looks hard at her interracial body, seeing it now not as different but as handsome. She uses her own vision to find beauty and value in her visually inscribed racial identity. She then burns her head rags, symbol of Joe's attempts to deny her beauty and to hide her from the communal gaze while subjecting her to his own. Displaying her abundant hair, presumably another indication of her racially mixed heritage, brings her still closer to an affirmation of her visual self, a self that celebrates rather than denying the mark of race—of both races. Kaja Silverman asserts that the "eye can confer the active gift of love upon bodies which have long been accustomed to neglect and disdain. It can also put what is alien or inconsequential into contact with what is most personal and psychically significant" (227). Even before Janie gains the aid of Tea Cake's loving eye, her own eyes confer love upon her body as she begins to assimilate what has often seemed an alien world into her own psyche.

Janie transforms her understanding of color so that the sting of her original recognition of her photograph, "'Aw! aw! Ah'm colored!'" (9), can be alleviated and reversed by recognizing the visual beauty of color. The evening she meets Tea Cake, she watches the moon rise, "its amber fluid . . . drenching the earth" (95). This scene reveals the darkness of night to be full of color, transcending the stark blackness of the sky and whiteness of the moon. Hurston thus presents color as a full range of variation and beauty. Janie starts wearing blue because Tea Cake likes to see her in it, telling Pheoby not only that visual mourning should not last longer than grief, but that "'de world picked out black and white for mournin'" (107–08). By specifically associating mourning with black and white, Hurston subtly suggests that going beyond the color binary moves one from grief to happiness, from mourning and loss to fulfillment. She further challenges the black–white binary with the episode after the storm in the Everglades, when Tea Cake is forcibly conscripted into burying bodies. The white overseers insist that the workers "'examine every last one of 'em and find out if they's white or black'" (162). This ridiculous and horrific command inspires Tea Cake to comment, "'Look lak dey think God don't know nothin' 'bout de Jim Crow law'" (163). The suggestion that God needs the aid of coffins to "see" racial difference again highlights the absurdity of seeing the world only in terms of black and white. By tying vision so intricately to race, Hurston offers a way out of the oppositional hierarchy of both.[8]

Thus Hurston destabilizes the visual racial binary, and Janie learns a new respect for color and for her own image. She restores the image that was desecrated by the photograph, when Tea Cake tells her to look in the mirror so she can take pleasure from her looks. "Fortunately," says Silverman, "no look ever takes place once and for all" (223). As Hurston well understands, looking is not a static activity. To "transform the value," as Silverman puts it, of what is seen, one needs to use one's life-experience in order to see it better. Having stood up to her husband, survived the gossip implicating her in his death, taken over the business, and dared to consider a lover, Janie learns to transform her gaze into one that accepts and values her own image.

After learning to use her vision to value herself, Janie is ready to take the next step: using vision to find God. The title episode of the novel reveals the full importance of the power of sight and of being an active looker; watching God is an active rather than a passive enterprise.

> They sat in company with others in other shanties, their eyes straining against crude walls and their souls asking if He meant to measure their puny might against His. They seemed to be staring at the dark, but their eyes were watching God. (151)

Like Alice Walker in *The Color Purple*, Hurston re-visions the old white man with a long beard. Instead, one approaches God not just in darkness but by looking *through* darkness, to see God where others see blackness. In so doing, she enables a kind of vision that deifies darkness, replacing the emptiness with presence, presence in blackness. At the height of the storm,

Janie tells Tea Cake, "'If you kin see de light at daybreak, you don't keer if you die at dusk'" (151). Since she can "see" the light in darkness, neither it nor death holds any fear for her. By having her characters watch God in darkness, Hurston redefines rationalist and masculine control of the gaze, transforming scopophilia into spirituality. Her enabled gaze does not make women specularizable, for it takes place in darkness; rather, it makes God viewable and blackness visible. Similarly, in Toni Morrison's *Paradise*, the midwife Lone, trying to find out what the men plan to do to the women at the convent, sits in the dark to read the signs: "Playing blind was to avoid the language God spoke in. He did not thunder instructions or whisper messages into ears. Oh, no. He was a liberating God. A teacher who taught you how to learn, to see for yourself" (273). Learning how to see—particularly, learning how to see in darkness—takes on special meaning for African American women. One comes to God not through light but through the ability to see in the dark.

But Hurston's world is not solely visual; material bodies exist tactilly as well as visually, and color is not always beautiful, as the historical forces of slavery and oppression can be read on Janie's body. She is the product of two generations of rape, one of them interracial. She suffers physically for her interracial body when Tea Cake beats her to display his ownership in the face of Mrs. Turner's theories of Janie's superiority due to her light skin. The bruises, of course, are clearly evident precisely because of that light skin, as Sop-de-Bottom enviously remarks, "'Uh person can see every place you hit her'" (140). These marks inscribe both visually and physically the full implications of her racial identity as well as the violence that brought it into being. Just as black women cannot ignore the visual, neither can they escape the tactile, a physical language which highlights the material racist and sexist abuse of the body.[9] As Sharon Davie argues, Hurston's bodily metaphors "acknowledge the tactile, the physical, which Western culture devalues" (454). But Hurston does more than acknowledge the tactile; she reveals it. In Hurston's world, the mark of violence is seen, making the tactile visual. Though she celebrates the power of vision, she has no illusions that it can erase or replace the discourse of violence and racism. Rather, it documents, for all to see, the effects of brutality.

Janie's act of killing is an act of physical self-defense to protect the body that Tea Cake has restored to her. Yet even this highly tactile response has a visual component. She waits for a sign from the sky, a visual indication that God will relent and spare Tea Cake's life, but "the sky stayed hard looking and quiet" (169). I find it telling that this is a daytime supplication, as Janie seeks to find a message "beyond blue ether's bosom," waiting for a "star in the daytime, maybe, or the sun to shout." This daylight sky appears much less accessible to her searching eyes than the blackness of the storm. The God sought in darkness evokes a reaffirmation of love, but this light (skinned?) God forces murder. Lack of visual contact spells doom, and Tea Cake's vision consequently suffers to the point where the "fiend in him must kill and Janie was the only thing living he saw" (175). Thus Tea Cake's death both saves Janie's physical body and erases his false vision.

Her final test involves learning to integrate voice and vision in a different form of self-defense. The trial scene reconstitutes Janie as speaker rather than object. The spectators are there not to watch but to listen. Janie's verbal defense succeeds because she "makes them see," a phrase repeated three times in six sentences:

> She had to go way back to let them know how she and Tea Cake had been with one another so they could see she could never shoot Tea Cake out of malice.
>
> She tried to make them *see* how terrible it was that things were fixed so that Tea Cake couldn't come back to himself until he had got rid of that mad dog that was in him. . . . She made them *see* how she couldn't ever want to be rid of him. (178; emphasis added)

Despite critical concern with the narrator replacing Janie's voice at this crucial moment, we must recognize that Janie has made them see, as she has already made the reader see, that voice at this moment is subordinate to the ability to visualize, an effect that may be heightened by Hurston's deflection of Janie's story. We don't need to hear her, since we can see her story. She manages to refute the implications of the black male spectators, that "'dem white mens wuzn't goin tuh do nothin' tuh no woman dat look lak her'" (179), and they turn their anger against Mrs. Turner's brother who puts "himself where men's wives could look at him" (181). But Janie's looks have not been directed at him; she has been too busy learning to visualize to waste time specularizing.

Consequently, she returns home to discover "'dis house ain't so absent of things lak it used tuh be befo' Tea Cake come along'" (182). Having learned to make presence out of absence, she can now not only re-visualize Tea Cake, whose "memory made pictures of love and light against the wall," but can also call "in her soul to come and see" (184). In thus successfully employing a visualized voice, Janie becomes both spectator and participant in her own life. To speak the body, for an African American woman, means to recognize its visual racial difference as well as affirming its sexual identity. Hurston's mind-pictures and seeing-voices reclaim the physical world of pear trees and the beauty of the visible presence of blackness. As Hurston herself noted, pictorial language is of primary importance in black discourse, where everything is "illustrated. So we can say that the white man thinks in a written language and the Negro thinks in hieroglyphics" ("Characteristics" 24). By filling Janie "full of that oldest human longing-self revelation" (*Their Eyes* 6), Hurston presents a text of "revelation"—with all of its visual implications. Her hieroglyphics reflect a community of people whose world is their canvas and whose lives and bodies are pictured in living color.

She thus provides a model for reconciling voice and vision, for transforming black bodies from museum pieces or ethnographic objects into embodied voices, by recasting spectacle as visual, a move away from passive sensationalism to active participation. Hortense Spillers notes of the Du Boisian double-consciousness that "it is also noteworthy that his provocative claims . . . crosses [*sic*] their wires with the specular and spectacular: the sensation of looking at oneself and of imagining being seen through the eyes of another is precisely performative in what it demands of a participant on the other end of the gaze" (143). In Hurston's hands, looking is indeed a performative act. In fact, it becomes a linguistic performance which affirms bodily presence, reversing Fanon's claim that, in the white world, "consciousness of the body is solely a negating activity" (110). Hurston, as Priscilla Wald so aptly puts it, "redesignates 'color' as performance in a process that draws her readers into the dynamics of 'coloration'" (87). Through the use of hieroglyphics, she reconstitutes women as active and colored performers. Vision, so often a means of fixing and silencing African Americans, can also provide the means to foreground the body without surrendering the voice. As the title of Hurston's novel indicates, her concern goes beyond presenting an individual woman's journey to self-awareness; her accomplishment is nothing less than redefining African American rhetoric, rendering it verbal and visual.

Notes

1. Along with several studies cited within the text of my article, the following represent only a few of the many fine analyses of various aspects of voice and language in *Their Eyes*: Bond; Brigham; Callahan; Gates, "Zora"; Holloway; Kubitschek; McKay; Racine; Wall.

2. For more on the political power of the visual, see Rosi Braidotti, especially 73.

3. In this, Hurston differs markedly from Ralph Ellison, who focuses not so much on attaining vision as on the implications of invisibility. Whereas Ellison documents in intricate detail the confines of being invisible, Hurston examines the process of learning to see and be seen.

4. Indeed, in film theory, as Miriam Hansen points out, "an aesthetics of the glance is replacing the aesthetics of the gaze" (135). This reflects a move from the intensity of a gaze to the glance, "momentary and casual" (50), according to John Ellis, who notes that, with a glance, "no extraordinary effort is being invested in the activity of looking" (137). While this may result in a less controlling and hegemonic situation, it can also, as Hurston indicates, illustrate a lack of deep perception.

5. Film, both popular and documentary, has long specularized black bodies. According to Fatimah Tobing Rony, early-twentieth-century ethnographic films "incessantly visualized race" (267).

6. I am indebted to Lori Jirousek's 1999 Penn State dissertation "Immigrant Ethnographers: Critical Observations in Turn-of-the-Century America" for better understanding the significance of Boas to Hurston's fiction.

7. Indeed, vision can offer a challenge to the links which Homi Bhabha has traced between the scopic drive and colonial surveillance (28–29).

8. As Donna Haraway has suggested, "Vision can be good for avoiding binary oppositions" (188).

9. Again, we see further evidence in Morrison's work in Beloved's scar and Sethe's "tree"; like Hurston, Morrison demands that one read the body visually.

Works Cited

Awkward, Michael. *Inspiring Influences: Tradition, Revision, and Afro-American Women's Novels*. New York: Columbia UP, 1989.

Baker, Houston A. "Scene . . . Not Heard." Gooding-Williams 38–48.

Bhabha, Homi K. "The Other Question . . .: The Stereotype and Colonial Discourse." *Screen* 24.6 (1983): 18–36.

Bond, Cynthia. "Language, Speech, and Difference in *Their Eyes Were Watching God*." Gates and Appiah 204–17.

Braidotti, Rosi. *Nomadic Subjects: Embodiment and Sexual Difference in Contemporary Feminist Theory*. New York: Columbia UP, 1994.

Brigham, Cathy. "The Talking Frame of Zora Neale Hurston's Talking Book: Storytelling as Dialectic in *Their Eyes Were Watching God*." *CLA Journal* 37.4 (1994): 402–19.

Butler, Judith. "Endangered/Endangering: Schematic Racism and White Paranoia." Gooding-Williams 15–22.

Callahan, John F. *In the African-American Grain: The Pursuit of Voice in Twentieth-Century Black Fiction*. Urbana: U of Illinois P, 1988.

Davie, Sharon. "Free Mules, Talking Buzzards, and Cracked Plates: The Politics of Dislocation in *Their Eyes Were Watching God*." *PMLA* 108 (1993): 446–59.

Doane, Marianne. *The Desire to Desire: The Woman's Film of the 1940s*. Bloomington: Indiana UP, 1987.

Ellis, John. *Visible Fictions: Cinema, Television, Video*. Boston: Routledge & Kegan Paul, 1982.

Fanon, Frantz. *Black Skin, White Masks: The Experiences of a Black Man in a White World*. Trans. Charles Lam Markmann. New York: Grove P, 1967.

Gaines, Jane. "White Privileging and Looking Relations: Race and Gender in Feminist Film Theory." *Screen* 29.4 (1988): 12–27.

Gates, Henry Louis, Jr., "Zora Neale Hurston and the Speakerly Text." *Southern Literature and Literary Theory*. Ed. Jefferson Humphries. Athens: U of Georgia P, 1990. 142–69.

Gates, Henry Louis, Jr., and K. A. Appiah, eds. *Zora Neale Hurston: Critical Perspectives Past and Present*. New York: Armistad P, 1993.

Gooding-Williams, Robert, ed. *Reading Rodney King, Reading Urban Uprising*. New York: Routledge, 1993.

Hansen, Miriam. "Early Cinema, Late Cinema: Transformations of the Public Sphere." *Viewing Positions: Ways of Seeing Film*. Ed. Linda Williams. New Brunswick: Rutgers UP, 1995. 134–52.

Haraway, Donna. "Situated Knowledges: The Science Question in Feminism and the Privilege of Partial Perspective." *Simians, Cyborgs, and Women: The Reinvention of Nature*. London: Free Association Books, 1991. 183–201.

Henderson, Mae G. "Response" to Houston A. Baker, Jr.'s "There Is No More Beautiful Way: Theory and the Poetics of Afro-American Women's Writing." *Afro–American Literary Study in the 1990s*. Ed. Houston A. Baker, Jr., and Patricia Redmond. Chicago: U of Chicago P, 1989. 155–63.

Holloway, Karla F. C. *The Character of the Word: The Texts of Zora Neale Hurston*. Westport: Greenwood P, 1987.

hooks, bell. *Black Looks: Race and Representation*. Boston: South End P, 1992.

Hurston, Zora Neale. "Characteristics of Negro Expression." 1934. *Negro: An Anthology*. Ed. Nancy Cunard. Ed. and abridged by Hugh Ford. New York: Frederick Ungar, 1970. 39–46.

———. "Drenched in Light." 1924. *Zora* 940–48.

———. "The Gilded Six-Bits." 1933. *Zora* 985–96.

———. *Jonah's Gourd Vine*. 1934. *Zora* 1–171.

———. "Sweat." 1926. *Zora* 955–67.

———. *Their Eyes Were Watching God*. 1937. New York: Harper, 1990.

———. "What White Publishers Won't Print." 1950. *I Love Myself When I Am Laughing . . . And Then Again When I Am Looking Mean and Impressive*. Ed. Alice Walker. Old Westbury: Feminist P, 1979. 169–73.

———. *Zora Neale Hurston: Novels and Stories*. New York: Library of America, 1995.

Johnson, Barbara. "Metaphor, Metonymy and Voice in *Their Eyes Were Watching God*." *Black Literature and Literary Theory*. Ed. Henry Louis Gates, Jr. New York: Methuen, 1984. 205–19.

Kaplan, Carla. "The Erotics of Talk: 'That Oldest Human Longing' in *Their Eyes Were Watching God*." *American Literature* 67.1 (1995): 115–42.

Kubitschek, Missy Dehn. "'Tuh de Horizon and Back': The Female Quest in *Their Eyes Were Watching God*." *Black American Literature Forum* 17 (1983): 109–15.

Lakritz, Andrew. "Identification and Difference: Structures of Privilege in Cultural Criticism." *Who Can Speak?: Authority and Critical Identity*. Ed. Judith Roof and Robyn Wiegman. Urbana: U of Illinois P, 1995. 3–29.

Lorde, Audre. *Sister Outsider*. Trumansburg, NY: Crossing P, 1984.

Loft, Eric. *Love and Theft: Blackface Minstrelsy and the American Working Class*. New York: Oxford UP, 1993.

Lubiano, Wahneema. "Don't Talk with Your Eyes Closed: Caught in the Hollywood Gun Sights." *Borders, Boundaries, and Frames: Cultural Criticism and Cultural Studies*. Ed. Mae Henderson. New York: Routledge, 1995. 185–201.

McKay, Nellie. "'Crayon Enlargements of Life': Zora Neale Hurston's *Their Eyes Were Watching God*." *New Essays on Their Eyes Were Watching God*. Ed. Michael Awkward. Cambridge: Cambridge UP, 1990.

Morrison, Toni. *Paradise*. New York: Knopf, 1998.

Mulvey, Laura. *Visual and Other Pleasures*. Bloomington: Indiana UP, 1989.

Racine, Maria J. "Voice and Interiority in Zora Neale Hurston's *Their Eyes Were Watching God*." *African American Review* 28 (1994): 283–92.

Rony, Fatimah Tobing. "Those Who Squat and Those Who Sit: The Iconography of Race in the 1895 Films of Felix-Louis Regnault." *Camera Obscura* 28 (Jan. 1992): 263–89.

Silverman, Kaja. *The Threshold of the Visible World*. New York: Routledge, 1996.

Spillers, Hortense J. "'All the Things You Could Be by Now, If Sigmund Freud's Wife Was Your Mother': Psychoanalysis and Race." *Female Subjects in Black and White: Race, Psychoanalysis, Feminism*. Ed. Elizabeth Abel, Barbara Christian, and Helene Moglen. Berkeley: U of California P, 1997. 135–58.

Stepto, Robert. *From Behind the Veil*. Urbana: U of Illinois P, 1979.

Wald, Priscilla. "Becoming 'Colored': The Self-Authorized Language of Difference in Zora Neale Hurston." *American Literary History* 2.1 (1990): 79–100.

Wall, Cheryl. "Zora Neale Hurston: Changing Her Own Words." *American Novelists Revisited: Essays in Feminist Criticism*. Ed. Fritz Fleischmann. Boston: Hall, 1982. 371–93.

Wallace, Michelle. *Invisibility Blues: From Pop to Theory*. New York: Verso P, 1990.

———. "Modernism, Postmodernism and the Problem of the Visual in Afro-American Culture." *Out There: Marginalization and Contemporary Cultures*. Ed. Russell Ferguson, Martha Gever, Trinh T. Minh-ha, and Cornel West. Cambridge: MIT P, 1990. 39–50.

———. "Race, Gender, and Psychoanalysis in Forties Films: *Lost Boundaries, Home of the Brave*, and *The Quiet One*." *Black American Cinema*. Ed. Manthia Diawara. New York: Routledge: 1993. 257–71.

Washington, Mary Helen. "'I Love the Way Janie Crawford Left Her Husbands': Emergent Female Hero." Gates and Appiah 98–110.

Wolff, Maria Tai. "Listening and Living: Reading and Experience in *Their Eyes Were Watching God*." Gates and Appiah 218–29.

Young, Lola. *Fear of the Dark: "Race," Gender and Sexuality in the Cinema*. New York: Routledge, 1996.

RYAN SIMMONS

"The Hierarchy Itself": *Hurston's* Their Eyes Were Watching God *and the Sacrifice of Narrative Authority*

The authoritarian relation between the one who commands and the one who obeys rests neither on common reason nor on the power of the one who commands; what they have in common is the hierarchy itself, whose rightness and legitimacy both recognize and where both have their predetermined stable place. (Arendt 93)

There was something about Joe Starks that cowed the town. It was not because of physical fear. He was no fist fighter. His bulk was not even imposing as men go. Neither was it because he was more literate than the rest. Something else made men give way before him. He had a bow-down command in his face, and every step he took made the thing more tangible. (Hurston, *Their Eyes* 44)

Ａs both Hannah Arendt and Zora Neale Hurston recognized, and indeed as most contemporary political scientists and literary critics would agree, authority figures are able to exercise power for reasons that are complex; authority is not a simple matter of physical or intellectual coercion. The social and psychological complexities of power, however, are difficult to articulate. Hurston's *Their Eyes Were Watching God* is one extended attempt to articulate these complexities. Even more importantly, *Their Eyes* offers a critique of

From *African American Review*, vol. 36, no. 2, pp. 181–193, © 2002 by Ryan Simmons.

more than one model of political authority. Though the novel shows Hurston
to be sympathetic to the felt need for African American leadership (about
which W. E. B. Du Bois, for example, felt strongly), and even to concede that
improved material conditions for African Americans could be bought by
adherence to strong leadership, Hurston indicates that the cost of traditional
authority is too great. In subscribing to traditional Anglo-American
authority patterns, African Americans risk replicating the very means of
their oppression, Hurston perceived. *Their Eyes*, then, represents a troubled
search for a "third way," a method for breaking out from the accommodating
and replicating patterns of, respectively, Logan Killicks and Joe Starks.[1]

The many recent critics of *Their Eyes* have frequently read the novel as a
celebration of Janie's ability to free herself from the confinement represented
by her first two husbands and, after the death of her third husband, Tea
Cake Woods, to attain a new form of cultural power, the ability to shape her
own story. Henry Louis Gates, for example, claims that Janie discovers her
own narrative power when she rhetorically "kills her husband" Joe (192), and
that Joe's methods are supplanted by Janie's development of a "communal
narration"—one that is inclusive rather than exclusive of the voices within the
listening community—which is also Hurston's major innovation in this novel
(200, 214). Others who have found in Janie a model of political self-assertion
include Alice Walker, Susan Willis, Glynis Carr, SallyAnn Ferguson, Wendy
J. McCredie, Jerome E. Thornton, and Robert Hemenway. On the other
hand, some critics have found that Hurston illustrates with this novel Janie's
highly *limited* potential for political assertion. Robert Stepto raised this issue
at a session at the 1979 MLA convention (Washington, Foreword xi) and
does so again in his book *From Behind the Veil*: "Hurston's curious insistence
on having Janie's tale ... told by an omniscient third person, rather than
by a first-person narrator, implies that Janie has not really won her voice
and self after all" (166). Mary Helen Washington concurs in part, agreeing
with Stepto that Janie is not empowered but contending that Hurston is
intentionally illustrating "women's exclusion from power, particularly from
the power of oral speech" ("'I Love'" 98).

Members of both camps—those who regard Janie, in the end, as
empowered or defeated—have noticed that Hurston is critiquing the
assumptions traditionally held by writers and readers about the uses of
narrative prose. One member of the former camp is Sharon Davie. While
conceding that Hurston necessarily speaks from "within" the culture she is
critiquing, Davie admires Hurston's ability to "create for readers a glimpse
of a 'force' excluded from ideologies or languages that assume a binary and
hierarchical model of reality," even as this force is "excluded from [Hurston's]
ideology and language" (447). For Davie, Hurston suggests this nearly
indescribable force when she describes Janie's signifying rebuttal to Joe's

abusive words, and when she uses physical experience (in the Tea Cake section especially) "as a reminder that human beings cannot know, much less control, everything with their rational minds" (456). Writing from the latter camp, Michael Awkward doubts that power arises from "an independent voice such as Janie's individual (first-person) narration" (45), but contends nonetheless that "Hurston's narrative strategies demonstrate not a failure of the novelist's art, but her stunning success in *denigrating* the genre of the novel" (17). Whether or not one feels that Janie is able to use self-expression to overcome her confinement as an African American woman, most critics agree that Janie's author manages to achieve, or at least suggest, liberating possibilities for narrative, and that she does this by exposing the limits of rigidly hierarchical expectations for narrative prose.

It cannot be emphasized enough, however, how difficult and uncertain a task Hurston recognizes the revision of her readers' narrative expectations to be. Davie notes the salient question: "How are moments that disrupt the expectation of a hierarchy of meanings—the expectation that one meaning will stand still on top—politically useful?" (456). How did Hurston reconcile her central argument about authority—that aspiring to be a "big voice," as Joe does, is oppressive to others and self-defeating—with her own aspiration to write a novel, and a politically-oriented one at that? Although I agree with the common critical perceptions that Hurston attempts to replace traditional authorship and its rigid, hierarchical language with alternative forms of narration and power, my discussion of *Their Eyes* will also attempt to articulate Hurston's sense of loss in her attempt to demolish the authority of a leader and author such as Joe. In sacrificing traditional notions of authorship, one gives something up in the hope of leading to something better—a strategy that, at best, is no guarantee of success. And the success Hurston realized in producing this book has come, for the most part, after many years and great personal sacrifice for the writer herself. For decades a nearly forgotten figure of the Harlem Renaissance, Hurston died in obscurity, and the importance of her writing has been recognized only by means of a long and complicated process of recovery.

Despite the recent proliferation of scholarship on *Their Eyes*, surprisingly little close attention has been given to the character of Joe ("Jody") Starks, the mayor of the innovative all-black town of Eatonville, Florida.[2] Yet Joe, and what he represents in the book, is an important component of Hurston's political message and of her own self-conception as an author. For all his faults, Joe is not merely what Janie and Hurston define themselves against. He also represents a type of power that, Hurston suggests, must be sacrificed only with regret. Gates is—as far as I know—alone in pointing to Joe's major significance to Hurston's conceptions of narrative and authorship: He writes,

"Joe is the text's figure of authority and voice, indeed the authority of voice. . . .
Joe is the figure of the male author" (206).

Though Gates does not fully elaborate this reading of Joe Starks,
the concept of authorship—and its companion term, authority—that Joe
represents is worth exploring, especially since much of the recent attention
to the novel has, appropriately, been to Hurston's restructuring of narrative
technique and of the authority to define the self. Furthermore, Joe is very
much like many of the other authority figures encountered in American
political texts since Henry Adams's *Democracy*. Hurston, it appears, is slyly
critiquing the figure of authority that some white and black novelists rather
uncritically promote. Although there are intimations that Joe has had a
difficult life filled with labor, his supreme confidence and seemingly natural
political ability allow him relatively easy access to power: He becomes the
unquestioned leader of Eatonville literally overnight. Joe states that "'in de
very first beginnin'. . . Ah aimed tuh be uh big voice'" (43); by the time he
appears in the novel, however, he is clearly already a big voice, dominating
the town's discourse from the first moment he enters it. In these respects
he is like many of the characters in politically oriented American fiction,
including Silas P. Ratcliffe of *Democracy* and a later invention, the similarly-
named Willie Stark of *All the King's Men*.[3] These are characters who, despite
questionable methods, use their immense (and seemingly innate) political
talents to break open stagnant political situations and get things done
that help people. Joe, for example, within days of his arrival in Eatonville,
purchases additional land for the town, organizes the clearing of roads, builds
a store and post office so that residents will no longer have to travel long
distances for provisions, and installs a street lamp (36–41). He is the sort of
politician who makes civic prosperity and personal profit one and the same;
as with Ratcliffe and Willie Stark, it quickly becomes difficult to separate the
well-being of the town from the interests of Joe Starks.

In common with Du Bois, Henry Adams and Robert Penn Warren
express anxiety about the leadership of such a politician, and the potential for
corruption and abuse of power, but seem scarcely able to imagine an effective
political landscape without such a leader. The choice they represent is between
corruption and chaos; whereas corruption is lamentable, chaos is unthinkable.
For her part, Hurston recognizes the positive aspects of Joe's authority, but
indicates that what is gained in material prosperity is overwhelmed by what
is lost in personal freedom when an individual amasses too much power. Joe's
authority, she shows, replicates the authority by which whites have oppressed
African Americans:

> [Janie] slept with authority and so she was part of it in the
> town mind. She couldn't get but so close to most of them in

spirit. It was especially noticeable after Joe had forced through a town ditch to drain the street in front of the store. They had murmured hotly about slavery being over, but every man filled his assignment.... Take for instance that new house of his. It had two stories with porches, with banisters and such things. The rest of the town looked like servants' quarters surrounding the "big house." (44)

Though most of Joe's visible faults lie in his domineering and abusive attitude toward Janie, it is clear from the outset that he compromises the ability of all of Eatonville's residents to achieve personal fulfillment, despite the prosperity that he offers.

Joe's enterprise—becoming mayor and building the town store—is justified by his belief that "'everything is got tuh have uh center and uh heart tuh it'" (38). The store, in fact, is intended to be a location for dialogue, a place where the community can shape discursively the issues of the day: This is the role the store in Eatonville plays in numerous Hurston books, such as *Mules and Men* and the long-unpublished collaboration with Langston Hughes, *Mule Bone*, as well as in *Their Eyes*. In this sense, Joe's project of bringing a "center" to Eatonville is actually successful: The communal, dialogic narrative at the store replaces the scattered individual narratives that seemed, when Joe and Janie arrived, to go nowhere. Joe, however, makes the mistake of displacing himself from this community dialogue. He purposely sets himself and Janie apart from the other Eatonville residents by displaying material possessions, such as expensive cigars and a fancy chair. "What with him biting down on cigars and saving his breath on talk and swinging round in that chair, it weakened people" (44). Although the townspeople are undoubtedly more prosperous than they were before Joe came, his complete subscription to bourgeois, material values—represented by his purchase of expensive, decorative spittoons for himself and Janie—demoralizes them: "It sort of made the rest of them feel that they had been taken advantage of. Like things had been kept from them. Maybe more things in the world besides spitting pots had been hid from them" (45).

Joe's materialism is not isolated from his other flaws as a leader. The relationship Joe stipulates between himself and the other residents of Eatonville (and especially Janie), by means of his displays of wealth and by means of his speech, illustrates that the idea of Eatonville—designed as an alternative to the oppression its residents faced in white-dominated society—is severely compromised by Joe's presence. As one resident, Sam Watson, states: "'Some folks needs thrones and ruling-chairs and crowns tuh make they influence felt. He don't. He's got uh throne in de seat of his pants'" (46). Joe unconsciously expects that, upon his ascent to power, his real work has been finished—when in fact it should just be beginning. As long as his displays of voice and prosperity include the town—as they still do when he displays the new street lamp in his store for a week before ceremoniously installing it (41–42)—he seems an effective, popular leader. In gradually withdrawing himself from the concerns of the town, however, Joe strives for an unattainable sort of timelessness—a semblance of immortality, the expectation that his reign will forever remain unchallenged—that is anathema to dialogue, which must always occur across time.

Hurston contrasts the stasis represented by his "gloaty, sparkly white" house (44) to the continuing dialogue of the town, of which Joe is no longer a part: "As time went on and the benefits he had conferred upon the town receded in time they sat on his store porch while he was busy inside and discussed him" (45). Again, the dialogue at the store offers the residents an opportunity to discuss current issues and come to some sort of consensus, as when they debate Joe's banishment of a man who has stolen from him (45–46). But Joe's continuing, domineering presence causes the town's political reality to remain stagnant, cyclical rather than forward-moving: "The town had a basketful of feelings good and bad about Joe's positions and possessions, but none had the temerity to challenge him. They bowed down to him rather, because he was all of these things, and then again he was all of these things because the town bowed down" (47).

As the narrator's remarks here suggest, the town is ripe for a revolt against Joe's reign. Importantly, it is Janie who initiates Joe's downfall. Although Janie's oppression by Joe is distinct from the other residents' because she is a woman and a wife (almost every other Eatonville resident depicted in the Joe Starks chapters is male), she also represents the community as an embodiment of their suffering and dissatisfaction. Despite the distance between Janie and the other community members—a distance imposed by both Joe and the other men of Eatonville—Janie in many ways speaks for the townspeople. As we will see, Hurston uses the oppression of Janie, as both an African American and a woman, as an emblem of the oppression of African Americans generally; however, the appropriate response to such oppression arises from narrative strategies that Hurston codes female. In other words, the men of Eatonville are able to help neither Janie nor themselves combat their mutual subjugation; Janie, in contrast, *does* arrive at positive methods for (narrative and political) leadership, even though these methods are not immediately valued by her community.

What Mary O'Connor has written of Alice Walker's *The Color Purple* could equally be said of *Their Eyes*: It "could well be plotted by the heroine's growing awareness of the languages that surround her" (203). Even though Janie is forbidden by Joe to "indulge" in the talk occurring at the storefront, she clearly is fascinated by it (*Their Eyes* 50–51). Finally, she succumbs to the temptation to speak out after Joe frees Matt Bonner's long-suffering mule. Her words are communal in that they continue the "mule talk" that has preoccupied the community for several days, but they also are an example of discursive leadership. They express a community sentiment in a way that the other individual community members apparently never thought of; Janie's words are an articulation of an idea that was already present in the community but that had formerly been shapeless. Janie says:

> "Jody, dat wuz a mighty fine thing fuh you tuh do. 'Tain't everybody would have thought of it, 'cause it ain't no everyday thought. Freein' dat mule makes uh mighty big man outa you. Something like George Washington and Lincoln. Abraham Lincoln, he had de whole United States tuh rule so he freed de Negroes. You got uh town so you freed uh mule. You have tuh have power tuh free things and dat makes you lak a king uh something."

As one listener, Hambo, says, "'Yo' wife is uh born orator, Starks. Us never knowed dat befo'. She put jus' de right words tuh our thoughts'" (55). For his part, Joe "beam[s]" at Janie's speech, which is an only partly ironic account of his leadership abilities and methods.

The seeds of Joe's destruction are sown by Janie's oration, however. As numerous critics point out, Joe's death from kidney failure immediately follows, and even seems prompted by, Janie's signifying rebuttal to Joe's insults. As Gates notes, "Janie Signifies upon Jody's manhood, thereby ending his dominance over her and over the community, and thereby killing Jody's will to live" (201). The forcefulness of Janie's words strikes Gates so strongly that he describes Joe's cause of death as "displaced 'kidney' failure," accentuating with quotation marks his suspicion that her words are the real cause (193). We must not, however, jump too quickly to the conclusion that Janie arrives at a position of power simply by deciding to assert her latent voice. By no means is Hurston suggesting that narrative power arrives easily, or without struggle. In the years between Janie's mule oration and her apparently deadly rebuttal to Joe, she strives fruitlessly to make the hierarchical marriage relationship work for her. She recognizes that both she and Joe are harmed by the distance Joe keeps between himself and the community, and by the distance he keeps between himself and her, making it impossible for them to be "'natural wid one 'nother'" (43). She also seems to recognize that, without Joe, she is vulnerable to the whims of an uncaring and often dangerous world.

Janie struggles to save Joe, and save their marriage, by encouraging him to take part in the discourse of the community: "'Everybody can't be lak you, Jody. Somebody is bound tuh want tuh laugh and play.'" In response, Joe

makes clear that he believes that control and prosperity—which he regards as
the outcomes of successful leadership—are incompatible with laughter and
narrative "play":

> "I god, Ah don't make out no such uh lie [that I don't like to
> laugh and play]! But it's uh time fuh all things. But it's awful
> tuh see so many people don't want nothin' but uh full belly and
> uh place to lay down and sleep afterwards. It makes me sad
> sometimes and then agin it makes me mad. They say things
> sometimes that tickles me nearly tuh death, but Ah won't laugh
> jus' tuh dis-incourage 'em."

Janie disagrees, but as usual Joe cuts her off, making clear that he will not
hear her dissent. Hurston writes, "Janie took the easy way away from such
a fuss. She didn't change her mind but she agreed with her mouth" (59).
Although Janie's dissenting voice, if heard rather than withheld, might help
draw Joe back into his community and his marriage, Joe cuts himself and his
wife off from the other residents' discourse. When, inevitably, Janie speaks
out publicly a second time, once again Joe perceives a threat in Janie's voice
and attempts to cut her off: "'You gettin' too moufy, Janie. . . . Go fetch me
de checker-board *and* de checkers. Sam Watson, you'se mah fish'" (71).

Finally comes the watershed moment. In response to Joe's constant,
cutting remarks about Janie's aging, Janie says: "'You big-bellies round here
and put out a lot of brag, but 'taint nothin' to it but yo' big voice. Humph!
Talkin' 'bout me lookin' old! When you pull down yo' britches, you look lak
de change uh life.'" Explains the narrator,

> Then Joe Starks realized all the meanings and his vanity bled
> like a flood. Janie had robbed him of his illusion of irresistible
> maleness that all men cherish, which was terrible. The thing
> that Saul's daughter had done to David. But Janie had done
> worse, she had cast down his empty armor before men and they
> had laughed, would keep on laughing. When he paraded his
> possessions hereafter, they would not consider the two together.
> They'd look with envy at the things and pity the man that owned
> them. (75)

Although, in doing to Joe rhetorically what he has done to her for years,
Janie creates for herself an eventual path to escape, at first she regards Joe's
devastation and death not with relief, but with regret. In the aftermath of
Janie's remarks, "anybody that didn't know would have thought that things
had blown over, it looked so quiet and peaceful around. But the stillness

was the sleep of swords. So new thoughts had to be thought and new words said. She didn't want to live like that" (77). The vagueness of the narrative strategies now available to Janie—"new thoughts had to be thought and new words said"—suggests once again that her position is one of uncertainty. In rhetorically defeating Joe, Janie has by no means arrived at a safe or protected position; nor has she discovered a clear path to narrative power.

Despite his undeniably oppressive presence during their years of marriage, Janie finally experiences strong feelings of pity when Joe dies:

> "Dis sittin in de rulin' chair is been hard on Jody," she muttered out loud. She was full of pity for the first time in years. Jody had been hard on her and others, but life had mishandled him too. Poor Joe! Maybe if she had known some other way to try, she might have made his face different. But what that other way could be, she had no idea.

Joe's death scene is a powerful early evocation of the "death of the author" in the twentieth century. Metaphorically, Hurston suggests that, while the loss of the "big voice" associated with the Western, white male author is regrettable in some ways, nonetheless it must be demolished in the name of a new type of narrative, despite the fact that such an "other way" is difficult to describe or achieve. Like Joe, the "author" sanctioned by modernist aesthetics is too intent on achieving some timeless form of control to heed the call for responsiveness to dialogue. Authorship, for Hurston, is a type of authority, a method for preserving the cultural power of those who have been privileged since time immemorial, and she expresses doubt that the traditional mode of authorship offers the potential of liberation for African Americans or for women; indeed, she doubts that it is even capable of sustaining *itself* indefinitely. Instead, she enacts with her book (as numerous critics—including Davie, Gates, and Awkward—also describe) an experimental form of narrative that attempts to break down readers' expectations and assumptions about reading fiction. Naturally, the experiments of the book have been difficult for many readers to take, which accounts for the initial hostility and long-term neglect the novel encountered. But Hurston offers faith that, even if the readership of her novel will not be prepared right away for its narrative implications, eventually the new possibilities that have been implanted in the text may be recovered.

In the often explicated opening lines of *Their Eyes*, Hurston's narrator says:

> Ships at a distance have every mans wish on board. For some they come in with the tide. For others they sail forever on the

> horizon, never out of sight, never landing until the Watcher
> turns his eyes away in resignation, his dreams mocked to death
> by Time. That is the life of men.
>   Now, women forget all those things they don't want to
> remember, and remember everything they don't want to forget. The
> dream is the truth. Then they act and do things accordingly. (1)

In the first paragraph quoted here, Hurston conflates the creativity, or
"dreaming," of males and the power of God to watch over the world,
suggested by the capital letter used to describe the frustrated male "Watcher."
Even when the man is incapable of enacting his dreams, his positioning as
the "Watcher" gives him a type of power: By making himself a God, with
the power to shape his experiences imaginatively, the man compensates for
his inability to shape the physical and material worlds. This, in short, is the
power of the author: Rather than changing the physical world, one shapes the
imaginative one, the structures by means of which experiences are interpreted.
Yet women, the novel's opening suggests, are not bestowed this option. For
them, neither material nor interpretive realities are easily overcome: While
they, too, are capable of dreaming (of creativity), it seems incapable, in
their case, of shaping reality. Nonetheless, Hurston suggests, women also
make narratives with the intent of shaping their immediate environment,
even if this means only selectively "forgetting" certain experiences, a sort of
coping ritual. The methods available to women for changing political (less
immediate) realities are much harder to articulate; Hurston's narrator must
rely on the vague claim that women "act and do things accordingly." Du Bois,
in his own political novel, *Dark Princess*, insists that art must move beyond
the task of reflection and must produce *action*, but here Hurston shows that
to *act* politically is more problematic than it may initially appear.

    In her portrayal of Janie's first two marriages, Hurston reenacts the
much-discussed struggle over the direction of African American leadership
between Booker T. Washington and Du Bois. Logan Killicks, who attains
modest financial success and respectability as a farmer, models the path
advocated by Washington: gradual progress that would neither threaten
whites nor complicate the capitalist infrastructure they had built. Although
Hurston satirized the view of "the better-thinking Negro" that Washington
"was absolutely vile for advocating industrial education" (*Dust Tracks* 189),
and similarly criticizes Mrs. Turner's disavowal of Washington in *Their
Eyes*—allowing Janie to voice the response that "'Ah was raised on de notion
dat he wuz uh great big man'" (136)—she also seems to suggest that the
appeal of Washington's approach is mainly felt by the dying generation of
Janie's grandmother, Nanny. Just as Nanny contends that Janie's happiness
must remain subordinate to "protection" through marriage to the unattractive

Killicks (14), many believed that Washington's gradualist approach called on blacks to sacrifice the struggle for liberty in the interest of modest prosperity.

One such critic was Du Bois, whose critique of Washington seems to be echoed in Joe's initial appeal to Janie: "'You behind a plow! You ain't got no mo' business wid uh plow than uh hog is got wid a holiday! You ain't got no business cuttin' up no seed p'taters neither'" (28). Just as Joe implies the possibility of a freer, better life that—we learn before long—he cannot deliver, so Hurston seems to be suggesting that Du Bois's less compromising, more assertive attitude is not capable, as it claims to be, of leading blacks to positions of real leadership. Joe fails Janie and Eatonville because he subscribes too readily to white, bourgeois values and tastes, and because his style of leadership replicates the domination of the few over the many—criticisms that have been leveled against Du Bois and his "Talented Tenth" as well. In Hurston's implied analysis, neither the accomodationist model propounded by Washington nor the more assertive, Modernist elitism of Du Bois offers an appealing approach for African Americans.

In short, by the time of her third marriage, Janie is in desperate need of a "third way." Certainly, this undefined new "way" does not necessarily mean a marriage. Consistently, Janie makes clear that she is willing to risk uncertainty in resisting confinement. In leaving her first marriage, Janie reasons that, even if Joe has lied to her, any possible future is preferable to her past with Logan: "A feeling of sudden newness and change came over her.... Even if Joe was not there waiting for her, the change was bound to do her good" (31). When Janie contemplates a relationship with Tea Cake, she knows full well that the safe, "rational" choice would be to steer clear of him (96, 100–01). Janie's endurance of Joe for twenty years and her marriage to Tea Cake reflect her faith that self-knowledge and "voice" are compatible with marriage, but not dependent upon it. In every marriage relationship depicted in the novel, Hurston shows that, while it is unclear whether a culturally disempowered woman like Janie can create a successful life for herself alone, the presence of men is not itself the antidote to the vulnerability of women. No man can keep Janie safe—men can protect neither her body nor her voice—and therefore, *if* a successful narrative is to be achieved by Janie, it will be a result of her own decisions and actions, whether or not she makes these in the company of a man.

Numerous critics have questioned the common assumption that Tea Cake is an emblem of Janie's liberation. Michael Awkward, for example, contends that Tea Cake is a barrier to Janie's fulfillment: "Janie ... is [with Tea Cake] a submissive woman, suppressing her will to fit the needs of an exceedingly charming, but nonetheless frequently domineering, husband" (37). Deborah G. Plant takes the argument further, agreeing that "the freedom Janie gains is circumscribed by Tea Cake's desire to dominate her" (168), and using his presence in the book to support her argument that Hurston "idealiz[ed] male authority" (172). I would agree with such critics that the text can hardly be used to support any claim that Tea Cake rescues Janie. She cannot depend on Tea Cake's protection. Notably, Tea Cake does not approach Janie until she is alone—the rest of the town has gone to a ball game (90–91)—when his courtship will be safe from approbation. Just as the men of Eatonville uncomfortably witness Joe's abuse of Janie but are unable to do anything about it (74), so Tea Cake is unable to protect Janie from the narrow attitudes of conventional society, and responds to Eatonville's hostility toward their relationship by asking Janie to move to Jacksonville (105–11). Furthermore, as Maria J. Racine points out, Tea Cake's act of violence toward Janie demonstrates his own "inability to articulate—or lack of a voice" (289). That Janie stays with him despite the sexism and the violence he exhibits toward her suggests that she makes a conscious decision, in the absence of compelling economic or safety reasons, to remain—even though, from a contemporary standpoint, many of us might question her decision. Both in her marriage to Tea Cake and in her apparently isolated position back in Eatonville after his death, Janie embraces risk rather than approval and protection.

Tea Cake does, however, offer important consolation and support to Janie. As Maria Tai Wolff contends, Tea Cake helps Janie recognize qualities that are already present in herself: "Rather than telling her who or what she is, he directs her only to recognize it for herself. . . . He becomes a mirror for her, but one which refers her back to her own experience" (223). In taking on this role, Wolff suggests, Tea Cake offers to Janie the possibility of being understood on terms that are personal and immediate rather than sterile and imposed from outside: "From her grandmother, Logan Killicks, and Joe Starks, Janie receives a ready-made text, a definition of her role. She is expected to conform to it. From Tea Cake, on the other hand, she receives an invitation to live a text, to formulate a role" (224). By opening up new interpretive possibilities—allowing Janie to break out of the "texts" that have been imposed on her—Hurston calls on the reader of *Their Eyes* to become involved in the making of her story, Wolff states: "The reader's own experiences and dreams will lead him or her to interpret the text in an individual way, to transform it into a personal image" (228).[4]

Tea Cake, in short, is Janie's best "reader" in the book—even though he is also, at times, a self-centered and neglectful one—and thus he is a figure of the reader Hurston *hopes* to encounter outside of the book. However, Hurston makes clear that she does not require the approval of readers. Or, rather, the success of her (and Janie's) narrative *does* depend to an extent on having good readers, but even if these implied readers are not available—if those who encounter this text are not yet prepared for it—the writing of the text is important for other reasons as well. For Hurston, language is not simply a method for communication; the process of articulating experience in words is a way of shaping, of making sense of, the self—and the audience to which this articulation is directed may be real and physically present, or it may be an implied audience—an ideal, imagined listener who is responsive to the varied dialogues that make up the self. As Racine points out, Janie's attainment of a "voice" before the white jury that tries her after she kills Tea Cake is "insignificant" in her project to discover herself, which is one reason that here we do not have access to Janie's words (291). The jurors are attentive listeners, but the "truth" they are listening for is purely exterior—they evaluate the extent to which Janie's actions do or do not fit the legal definition of murder—and there is no evidence that they come to a fuller understanding of Janie's individuality or, on the other hand, the larger issue of racial oppression (and their own complicity in it).[5] Janie must re-narrate her story to her sympathetic friend Pheoby—which appears to be, approximately, the story Hurston's narrator relates to the book's readers. Even in this case—as I will explain momentarily—Janie's dialogic narration of her story and her "self" is only relatively successful; we have not yet located a narrative ideal.

The purpose of dialogue, as Hurston illustrates in this book, is not simply to achieve the elusive (perhaps unattainable) goal of self-understanding. Since authoritative (or monologic) discourse—that which allows Janie's oppression—is characterized by stasis, by its textual stability, then dialogic discourse must work to break down the language of the empowered. The voice articulated by Janie—and that of Hurston, which (as Gates notes) is often indistinguishable from Janie's (196)—is disruptive in that it cannot be rendered useful to the community, unless the community changes its own attitudes and practices. The would-be listeners to Janie's tale after her return to Eatonville, Janie knows, will be affronted by her story unless they can learn "'dat love ain't somethin' lak uh grindstone dat's de same everywhere and do de same thing tuh everything it touch'" (182). Similarly, *Their Eyes* itself is an affront to its modernist readers, who struggle with its perceived shapelessness and confusing message. Evidence of the disruption offered by *Their Eyes* can be seen in its varied readings and misreadings; even sympathetic readers of Hurston almost invariably are troubled by some aspect of her narrative that sticks out funny, that their interpretation cannot cleanly account for. As Alice Walker writes, Hurston "was quite capable of saying, writing, or doing things *different* from what one might have wished"—which itself is part of her appeal ("On Refusing" 1). *Their Eyes* is, despite its readability, a truly *surprising* text, one that continually subverts any expectations a reader might put upon it; and this, I suggest, is integral to the point Hurston is making about language: It must change us, rather than allowing us easily to push it into a pre-constructed box.

I do not wish to suggest that *Their Eyes* is uninterpretable, but only that any interpretation must be seen as something other than the final one. Hurston designed *Their Eyes* to accentuate the degree to which, upon each new reading of the novel, its meaning changes. Pheoby, the listener of Janie's story, represents one response Hurston hoped to elicit among her readership; as the implied audience of the narration of most of the novel, she stands for us as we read the book. After Janie's tale is complete, Pheoby says, "'Lawd! . . . Ah done growed ten feet higher from jus' listenin' tuh you, Janie. Ah ain't satisfied wid mahself no mo'" (182–83). If Tea Cake is Janie's "best" reader, then Pheoby is her second-best. Although (in contrast to Tea Cake) Pheoby seems capable of contributing only slightly to her friend's psychic survival, there is some compensation in the fact that *Pheoby* benefits from hearing Janie's tale, even if Janie does not otherwise benefit from the telling of it. An ideal narrative, in short, would be one that nurtures both the teller and the listener. Hurston indicates that such an ideal, in the absence of extraordinarily sympathetic and responsive "readers" like Tea Cake, is nearly impossible. Nonetheless, narrative is crucial because, given enough time and enough readings, it can change the world, one reader—one connection—at a time.

Although the achievement of a "connection" between writer and reader does not immediately appear revolutionary—it is, after all, an effect commonly experienced by readers of the most traditional and canonical texts—Hurston insists on offering potential connections that are capable of changing the reader politically. *Their Eyes* valorizes neither the coherent, authorial self nor the identity imposed by community, even though Hurston values both self and community. *Their Eyes* is an expression of "feminist dialogics" (as Dale M. Bauer describes the concept) because, despite the value of self and community, Hurston is willing to sacrifice the possibility of attaining a coherent version of either, recognizing that, in a patriarchy, the coherence of one necessarily means the sacrifice of the other. A dialogic feminism, Bauer writes, "warns against a critical short-sightedness women have in patriarchal culture: the myth of a unified subject under patriarchy. And, . . . it also cautions against the perils of insertion into a community which might drown out one's voice the moment one agrees to enter into it" (x). Hurston hopes to provide, in her novel, an account of a "self" and a potential community that will sustain readers and provoke them to act against oppression, but she does not attempt simply to replace one "unified subject under patriarchy" with another—to do so would be to replicate the very means of oppression, which is Joe's fatal error. Instead, she offers, in representing Janie, segments of a self that is fragmented, that may be recovered by readers over time; and this process of recovery offers, itself, the potential of forming a new community.

In exposing the oncoming "death of the author," and in writing a text that does not subscribe to the expectations of a critical, anti-racist elite (such as Richard Wright, who castigated the book), Hurston risks sacrificing critical and material "success" in the hope of creating a voice that will continue to echo long after her death, even though she recognized that the echoing might not be audible in time to save the author herself from obscurity and impoverishment. She does this for the same reasons that Janie embraces risk throughout the novel: No matter how much Janie tries to save Joe, the authority figure, and protect herself, and no matter how capable she may be of speaking to the genuine needs of her immediate, disempowered community, there simply is no way to alter the contexts of her reception except—possibly—across time. Janie, in other words, takes risks because, as an African American woman, she has to. Writes DuPlessis, "Janie is in incessant dialogue with the meanings of 'colored,' of which she is not in control. To construct Janie's dialogue, Hurston has treated many of these social determinants (such as class, sexuality, and gender role) as if they were matters of choice and risk for her character, not fixed and immobilized" (96). It would be inadequate, given Hurston's awareness of oppression, to read *Their Eyes* as claiming that an African American woman can produce personal freedom simply by demanding it. It would be equally inadequate, however, to read Hurston or her character, Janie, as utterly confined by the demands of traditional discourse, since creatively to break out of such confinement is very much part of Hurston's intent.

Necessarily, "breaking out" is a process in which not only the author, but also her readers, participate; this is visibly true to an unusual extent in Hurston's case. *Their Eyes* and Hurston's other books fell into obscurity for a variety of reasons, but especially due to two factors—Hurston's refusal to advocate similar views to those of the Civil Rights "elite," and the general apathy and insensitivity of white critics toward African American fiction for much of this century. Hurston's work has been returned to us largely due to the concerted efforts of three critics: Mary Helen Washington, who has written and spoken extensively about Hurston, in both traditional academic settings and popular ones such as the magazine *Black World*, since the early 1970s; Alice Walker, who discovered Hurston for herself and shared this discovery in a 1975 *Ms.* article and elsewhere; and Robert Hemenway, whose well-received biography of Hurston helped launch her books back into print. The title of Walker's *Ms.* article, "Looking for Zora," is appropriate to the ongoing project Hurston set out for her readers: When we think we have "found" Zora is when her contribution will truly have been lost.

Hazel Carby, in a strong critique of the contemporary Zora Neale Hurston "industry," suggests that this unfortunate moment may already have arrived:

> Clearly, a womanist- and feminist-inspired desire to recover the neglected cultural presence of Zora Neale Hurston initiated an interest in her work, but it is also clear that this original motivation has become transformed. Hurston is not only a secured presence in the academy; she is a veritable industry, and an industry that is very profitable.

Questions Carby, "How is she being reread, now, to produce cultural meanings that this society wants or needs to hear?" (72). She concludes that many of Hurston's recent critics share with her a desire to describe, and make use of, "black cultural authenticity" while avoiding implication in actual, material issues affecting the romanticized "folk" (89). Hurston wrote Janie, and we read her, to exhibit interest in the social problems alluded to in *Their Eyes* without actually having to do anything about them, in Carby's view. Although I can only partly agree with Carby's conclusions, I think the point she raises is worth contemplating: One of the disadvantages of writing a dialogic novel is, clearly, that an extended, communal response *across time* may not be enough. If we do not become more fully connected than a loose assemblage of monadic readers is likely to become, then the political effect of Hurston's writing will be highly restricted, if it exists at all.

Hurston sacrifices the authority to *direct* her readers, clearly and efficiently, to any specific conclusion. She does so knowingly, I believe, recognizing that to assert the power to direct us would be to perpetuate a myth, one that is harmful to her and to others. As Barbara Johnson asserts, Hurston writes "out of a knowledge of the standards of male dominance that pervade both the black and white worlds" (169). Janie becomes detached from the black community from which she comes, and which she appears to understand with a near-artistic sensitivity, not by her own choice: Not only Joe, but the other men and women of Eatonville (as their presence at Janie's trial shows) resist any understanding of Janie. Similarly, Hurston moved "away from the community that produced her[, while attempting] to reproduce" it textually (Carby 85), not out of a desire to redirect "black cultural authenticity" toward selfish ends but because that was virtually the only option available to her. Like any text, *Their Eyes* depends upon its readership in order to achieve its narrative ends. To an unusual degree, however, that dependence is foregrounded by the author of this novel. And Hurston's prescience of her readership's inevitable shortcomings—shortcomings that Carby ultimately enumerates—accounts for the tone of regret and of sacrifice that complicates the joy of the book.

Notes

1. Similarly, Henry Louis Gates, Jr., describes Hurston's attempt to find a "third term"—between "a profoundly lyrical, densely metaphorical, quasi-musical, privileged black oral tradition on the one hand, and a received but not yet fully appropriated standard English literary tradition on the other hand" (174).

2. Eatonville was a real town where Hurston grew up; the character of Joe Starks is clearly based, at least in part, on the historical Joe Clarke, the leader of the new town before Hurston was born. See Hurston's autobiography *Dust Tracks on a Road* 5–6.

3. One can only speculate as to whether Robert Penn Warren might have been familiar with Hurston's book and have been influenced by Hurston in naming his own Willie Stark.

4. Wolff insists that "Janie's search for identity is not a temporal, progressive process" (220), which I find a strange conclusion within a sensitive and enlightening reader-response approach. In my view, part of Hurston's point is that the meaning of the book is temporal, does emerge across time: In opposition to the Modernist aesthetic of timeless, unified meaning, Hurston proposes (for example, in the book's opening two paragraphs) that the development of an identity is ongoing, a form of dialogue in which the interior self and outside communities—including both the community populating the book and the community of readers—mutually participate.

5. Rachel Blau DuPlessis notes that, in acquitting Janie, the jurors "are right for possibly the wrong reasons. Being fascinated by the 'whiteness' of this black woman, and by her 'romance,' but also wanting to put black men in their place, they judge her not guilty" (105).

Works Cited

Adams, Henry. *Democracy: An American Novel*. 1880. New York: NAL, 1988.

Arendt, Hannah. "What Is Authority?" *Between Past and Future: Eight Essays in Political Thought*. New York: Viking, 1968. 91–141.

Awkward, Michael. *Inspiriting Influences: Tradition, Revision, and Afro-American Women's Novels*. New York: Columbia UP, 1989.

Bauer, Dale M. *Feminist Dialogics: A Theory of Failed Community*. Albany: SUNY P, 1988.

Carby, Hazel V. "The Politics of Fiction, Anthropology, and the Folk: Zora Neale Hurston." *New Essays on Their Eyes Were Watching God*. Ed. Michael Awkward. New York: Cambridge UP, 1990. 71–93.

Carr, Glynis. "Storytelling as Bildung in Zora Neale Hurston's *Their Eyes Were Watching God*." *CLA Journal* 31 (1987): 189–200.

Davie, Sharon. "Free Mules, Talking Buzzards, and Cracked Plates: The Politics of Dislocation in *Their Eyes Were Watching God*." *PMLA* 108 (1993): 446–59.

Du Bois, W. E. B. *Dark Princess: A Romance*. 1928. Jackson: Banner, 1995.

DuPlessis, Rachel Blau. "Power, Judgment, and Narrative in a Work of Zora Neale Hurston: Feminist Cultural Studies." *New Essays on Their Eyes Were Watching God*. Ed. Michael Awkward. New York: Cambridge UP, 1990. 95–123.

Ferguson, SallyAnn. "Folkloric Men and Female Growth in *Their Eyes Were Watching God*." *Black American Literature Forum* 28 (1987): 185–97.

Gates, Henry Louis, Jr. *The Signifying Monkey: A Theory of African-American Literary Criticism*. New York: Oxford UP, 1988.

Gates, Henry Louis, Jr., and K. A. Appiah, eds. *Zora Neale Hurston: Critical Perspectives Past and Present*. New York: Amistad, 1993.

Hemenway, Robert. *Zora Neale Hurston: A Literary Biography*. Urbana: U of Illinois P, 1977.

Hurston, Zora Neale. *Dust Tracks on a Road*. 1942. New York: Harper, 1991.

———. *Their Eyes Were Watching God*. 1937. New York: Harper, 1990.

Johnson, Barbara. "Metaphor, Metonymy and Voice in *Their Eyes Were Watching God*." *Modern Critical Views: Zora Neale Hurston*. Ed. Harold Bloom. New York: Chelsea House, 1986. 157–73.

McCredie, Wendy J. "Authority and Authorization in *Their Eyes Were Watching God*." *Black American Literature Forum* 16 (1982): 25–28.

O'Connor, Mary. "Subject, Voice, and Women in Some Contemporary Black American Women's Writing." *Feminism, Bakhtin, and the Dialogic*. Ed. Dale M. Bauer and Susan Jaret McKinstry. Albany: SUNY P, 1991. 199–217.

Plant, Deborah G. *Every Tub Must Sit on Its Own Bottom: The Philosophy and Politics of Zora Neale Hurston*. Urbana: U of Illinois P, 1995.

Racine, Maria J. "Voice and Interiority in Zora Neale Hurston's *Their Eyes Were Watching God*." *African American Review* 28 (1994): 283–92.

Stepto, Robert B. *From Behind the Veil: A Study of Afro-American Narrative*. 2nd ed. Urbana: U of Illinois P, 1991.

Thornton, Jerome E. "'Goin' on de Muck': The Paradoxical Journey of the Black American Hero." *CLA Journal* 31 (1988): 261–80.

Walker, Alice. "Looking for Zora." Walker, *I Love* 297–313.

———. "On Refusing to Be Humbled by Second Place in a Contest You Did Not Design: A Tradition by Now." Walker, *I Love* 1–5.

Walker, Alice, ed. *I Love Myself When I Am Laughing . . . And Then Again When I Am Looking Mean and Impressive: A Zora Neale Hurston Reader*. Old Westbury: Feminist P, 1979.

Warren, Robert Penn. *All the King's Men*. 1946. San Diego: Harvest/HBJ, 1982.

Washington, Mary Helen. Foreword. *Their Eyes Were Watching God*. By Zora Neale Hurston. New York: Harper, 1990. vii–xiv.

———. "'I Love the Way Janie Crawford Left Her Husbands': Emergent Female Hero." Gates and Appiah 98–109.

Willis, Susan. "Wandering: Hurston's Search for Self and Method." Gates and Appiah 110–29.

Wolff, Maria Tai. "Listening and Living: Reading and Experience in *Their Eyes Were Watching God*." Gates and Appiah 218–29.

SHAWN E. MILLER

"Some Other Way to Try": From Defiance to Creative Submission in
Their Eyes Were Watching God

Since 1979, by which time *Their Eyes Were Watching God* (1937) had established itself as "the most privileged text in the African-American literary canon" (Washington xii), some Hurston critics have been of two minds about her best-known book.[1] Citing various unresolved textual problems, some cautious skeptics have asked whether the novel's preeminence, won through nearly universal praise from Alice Walker and other first-generation advocates, is premature, and perhaps even unwarranted.[2] In the early days of the Hurston revival, one might have expected enthusiasts to regard such questions as hostile, and to respond in the mode of spirited defense; they were, after all, engaged in a delicate operation to recuperate a mostly forgotten writer who did not exactly fit the extraliterary profile of Herman Melville and other previously successful candidates. When the question was whether Hurston would be remembered at all, one can hardly blame her advocates for their wagon-circling against rigorous interrogation by critics of uncertain loyalties. But now, with the revival an accomplished fact, *Their Eyes Were Watching God* not only competes with, but even overshadows and threatens to eclipse, most other modern novels. Not surprisingly, questions about its worth have become more frequent and insistent, even from some of the book's early admirers. Such questions now are not so much measures of the book's precarious status, as they are of its ubiquity.

From *Southern Literary Journal*, pp. 74–95. © 2004 by the *Southern Literary Journal* and the University of North Carolina at Chapel Hill Department of English.

Understanding this latter-day reception history may help us get to the bottom of more recent questions (and answers) about the book's purported inconsistency; indeed, reception politics may even explain why they have been raised to begin with. When Hurston's position in the canon seemed uncertain, little deviation from the fundamental feminist interpretation was possible without hazarding the success of the recovery effort. Gradually, this initial interpretation became standard, then assumed, even after the book had become a fixture in high school and undergraduate curricula across the country. Few now seriously ask whether the interpretation advanced by first-generation critics is valid; even the novel's detractors simply assume that it is, then point out all the ways the book contradicts it. When William M. Ramsey charges that *Their Eyes Were Watching God* is "not a fully finished or conceptually realized text" (36), he means that substantial textual evidence does not accord with, and at times contradicts, the widely-assumed feminist interpretation of the novel. He concludes that perhaps *Their Eyes Were Watching God* is not as good as we had thought, but an alternate conclusion is of course possible: perhaps the conventional interpretation of *Their Eyes Were Watching God* is not as right as we had thought. Rather than acknowledge the necessity of either conclusion, Hurston advocates have often addressed the concerns of readers like Ramsey with ever more fanciful explanations of why the standard interpretation is nevertheless still adequate to its task, an activity which Joseph R. Urgo laments "only emphasizes the assumption of textual weakness" (42). The reader who craves unity of effect is left with the notion that something is still awry.

A more helpful strategy for assessing the book might lie in reconsidering our allegiance to certain assumptions that undergird the traditional feminist interpretation, especially now that Hurston and her work are widely known and respected. In brief, this interpretation posits Janie Crawford as an internally static feminist hero seeking liberation from masculine oppression as a necessary prerequisite to self-actualization. Her first two marriages fail because Logan Killicks and Joe Starks insist too severely on Janie's obedience to them and to conventional sex-role and class-role stereotypes. Janie heroically defies the roles imposed upon her, and eventually finds the love she had first envisioned under the pear tree when she marries Tea Cake Woods. Their marriage, unlike her first two, is egalitarian and liberating. She thus completes her journey from object to subject. Though this interpretation in its more fleshed-out form is still the standard in Hurston criticism, many of its adherents are bothered by certain aspects of the text that seem not to measure up to it, including a questionable choice of point of view (Washington xi), an "uncritical depiction of violence toward women" (Washington xiv), the "ambiguities" of Hurston's characterization of Tea Cake (Lupton 49), and, of course, the novel's ending. Some have been content to label these oddities flaws, but we also might entertain the notion that they perform substantive functions that the standard interpretation cannot yet sufficiently explain. When we do, a modified interpretation emerges, within which many of the conventional assumptions about the book cannot be sustained. As Tea Cake's "ambiguities" begin to look more like character traits he shares with Killicks and Starks, who meanwhile begin to appear more human than monstrous, we must locate a different rationale for the failures and achievements of Janie's quest, one that does not depend too greatly on the attitudes of her husbands. Such ruminations lead inevitably, I believe, to the conclusion that Janie is more dynamic than we have previously realized, and that her final triumph has more to do with her mastery of conventional marriage than with her escape from it.

AN UNDERACKNOWLEDGED PATTERN

Many have observed that Hurston's novel is at the core a quest narrative whose object is love, a marriage capable of sustaining Janie's vision of bee and pear tree blossom. In presenting a succession of three marriages, the first wholly unsuccessful, the second mostly unsuccessful, and the third successful but for the outrages of fortune, Hurston invites a misreading of Janie's predicament. This common misreading, which assumes that Janie's triumph is solely over external obstacles, has tempted some to compare the book to *The Odyssey* (Lupton 48) and the traditional literary romance (Daniel 66). Logan Killicks and Joe Starks are merely impediments, Janie's Cyclops and Circe, who but for her heroism would deny the object of her quest. Janie is the steadfast hero, unwavering in her resolve to see the quest to its end. Undoubtedly, Janie sees herself as this kind of figure throughout much of her life, and this self-perception has added to the confusion, perhaps as Hurston intended; external circumstances often mask the inner struggle of the modern hero. But even if the unchanging protagonist beset solely by external forces were a common figure in the work of Hurston's contemporaries, the balance of the evidence in this book points in another direction. As Urgo has rightly pointed out, to read the novel "as a progression from bad to mediocre to best mate for Janie is to miss the repetition of treatment Janie receives from each man" (52).

This repetition of treatment underlies the discomfort many readers have with Tea Cake. Initially, critics such as S. Jay Walker viewed Janie's romance with Tea Cake as a "blurring of sex-role stereotypes within an intensely sexual relationship" (527). In her previous marriages, Janie had been kept in her place, either as domestic servant to Killicks or as Starks's ornament, and in both cases had suffered the oppressions of a narrowly-defined sex role. Her marriage to Tea Cake, on the other hand, is egalitarian;

both Janie and Tea Cake work in the field, both fix supper, both go shooting, both play checkers, and so on. This argument, of course, has its problems. From a feminist perspective, it takes agency away from Janie and makes her happiness a function of her relationships with men. It also conveniently ignores that Janie often chooses to occupy these roles. When Killicks orders her to help him shovel manure before the day gets hot, noting that she might "take a bit of interest in dis place" rather than "foolin' round in dat kitchen all day long," Janie responds, "You don't need mah help out dere, Logan. Youse in yo' place and Ah'm in mine" (30). As Karen Jacobs argues, while "on the muck, [Janie] may interpret her husband's invitation to share the spheres of work and domesticity as an opportunity for gender and class parity . . . she greets Killicks's intention to buy her a mule of her own as a violation of her newly won status as a woman who does not have to work" (344). Shortly thereafter, Janie leaves Logan of her own volition, already captivated by Joe Starks's image of her as "A pretty doll-baby . . . made to sit on de front porch and rock and fan [herself] and eat p'taters dat other folks plant just special for [her]" (28). Janie's own desire to occupy these roles aside, this common view of her final marriage also ignores the many characteristics all of her husbands, including Tea Cake, share.

More recently, critics have begun to recognize these shared characteristics. Under Killicks and Starks, Janie's oppression takes a number of specific forms. Though Janie's interlude with Killicks is brief, Hurston here manages to set the basic pattern. First, Killicks intends to exploit his wife by putting her to work plowing his fields. Janie is completely powerless to assert her will, for as Killicks claims, Janie "ain't got no particular place. It's wherever [he needs her]" (30). Killicks silences Janie whenever she tries to assert herself, scorning her family when Janie tries to confront him about their marriage (29) and again when she refuses to shovel the manure (30). When Janie resists this silencing, Killicks resorts to threats of physical violence: "Don't you change too many words wid me dis mawnin', Janie, do Ah'll take and change ends wid yuh! . . . Ah'll take holt uh dat ax and come in dere and kill yuh!" (30).

Likewise, Joe Starks insists on placing Janie where he wants her to be. Though he, too, puts Janie to work minding the store, Janie seems to be bothered most by the "high stool" Joe insists she sit on, as she tells Pheoby after his death (109). Silence is, again, an integral part of Janie's role. The first time Starks leaves Janie "feeling cold," the first time he "[takes] the bloom off of things," is when he refuses to allow her to make a speech at his election. When Tony Taylor requests "uh few words uh encouragement from Mrs. Mayor Starks," Joe takes the floor and says, "mah wife don't know nothin' 'bout no speech-makin'. Ah never married her for nothin' lak dat. She's uh woman and her place is in de home" (40–41). He again makes Janie "sullen" (58) when he refuses to allow her to attend the funeral of Matt Bonner's mule:

"*you* ain't goin' off in all dat mess uh commonness. Ah'm surprised at yuh fuh askin'" (56). Joe's motive in silencing Janie seems to be, as Haurykiewicz has noted, his "sexual jealousy" (56), and the pattern continues through his making Janie wear the head-rag (51), his refusing her the right to join in the mule-talk and checker-playing of the store porch (50), and his insisting that Janie is "gettin' too moufy" (71) whenever she challenges him, all the way up to the day of his death, when he commands her to "Shut up!" (82). Starks, like Killicks, resorts to scorn whenever Janie tries to assert herself, often disparaging her looks or intelligence. The threat of violence under Killicks turns into Starks's actual violence when he beats her for a poorly-cooked dinner (67) and for insulting his sexual prowess, when he "[strikes] Janie with all his might and [drives] her from the store" (76). Just as Killicks on his last day with Janie threatens to kill her, so Starks, bedridden and helpless before Janie's verbal assault, wishes "thunder and lightnin' would kill [her]!" (82).[3]

Killicks and Starks have been charged with patriarchal domination, treating Janie as little more than chattel (no better than a mule, according to Julie Haurykiewicz [54]), yet Hurston's narrator notes that Tea Cake also displays "all those signs of possession" (105). The source of this domination, according to most readings of the novel, is the husband's exacting insistence on conventional sex roles (the complication of Killicks's intent to take Janie out of the kitchen notwithstanding), combined with his sexual jealousy. Tea Cake, again, shows all of these flaws Killicks and Starks have been faulted with, and his treatment of Janie is remarkably similar to theirs once we see beyond the difference in Janie's reactions to the treatment. Tea Cake insists, for instance, on a traditional economic arrangement; Janie is to rely solely on Tea Cake as bread-winner, and leave her own money useless in the bank: "Ah no need no assistance tuh help me feed mah woman. From now on, you gointuh eat whutever mah money can buy yuh and wear de same. When Ah ain't got nothin' you don't git nothin'" (122). Though Tea Cake's invitation to Janie to work in the fields has been much-discussed as a site where sex roles break down, its significance pales when we realize that Tea Cake is only asking Janie to do what "de rest uh de women" do (127), and though his words are gentler than Killicks's, the substance of what he is asking Janie to do is the same.[4] Further, Tea Cake prevents Janie from being in situations inappropriate to her sex and class; just as Starks does not allow Janie to mingle in the "commonness" of the mule's funeral, so Tea Cake insists that Janie stay away from his gambling: "dis time it's gointuh be nothin' but tough men's talkin' all kinds uh talk so it ain't no place for you tuh be" (119).[5] The place for Janie to be is, in fact, solely Tea Cake's prerogative; just as Killicks tells Janie that her place is "wherever Ah need yuh" (30), so Tea Cake brags to Sop-de-Bottom, "Janie is wherever *Ah* wants tuh be" (141). Hurston is so careful to highlight evidence that Tea Cake rules in this marriage that one must wonder how S. Jay Walker could ever have dubbed it "a relationship between acknowledged equals" (521).

As Ramsey has noted, Tea Cake displays all the traits of the "man's man" (45). He boasts of his sexual prowess ("Ah'm de Apostle Paul tuh de Gentiles. Ah tells 'em and then again Ah show's 'em" [100]). As Lupton notes, he exhibits plenty of other negative masculine traits as well: "fist-fighting, getting slashed with a knife after a gambling win, hitting Janie, hostility toward her greater economic power, taking Janie's two hundred dollars without permission and not inviting her to the party he throws with it, and so forth" (50). Like Starks and Killicks, Tea Cake is sexually jealous of Janie, commanding her to "keep [Mrs. Turner] from round dis house" (137) and "treat her cold" (138) out of fear that Janie might succumb to Mrs. Turner's unflattering comparisons of Tea Cake with her brother. Out of sexual jealousy, Tea Cake beats Janie in order to "[reassure] him in possession" and "show he was boss" (140). As if Tea Cake's masculinity needs emphasizing, Hurston drags before the reader the pitifully effeminate Mr. Turner with his "powerless laugh" (138), a "vanishing-looking kind of man as if there used to be parts about him that stuck out individually but now he hadn't a thing about him that wasn't dwindled and blurred" (137). As Hurston indicates, the proper sentiment toward such a castrated male who is not the boss and not in possession of his wife is pity.[6]

THE DYNAMICS OF OPPRESSION

This is the problem for those who celebrate Tea Cake as Janie's liberator: he displays all the nasty characteristics of her oppressors. Skeptics want to see this pattern as proof of Hurston's unexamined ambivalence toward Tea Cake and of textual inconsistency. Apologists respond with a variety of explanations. Some feminist critics, who have become troubled by Tea Cake, insist nevertheless that he is part of Janie's progression toward autonomy, if not its end; once he has done all he can for Janie, Hurston rids her of him through the hurricane device, freeing her to experience "a special fate that lies beyond a happy marriage" (Lillios 93), an "alternative to heterosexuality" (Batker 211). Urgo, who admits a consistency of treatment among the three husbands, explains that Killicks and Starks merely get "the words all wrong" (47), raising an interesting possibility. Certainly Tea Cake looks and sounds the part of Janie's ideal husband more than the other two. Killicks is old, with a misshapen head and neck, and says exactly what he means (at least once he stops talking in rhymes to Janie). Starks also is older than Janie, with a growing belly, and he, too, is no diplomat. Both men demand obedience. Tea Cake, on the other hand, is young and handsome, and achieves what he wants by saying what he does not mean. Unlike Killicks, for instance, who says directly to Janie that she will do the work he tells her to do, Tea Cake invents charming reasoning for his wanting Janie to pick beans with him. In short, he allows her to bow down without losing face. If we accept this explanation as sufficient address to the problem, we ought to recognize the consequences for our reading of Janie: in her relationship with Tea Cake, she is deceived into obedience, struck powerless by a handsome face and charming words that flatter her own pride. Hardly the makings of a feminist hero—or of any other kind.

But that does not have to be the end of the explanation. Both Urgo's assertion and claims of ambivalence and inconsistency rest on two related but erroneous assumptions: that Hurston intends Tea Cake as Janie's liberator and that she intends her first husbands wholly as villains. As the previous discussion shows, the first of these assumptions simply cannot be sustained without admitting Hurston's inconsistency. The second assumption can easily be challenged using evidence from the text as well, for Hurston indicates that Killicks and Starks are not to be taken as the mere villains those who read the book in terms of epic or romance quest claim they are. Some critics have noted the oddity of telling Janie's story in the core narrative in third person; why not allow Janie to tell her own story? The answer lies in what this technique allows Hurston to do that a first person narrative would not. One thing it allows her to do is get behind how Janie perceives Killicks and Starks to expose their motives for acting the way they do; in short, a third-person narrative allows Hurston to humanize these men.

We see in both of these marriages Janie's ability to hurt her husbands as they have the ability to hurt her. When Janie confronts Killicks about their marriage, he silences her with scorn not out of a desire to oppress, but as a response to fear. Janie's indication that she might run away from Killicks sends fear coursing through his body: "There! Janie had put words in his held-in fears. She might run off sure enough. The thought put a terrible ache in Logan's body, but he thought it best to put on scorn" (29). Janie's words have hurt him, and he responds in kind. As he feigns sleep, "resentful in his agony," Hurston tells us that "he hoped that he had hurt her as she had hurt him" (29). Killicks's threatening to kill Janie is also a response to hurt and fear, as Hurston notes that his speech is "half a sob and half a cry" (30). Janie's marriage to Joe Starks illustrates even further that much of her oppression results from her actual or perceived attack on her husband. The narrowly-avoided "fuss" following the funeral of Matt Bonner's mule originates with Janie, for though Starks returns to the store "full of pleasure and good humor," Janie's "sullen" demeanor makes him resentful (58). The argument over the bill of lading, during which Joe insults Janie's intelligence, also begins with her. After having to wait on a customer despite her wish to hear the end of the play-acting on the porch, Janie returns "with her bristles sticking out all over her and with dissatisfaction written all over her face. Joe [sees] it and [lifts] his own hackles a bit" (66). Likewise, when Joe strikes Janie and drives her from the store, Hurston does not allow the reader to take this act simply as an over-reaction to Janie's insult; in fact, she provides an in-depth look at what goes through Joe's head:

> Janie had robbed him of his illusion of irresistible maleness that all men cherish, which was terrible. . . . There was nothing to do in life anymore. Ambition was useless. And the cruel deceit of Janie! Making all that show of humbleness and scorning him all the time! Laughing at him, and now putting the town up to do the same. Joe didn't know the words for all this, but he knew the feeling. (75–76)

By presenting Joe's perspective, Hurston makes this incident less about Joe's insistence on domination and more about his response to hurt. She does the same throughout this part of the narrative, providing us with information that Janie is not privy to, telling us, for instance, that Janie resents the head-rag only because she does not know of Joe's jealousy of her, which Hurston implies would have made the whole thing "sensible" to Janie, "But he never said things like that. It just wasn't in him" (51–52).

That Killicks and Starks are human does not, of course, wholly exculpate them. In most instances, Janie acts as she does because she believes her husbands are trying to dominate her. But fingering the correct perpetrator is not so important, perhaps, as understanding the dynamic at work in these exchanges. Janie receives a command that she thinks unfair; in reply, her fighting spirit asserts itself. This assertion, however, is always futile, as Janie herself recognizes: "Time came when she fought back with her tongue as best she could, but it didn't do her any good. It just made Joe do more. He wanted her submission and he'd keep on fighting until he felt he had it" (67). As Janie is weaker, the only possible outcome of her resistance is further escalation of conflict ending in defeat. Over the years, Janie tries to mask her fighting spirit to avoid conflict, but never really gives it up entirely. As Hurston notes, "The years took all the fight out of Janie's face. For a while she thought it was gone from her soul" (72), but Janie is mistaken. It asserts itself again when Janie figuratively castrates Joe Starks before his admiring public, ending any chance for the two to reconcile. Janie's final, seething conversation with Joe on his deathbed has been seen both as her triumph and as an insensitive attack (Lupton 47), but in any case an unmasking of the central problem of their marriage. Here we discover Joe's fault: he has not yet found out that "you got tuh pacify somebody besides yo'self if you wants any sympathy in dis world. [He] ain't tried tuh pacify *nobody* but [himself]" (82).

The reader has no qualms against accepting Janie's assessment of Joe, even if he thinks her speech insensitive given Joe's condition, but what often goes unrecognized is that this charge applies equally to Janie. In all instances, it is Janie's unwillingness to pacify Killicks and Starks that leads to their further oppression of her. That Janie herself suspects this to be true is evinced in her overwhelming sense of pity after Joe's death: "Poor Joe! Maybe if she had known some other way to try, she might have made his face different" (83).

Strangely, in her third marriage, Janie offers no resistance to Tea Cake's commands, which are often as patriarchal as those of Killicks and Starks; in fact, we usually see Janie in absolute submission to him. She wears what he wants her to wear, goes where he wants her to go, and accepts all manner of negative behavior from her new husband with a quiet passivity uncharacteristic of the Janie we have come to know. Janie's willingness to take a beating, for instance, makes Tea Cake the envy of the muck; Sop-de-Bottom congratulates his friend on his luck in finding such a submissive wife, a wife so much unlike his own, who is a shrew by comparison (140–141). But this development is not so strange if we understand Janie as a character who changes. The obstacles she overcomes are not solely outside of herself; she must also overcome her own impulse to demand that her marriages conform exactly to her immature understanding of what a marriage is (and surely it is reasonable to suggest that Janie's understanding has, by the time she is forty, progressed beyond that of a pubescent girl). In fact, expecting her husbands to conform is exactly what strips Janie of her power; once they do not, she is powerless to do anything but fight or run away. Janie must learn that she can have the marriage of her vision, but that it will not be provided to her by any man, no matter how promising he might seem. Hurston carefully manages events to underscore this theme. Two marriages fail, one succeeds, yet all three husbands treat Janie the same way. One might argue that Tea Cake's treatment is not so extreme, but, according to the logic provided by Janie herself as she describes how her resistance provokes escalation with Joe, one might respond that Janie does not allow it ever to become as extreme. She submits to Tea Cake, and the result is the growth of their relationship and Tea Cake's willingness to empower her; as Tea Cake explains to Sop-de-Bottom, his response to Janie's submission is "Ah love her for it" (141). By the time she marries Tea Cake, Janie has learned the true source of power in marriage and in this book, which Joseph Urgo correctly identifies when he asserts that "Power, in *Their Eyes Were Watching God*, is rooted in one's sense of vulnerability" (41). To find her vulnerability, Janie must first subdue her fighting spirit, which Hurston symbolically anticipates in the first checker match between Janie and Tea Cake; "Yuh can't beat uh woman," Tea Cake muses, "Dey jes won't stand fuh it. But Ah'll come teach yuh agin. You gointuh be uh good player, too, after while" (92).

A Feminist Hero?

This argument may seem to complicate the notion that Janie is a feminist hero. Hurston, by allowing Janie to achieve her vision of marriage by submitting to a man, has seemingly winked at an oppressive tradition. But we ought not simply ignore that Janie does achieve her goal. At the end of her story, she is undeniably the dignified, empowered woman that Hurston's feminist advocates have claimed she is. The current reading differs only in that it takes responsibility for that achievement out of Tea Cake's hands and puts it solely in Janie's; she gains her subject position as a result of her own subversive actions, and not because she fortunately meets the right man. It posits Janie as an internally dynamic, rather than internally static, character; she must abandon her "fighting spirit" in order to achieve her ideal marriage. Many critics, however, have misread Janie's quest for a marriage as a search for a suitable man. Comparing Janie to Chopin's Edna Pontellier, Alice Walker suggests that each "desires . . . a man who loves her and makes her feel alive. Each woman finds such a man" ("Saving" 6). In order to be free, Janie must locate the temporal circumstances (that is, the man) best suited for freedom. Walker refers explicitly to slave narratives, where "escape for the body and freedom for the soul went together" ("Saving" 5), as the appropriate paradigm for understanding *Their Eyes Were Watching God*. To Walker, Janie's situation is little different from that of escaped slaves in the Antebellum South heading for Canada; as with Janie, their freedom depends on getting to the right place. This interpretive scheme does not allow for submission because submission would necessarily entail defeat.

Fortunately, however, the slave narrative is not the only paradigm available to help us understand what is going on in this book. As Houston A. Baker, Jr., has shown, the strategy of direct resistance common in slave narratives, which he calls deformation of mastery, is only one of two strong currents running through African-American texts concerned with issues of race and power. The other, which Baker dubs mastery of form, seeks empowerment not through escape from conventional expectations, but rather through satisfaction of them. In *Their Eyes Were Watching God*, Hurston herself engages in deformation strategies regarding race—her use of African-American folklore would be one example—but Janie's strategy in negotiating oppression predicated on gender follows a different pattern. Clearly, Janie has pursued the strategy of deformation in her first two marriages—that is, "go[ue]rilla action in the face of acknowledged adversaries" (Baker 50)—leading some to believe that this is the strategy which allows her to achieve her final subject position. As the current discussion has shown, however, this strategy has always resulted in defeat because Janie is no go[ue]rilla. Her defeats do not vanquish Janie because she abandons direct resistance in favor of the mastery strategy, which "conceals, disguises, floats like a trickster butterfly in order to sting like a bee" (Baker 50).

In referring to the slave narrative tradition, Walker offers convincing, if circumstantial, evidence for the unchanging feminist hero theory. Janie fits into a long line of black characters whose physical circumstance is inextricably linked to larger issues of freedom; to suggest a Janie who wins freedom through submission is therefore counterintuitive. Yet, as Baker has shown, mastery of form is far from uncommon in African-American discursive practice. A Janie who uses submission as a strategy of resistance would be no newfangled Hurston invention; she would fit into a tradition of black activists and characters stretching from Booker T. Washington and Charles Chesnutt's Uncle Julius to Houston Baker's own father and Ishmael Reed's Uncle Robin.[7] All of these win power and freedom not by direct resistance or horizontal displacement, but by recognizing the realities and exigencies of their temporal situation and by using this keen insight within a context of covert resistance. In short, this strategy may be characterized as uncle-tomming with a purpose. It is not radical, therefore, to suggest that Hurston used a pattern of power through submission already available to her in literature dealing with race and applied it to her own story of gender and power in marriage.

The scope of the power Janie achieves through submission to Tea Cake is far-reaching. By appealing to his patriarchy, Janie flatters him. In order to justify his pride, he must constantly consult Janie for approval, most notably after she has taken the job in the fields ("You don't think Ah'm tryin' tuh git outa takin' keer uh yuh, do yuh, Janie, 'cause Ah ast yuh tuh work long side uh me?" [127]), and again during the storm ("Ah reckon you wish now you had of stayed in yo' big house 'way from such as dis, don't yuh? . . . 'sposing you wuz tuh die, now. You wouldn't get mad at me for draggin' yuh heah?" [151]). These passages show that Tea Cake's identity as the good husband relies on Janie; she must approve in order for him to maintain it. She has been so submissive to his will, such a good wife, that he begins to wonder if he really deserves her, and so he must demonstrate that he does in word and deed. In this way, Tea Cake's understanding of himself becomes a reflection of Janie's response; she is able to fashion his identity and guide his actions by appealing, directly or indirectly, to his pride in the role of benevolent patriarch.

We understand why this strategy might succeed when we remember the claims conventional marriage makes on the patriarch, who, like the submissive wife, has his own externally-imposed role to play. According to this tradition, men must give up absolute freedom to take on full executive responsibility for their families. They must be monogamous. They must work to provide economic support. As wives are incapable of performing complex tasks of the mind and providing for the future, husbands must hold full decision-making powers; they also must shoulder full responsibility when their decisions fail to achieve desired ends. To the extent that a husband is incapable of fulfilling these responsibilities, he is inadequate. To say that this ideal male has nowhere existed does not diminish his ability to shape community standards of masculine behavior. Husbands who rule unjustly are objects of ridicule, their wives innocent victims. If, as Nanny suggests, black women are the mules of the world, even literal mules in this book are considered by community standards to have certain rights, and their owners certain responsibilities; consider the town's harsh judgments of Matt Bonner. Luckily for Janie, none of her husbands is so shameless; she therefore has available to her the stereotype of the good husband for her own use. As marriage is somewhat of a contractual agreement, a wife who fulfills the role expected of her has the reasonable expectation that the other party will do the same; thus, submission becomes a way for a wife like Janie to demand that the other terms of the contract be satisfied as well, and a source of power in controlling her husband.

A number of passages in the book support this understanding of the force of contract in its matrimonial or other forms. Power, according to Hurston, may be achieved in two ways. If a subject is not willing to be ruled, then the would-be ruler must resort to coercion to achieve and maintain power. If, on the other hand, a subject submits willingly to rule, then a ruler's power derives directly from the subject's will. In the first case, resistance is futile if the subject is weaker, but in the second the subject maintains certain rights within the framework of a social contract. The most conspicuous (non-matrimonial) social contract in the book is that between the citizens of Eatonville and Mayor Joe Starks, and as such it is a telling example of how Hurston understands power to work. Joe's power does not derive from the direct use of force; as Hurston notes, the citizens have no "physical fear" of him (44). When he catches Henry Pitts with a load of his ribbon cane and makes him leave town, some of the citizens think the act unjust, and they begin to complain among themselves of how exacting Joe is with his citizens, of his haughtiness, of his love for obedience. Sam Watson acknowledges these things, noting that the citizens are but blades of grass bending before the wind that is Joe Starks, yet he also defends the Mayor: "at dat us needs him. De town wouldn't be nothin' if it wasn't for him" (46). Despite their feelings "good and bad" about Starks, the town does not challenge him. They willingly accept the costs of being subjects under Starks in order to gain the benefits. Hurston explains that this arrangement has consequences for Joe's identity and the way he exercises his power when she explains that he is who he is not only because of intrinsic character traits, but also "because the town [bows] down" (47); this ruler's identity and actions are both functions of his subjects' willingness to submit. As Joe is hardly capable of making the town submit under force, he surely must see his own self-interest in carefully preserving its citizens' willingness to be ruled. In this way Joe's self-interest becomes aligned with the interests of the citizens; he must become a ruler they understand to be just if he wishes to preserve his power.

Though Joe is certainly capable of using coercion to control Janie, the text suggests all along that he would prefer not to. He does not resort to coercion to force Janie to marry him, but rather argues that she should because he will treat her like a lady. Some who think his character wholly unredeemable may judge his flowery speeches to be little more than deception, but they still constitute the offer of a contractual agreement: "You come go wid me. Den all de rest of yo' natural life you kin live lak you oughta" (28). Further, just as Joe needs the town to think him just, so he demonstrates that he wants Janie to think the same. As Joe joins unthinkingly in the mirth attending the baiting of Matt Bonner's mule, Janie turns away in disgust, talking to herself about how cruel the men are being, saying finally, "Wisht Ah had mah way wid 'em all" (53). Here Janie wishes that she could assert herself on behalf of the mule—Hurston notes that she "wanted to fight about it" (54)—but she chooses instead to remain silent to avoid an argument, undoubtedly realizing that she is incapable of bending the men to her will by force. Unbeknownst to her, Joe has heard what she muttered to herself, and he orders the men to stop, buys the mule, and sets it free. Janie responds with a flattering speech of praise. Perhaps if she had known that Joe's act was a direct response to her own powerlessness and not the expression of something intrinsic to his character—he was, after all, laughing with the rest before he overheard her—she might have understood much earlier that dependency and submission can be more effective ways to exercise power than the direct application of force, especially when she is the weaker. She also might have understood that submission can act to fashion a husband into a ruler worthy of her praise.

If there is one woman in this book who understands that the traditional feminine role is in its own way a powerful one, it is surely Mrs. Bogle, who appears for a mere paragraph's duration in Chapter Six. In a novel filled with seemingly extraneous vignettes, it is easy to take little notice of her appearance, but the little information we do learn about her is highly relevant to Janie's predicament. This grandmother is a woman fully at home in the role of desire object; when she strides up to the store porch with "a blushing air of coquetry about her" that invokes visions of "magnolia blooms and sleepy lakes under the moonlight" (65), she obliterates the presence of the mere girls who preceded her. Unlike these girls, who elicit only hyperbolic overtures from the porch-sitters, Mrs. Bogle commands their notice because two men had already worked hard to be worthy of her:

> Her first husband had been a coachman but "studied jury" to win
> her. He had finally become a preacher to hold her till his death.
> Her second husband worked in Fohnes orange grove—but tried
> to preach when he caught her eye. He never got any further than
> a class leader, but that was something to offer her. It proved his
> love and pride. (65)

In both instances, Mrs. Bogle's husbands had sought for and won her
approval. Hurston likens her to "a wind on the ocean," a force which moves
men though "the helm determine[s] the port," a reference to conventional
patriarchy. If the helm does determine the port, we must at least admit that
Mrs. Bogle determines the helm; she recognizes that she is an object of
men's desire, and so she sets about using her desirability to make those men
into acceptable husbands. She does not rule in her marriages, but she makes
certain that her husbands conform to her notion of a just ruler; that is, one
who acts as she wishes.

Janie also insists that Tea Cake prove his intentions if he wishes
to win and keep her as wife. She has been training him carefully from
the days of their courtship, when she plays the role of defenseless widow
suspicious that Tea Cake might, in fact, be "uh rounder and uh pimp"
(100). He recognizes this suspicion and, in order to win the prize, must set
about demonstrating through his words and actions that Janie has nothing
to fear—though every piece of information we learn about his past might
suggest otherwise. The Tea Cake who wins Janie is, we suspect, not the
same man she meets that first day in the store. Nowhere is Janie's ability
to make Tea Cake bend to her vision of what she wants him to be more
evident than in their exchange following a night of fighting over Nunkie.
Here, Janie charges Tea Cake with still harboring feelings for Nunkie, not,
Hurston says, "because she believed it. She wanted to hear his denial. She
had to crow over the fallen Nunkie." Tea Cake, seeing his image tarnished
in Janie's eyes, answers quickly—and, one might say, obediently—"Whut
would Ah do wid dat lil chunk of a woman wid you around? She ain't
good for nothin' exceptin' tuh set up in uh corner by de kitchen stove and
break wood over her head. You'se something tuh make uh man forgit tuh
git old and forgit tuh die" (132). This speech is part of a larger pattern
of proving himself through affirmation and action in response to Janie's
putting "de shamery" (100) on him; to win and keep Janie, Tea Cake must
satisfy her need for "tellin' and showin'" (102) that she does hold the keys
to the kingdom. When Tea Cake admits that Janie has got him so he
can no longer help himself (116), we understand that she has become the
wind that drives him, even if he does determine the port. Janie is such the
ideal of the submissive wife, and Tea Cake of the benevolent patriarch,

that their relationship becomes the envy of every man and woman on the muck; the day following Janie's beating, the men in the fields "dream dreams" because of "the helpless way she [hangs] on [Tea Cake]," and the women "see visions" because of the way he pets and pampers her (140). As Tea Cake's goal has been to demonstrate his ownership of Janie to the world, one can only imagine how different the aftermath might have been had she put up a fight.

WHITHER HURRICANES AND OTHER AUDACITIES

Of course, the book does not leave Janie and Tea Cake together on the muck, and any evaluation must take account of the hurricane, Tea Cake's madness, and his death by Janie's hand. Hurston has left many wondering why this marriage must end in such a violent way, and here again conventional assumptions have caused confusion. Following her interpretation of the book as literary romance, Janice Daniel sees the hurricane as the "requisite 'dragon' of [Janie's] romance quest" (72). Lupton cites this final action sequence as part of her reading of the novel in terms of evolutionary theory; under stress from the natural world, a woman has been selected as the fittest over a man (53–54). Carla Kaplan asserts that Tea Cake's death is required by the narrative logic of the novel, liberating Janie "to continue her quest and, ultimately, to satisfy her 'oldest human longing—self-revelation' with someone who *can* listen [Pheoby]" (132). Here again, Hurston comes under fire from skeptics. Ramsey, who describes Janie's life on the muck as "implausibly Edenesque" (46), calls the hurricane "melodramatically gratuitous," Tea Cake's infection by rabies "fictionally arbitrary" (43), and concludes finally that Tea Cake's death is yet another mark of weakness, a way to duck several important questions: "Would Janie remain happy if tied to the seasonal cycles of grinding migrant work? Would she have money of her own that she could expect not to be taken? The novel ends conveniently before such issues arise to require resolution" (45). Even Urgo calls the novel's final sequence "wildly audacious" (53), fashioning a compliment out of the same material of Ramsey's accusation.

Recently, some have been content to label the hurricane mere plot device, and a derivative one at that, which serves solely to rid Janie of Tea Cake (or, according to Ramsey, to enact Hurston's revenge fantasy against the man she loved [46]) and titillate the reader (Lillios 91–92), but which is in any case insufficiently integrated with the novel's thematic concerns. Assuredly, the hurricane does function in these ways, but it is also more relevant to Hurston's themes than many have been willing to admit. It fits a pattern of incidents in which characters are powerless to overcome external obstacles by main force; survival depends on a careful understanding of the variables which can be controlled and those which cannot. A failed assessment leaves characters wholly at the mercy of fortune, as Motor Boat and Dick Sterrett are at the mercy of the hurricane. Other incidents fitting this pattern include Nanny's slavery experiences, Starks's bout with Death, Tea Cake's rabies, and Janie's trial. In some instances (as with Nanny and Motor Boat), fortune works in the character's favor; in others (as with Starks, Tea Cake, and Sterrett), fortune works against him, regardless of the dictates of cosmic justice. Janie's quest, if we accept that she is too weak to reverse single-handedly the sex role she is expected to play, also fits this pattern, a connection strengthened by her objective both in the quest and in escaping the hurricane waters. In both instances, Janie wishes to reach the high ground.

And here again, as with the technique of third-person narration, we must ask ourselves what the hurricane's aftermath allows Hurston to do that she otherwise could not. First, it allows her to dramatize in extreme fashion Janie's continued use of submission to control Tea Cake. During his bout with rabies, Janie never fails to answer Tea Cake's increasingly wild accusations and assertions of masculine privilege with pacifying submission: "All right, Tea Cake, jus' as you say" (172). Until the disease consumes him, her abject obedience still makes Tea Cake cry and feel ashamed of himself (171). Janie continues with her strategy of pacification to the verge of oblivion, but here Hurston is able to draw the line where submission must end; only after Tea Cake's pistol has twice clicked on an empty chamber does Janie, for the first time in their relationship, dare to command him: "Tea Cake, put down dat gun and go back tuh bed!" (175). Once Janie sees that her submission no longer functions to make her husband as she wishes him to be, she abandons the strategy entirely, shooting him with the rifle rather than follow him into death. But Janie's role-playing continues to serve her purposes, as it allows the judge in her trial to portray her as "a devoted wife trapped by unfortunate circumstances who really in firing a rifle bullet into the heart of her late husband did a great act of mercy" (179).

These events also allow Hurston to portray Janie without Tea Cake, and to re-emphasize that her happiness depends not on Tea Cake as he is, but on the Tea Cake of her dreams. As the novel comes to an end, and as Janie reflects on the sadness of what she has gone through, suddenly a vision of Tea Cake appears:

> Then Tea Cake came prancing around her where she was . . . Tea Cake, with the sun for a shawl. Of course he wasn't dead. He could never be dead until she herself had finished feeling and thinking. The kiss of his memory made pictures of love and light against the wall. Here was peace. (183–184)

The man Janie met in the store is dead, but the man whom she herself has fashioned out of his raw material still lives. Here Hurston brings the exposition of her novel full-circle; Janie is one of the women who "forget all those things they don't want to remember, and remember everything they don't want to forget. The dream is the truth" (1). This ability to fashion truth out of dreams regardless of temporal reality is what gives women like Janie their power; they are not like the pitiable men whose dreams are "mocked to death by Time" (1). Nanny, who envisions a ruling chair for Janie, has sought a future for her granddaughter where the substance of life accords with her dream of it. But, just as the ruling chair has been by custom reserved for men, so this insistence on the correspondence of dream and reality puts Janie's happiness in the hands of fortune, which Hurston notes is the predicament of the male "Watcher" of the horizon (1). Only when Janie gives up this insistence, only when she removes the fighting spirit from her soul to focus on achieving her dream through submission, is she able to become self-reliant; the reality of Tea Cake's domination of her becomes irrelevant, and so, finally, does his physical death, for despite these inconsistencies, Janie is able to make her husband into a dream-figure to serve her own needs.

CONCLUSION

I may here seem to portray a coldly calculating Janie, and to diminish the love she and Tea Cake share. Anyone who has read the book might protest, and rightly so, that there is no evidence for this characterization of Janie, no evidence that her love for Tea Cake and his love for her are anything but genuine. I agree with Alice Walker when she claims *Their Eyes Were Watching God* constitutes "one of the sexiest, most 'healthily' rendered heterosexual love stories in our literature" ("Zora" 17). I have not set out to challenge this claim; rather, the questions before me have been why this final marriage allows the survival of love, and why the first two do not. That traditionally-conceived sex roles are love-defeating in Janie's first two marriages is obvious; why they are not love-defeating in her third is questionable, as I have suggested. Perhaps, in answering Richard Wright's early criticisms of the book, we have been too tempted to discover the social protest he missed; Janie must therefore be the questing feminist who finds her own voice and autonomy in a marriage to a man who will allow her to actualize herself. Evidence from the text, however, suggests that Tea Cake is no such man. Further, it is unreasonable to expect him to be: he is a southern, working-class, uneducated wanderer much more likely to be within the traditional ideology of marriage prevalent in rural, early twentieth-century America. One must assume that he is not conversant with more enlightened ideas of marriage, which were necessarily unavailable to illiterate men, not to mention undesirable to them, until much later in the century. Janie, who is incapable of single-handedly unmaking conventional marriage, must find a way to appropriate it in order to achieve her own ends. She is not responsible for externally-imposed sex roles, nor should we interpret her submission to them as whole-hearted consent to their justice; however, she has learned in her first marriages that defiance, though just, though heroic, is quixotic if not wholly disastrous. Janie's purposes, which I would suggest tend much more toward love than toward autonomy anyway, are served only when she appeals to the force of contract within conventional marriage. She achieves both self-reliance and love in spite of, not through, her third husband.

Once we adjust certain of our long-held assumptions to account for evidence they cannot explain, we are left with a well-wrought text capable of sustaining close reading. We do not have to gloss over "inconsistency" or "ambivalence" to see Janie for the heroine she is, nor do we have to resort to strained explanations that flatter our own sensibilities. This novel is clearly not the straightforward critique of gender and power in marriage that some critics claim it is, but neither is it the flawed, unfinished work of an exhausted and emotionally conflicted Zora Neale Hurston, as Ramsey claims. If we let go of our assumptions of Tea Cake as liberator, of Killicks and Starks as villains, of Janie as the unchanging feminist hero, this text is capable of answering consistently each of our questions and concerns about it. Further, we are left with a reading capable of satisfying the advocates and gate-keepers alike. Janie does not have to remain unchanged and defiant for us to recognize her covert feminism, just as other apparently subservient characters throughout the African-American tradition do not have to defy their white masters for us to recognize their achievement of power despite an imposed racial hierarchy. Neither must we elect this book to the canon with a wink and a nudge, for charges of textual weakness, as I hope I have shown, are due to our own mistaken assumptions and not to Hurston's shoddy craftsmanship. Though one must agree with Urgo that "there is no longer any need to argue the importance of *Their Eyes Were Watching God* to American literature" (41–42), it would be best to stop coddling it. The best argument for this change in attitude is the text itself, for Hurston here demonstrates that her book has need of no one's patronage.

Notes

1. I gratefully acknowledge Donald Kartiganer, Wendy Pearce Miller, Jay Watson, and Ethel Young-Minor for their indispensable advice.

2. See, for instance, Mary Helen Washington on an exchange between Walker and Robert Stepto at the 1979 MLA convention (xi–xii), and on her own second thoughts about the book (xiii–xiv). See also Lupton, Urgo, Ramsey.

3. To focus exclusively on the elements that make this marriage disastrous for Janie is to ignore her early perceptions of its promise. Initially, Janie does think Joe is the "bee for her bloom"; "From now on until death," she thinks, "she was going to have flower dust and springtime sprinkled over everything" (31). Once the relationship sours, her reflections on the present indicate that things have not always been this way. When Janie thinks that "The bed was *no longer* a daisy-field for her and Joe to play in" (67, emphasis added), she tacitly admits that at one time she and Joe had been involved in a love-game. Likewise, when she learns—and only after seven years of marriage—that "She wasn't petal-open *anymore* with [Joe]" (67, emphasis added), that "She had *no more* blossomy openings dusting pollen over her man, neither any glistening young fruit where the petals *used to be*" (68, emphasis added), we know that the history of Janie's second marriage has been one of a romantic union compromised, and not a consistent history of unhappiness and oppression.

4. Though a doctrine of separate spheres follows Janie as she moves between class groups, sphere boundaries change. The role of a wife on the muck is to work in the fields with her husband; because Janie initially keeps to the quarters there, she is considered a "special case" (127).

5. We never witness Janie gambling, which seems wholly within the masculine sphere among working-class blacks like Tea Cake. His preventing her from joining him is roughly equivalent to Joe's insistence that she not join in the porch talk. From what we see, the porch talk is carried on solely by men; when women enter the scene, they are objects of judgment. In both cases, the husband acts to keep the wife out of sex- and class-inappropriate situations.

6. Some may object to my notion here that Hurston praises traditionally-conceived masculinity by pointing to other Hurston texts that seem to suggest otherwise. Sykes of "Sweat," whose assertions of masculine privilege over his wife Delia are undeniably unjust, comes readily to mind. The problem with Sykes, however, is not so much that he is too much the man as it is that he is not enough of one. His inability to provide for his wife's economic needs underscores this claim, as do the judgments rendered by the porch-sitters in that story. Sykes's death by rattlesnake, the self-chosen symbol of his phallic power, and over which he claims to have mastery, indicates that though he talks the talk of masculinity, he is more appropriately regarded as inadequate. I would suggest, therefore, that Delia's predicament in "Sweat" is not an appropriate analogue to Janie's predicament in *Their Eyes Were Watching God*.

7. Baker discusses Washington and Chesnutt as representatives of the mastery of form strategy at length in *Modernism and the Harlem Renaissance* (1987). See also passages relating directly to his own father's adoption of Washington's teachings (xvi–xvii, 100–103). Though Baker does not discuss Reed's *Flight to Canada* (1976), it is a particularly good illustration of both mastery of form and deformation of mastery. In this postmodern slave narrative, protagonist Raven Quickskill's escape from his master and subsequent guerilla tactics are contrasted with the covert resistance of Uncle Robin, who has mastered the stereotype of the good slave.

Works Cited

Baker, Houston A. *Modernism and the Harlem Renaissance*. Chicago: U of Chicago P, 1987.

Baker, Carol. "'Love Me Like I Like to Be': The Sexual Politics of Hurston's *Their Eyes Were Watching God*, the Classic Blues, and the Black Women's Club Movement." *African American Review* 32 (1998): 199–213.

Daniel, Janice. "'De Understandin' to Go 'Long wid It': Realism and Romance in *Their Eyes Were Watching God*." *Southern Literary Journal* 24 (1991): 66–76.

Haurykiewicz, Julie A. "From Mules to Muliebrity: Speech and Silence in *Their Eyes Were Watching God.*" *Southern Literary Journal* 29 (1997): 45–60.

Hurston, Zora Neale. *Their Eyes Were Watching God.* 1937. New York: Harper, 1990.

Jacobs, Karen. "From 'Spy Glass' to 'Horizon': Tracking the Anthropological Gaze in Zora Neale Hurston." *A Forum on Fiction* 30 (1997): 329–361.

Kaplan, Carla. "The Erotics of Talk: 'That Oldest Human Longing' in *Their Eyes Were Watching God.*" *American Literature* 67 (1995): 115–142.

Lillios, Anna. "'The Monstropolous Beast': The Hurricane in Zora Neale Hurston's *Their Eyes Were Watching God.*" *Southern Quarterly* 36 (1998): 89–93.

Lupton, Mary Jane. "Zora Neale Hurston and the Survival of the Female." *Southern Literary Journal* 15 (1982): 45–54.

Ramsey, William M. "The Compelling Ambivalence of Zora Neale Hurston's *Their Eyes Were Watching God.*" *Southern Literary Journal* 27 (1994): 36–50.

Urgo, Joseph R. "'The Tune Is the Unity of the Thing': Power and Vulnerability in Zora Neale Hurston's *Their Eyes Were Watching God.*" *Southern Literary Journal* 23 (1991): 40–54.

Walker, Alice. "Saving the Life That Is Your Own: The Importance of Models in the Artist's Life." *In Search of Our Mothers' Gardens: Womanist Prose.* San Diego: Harcourt, 1983. 3–14.

———. "Zora Neale Hurston: A Cautionary Tale and a Partisan View." *Alice Walker and Zora Neale Hurston: The Common Bond.* Ed. Lillie P. Howard. Westport: Greenwood, 1993. 13–19. Rpt. from Foreword. *Zora Neale Hurston: A Literary Biography.* By Robert E. Hemenway. Urbana: U of Illinois P, 1977.

Walker, S. Jay. "Zora Neale Hurston's *Their Eyes Were Watching God*: Black Novel of Sexism." *Modern Fiction Studies* 20 (1974–75): 519–527.

Washington, Mary Helen. Foreword. *Their Eyes Were Watching God.* By Zora Neale Hurston. New York: Harper, 1990. vii–xiv.

Chronology

1891	Born in Notasulga, Alabama, on January 7, the fifth of eight children, to John Hurston, a carpenter and sharecropper, and Lucy Potts Hurston, a former schoolteacher.
1904	Mother dies.
1917–1918	Attends high school at Morgan Academy in Baltimore.
1918–1919	Attends Howard Prep School, Washington, D.C.
1919–1924	Attends Howard University; receives an associate degree in 1920.
1921	Publishes her first story, "John Redding Goes to Sea," in *Stylus*, the campus magazine.
1924	Publishes "Drenched in Light," a short story, in *Opportunity*.
1925	Submits a story, "Spunk," and a play, "Color Struck," to *Opportunity's* literary contest. Both win second-place award; publishes "Spunk" in the June number.
1925–1927	Attends Barnard College, studying anthropology.
1926	Begins field work for Franz Boas in Harlem; organizes *Fire!* with Langston Hughes and Wallace Thurman; they publish only one issue, which includes Hurston's "Sweat." Publishes several other stories in literary magazines.
1927	Marries Herbert Sheen; first visits Mrs. Rufus Osgood Mason, seeking patronage; publishes "Cudjo's Own Story of the Last African Slaver" in the *Journal of Negro History*;

	signs a contract with Mason, enabling Hurston to return to the South to collect folklore.
1928	Receives a bachelor of arts degree from Barnard; publishes "How It Feels to be Colored Me" in *The World Tomorrow*.
1930	Works on the play *Mule Bone* with Langston Hughes.
1931	Publishes "Hoodoo in America" in the *Journal of American Folklore*; breaks with Langston Hughes over the authorship of *Mule Bone;* divorces Sheen; writes for a theatrical revue called *Fast and Furious*.
1932	Writes and stages a theatrical revue called *The Great Day*.
1933	Stages *From Sun to Sun* (a version of *Great Day*) at Rollins College; publishes "The Gilded Six-Bits" in *Story*.
1934	Publishes seven essays in Nancy Cunard's anthology, *Negro;* goes to Bethune-Cookman College to establish a school of dramatic arts; publishes *Jonah's Gourd Vine; Singing Steel* (a version of *Great Day*) performed in Chicago.
1935	Begins to study for a PhD in anthropology at Columbia University on a fellowship from the Rosenwald Foundation; joins the WPA Federal Theater Project as a "dramatic coach"; *Mules and Men* published.
1936	Awarded a Guggenheim Fellowship to study West Indian Obeah Voodoo practices; goes to Jamaica to do research.
1937	Writes *Their Eyes Were Watching God* in seven weeks; returns to Haiti on a renewed Guggenheim; *Their Eyes Were Watching God* published.
1938	Writes *Tell My Horse;* it is published the same year. Joins the Federal Writers Project in Florida to work on *The Florida Negro*.
1939	Publishes "Now Take Noses" in *Cordially Yours;* receives an honorary doctor of letters degree from Morgan State College; hired as a drama instructor at North Carolina College for Negroes at Durham; marries Albert Prince III; *Moses, Man of the Mountain* published.
1940	Files for divorce from Prince.
1941	Writes *Dust Tracks on a Road;* publishes "Cock Robin, Beale Street" in the *Southern Literary Messenger;* works as a story consultant at Paramount Pictures.
1942	*Dust Tracks on a Road* published.
1943	Awarded the Anisfield-Wolf Book Award in Race Relations

for *Dust Tracks*; on the cover of the *Saturday Review*; receives Howard University's Distinguished Alumni Award; publishes "The 'Pet Negro' Syndrome" in the *American Mercury*; divorced from Prince.

1944   Publishes "My Most Humiliating Jim Crow Experience" in the *Negro Digest*.

1945   Writes *Mrs. Doctor*; it is rejected by Lippincott.

1947   Goes to British Honduras to research black communities in Central America; writes *Seraph on the Suwanee*.

1948   *Seraph on the Suwanee* published.

1950   Publishes "Conscience of the Court" in the *Saturday Evening Post*, while working as a maid in Rivo Island, Florida; publishes "What White Publishers Won't Print" in the *Saturday Evening Post*; publishes "I Saw Negro Votes Peddled" in the *American Legion* magazine. Moves to Belle Glade, Florida.

1951   Publishes "Why the Negro Won't Buy Communism" in the *American Legion* magazine; publishes "A Negro Voter Sizes up Taft" in the *Saturday Evening Post*.

1952   Hired by the *Pittsburgh Courier* to cover the Ruby McCollum case.

1956   Receives an award for "education and human relations" at Bethune-Cookman College. Works as a librarian at Patrick Air Force Base in Florida.

1957–1959   Writes a column on "Hoodoo and Black Magic" for the *Fort Pierce Chronicle*.

1958   Works as a substitute teacher at Lincoln Park Academy, Fort Pierce.

1959   Suffers a stroke. Enters the St. Lucie County Welfare Home.

1960   Dies in the St. Lucie County Welfare Home on January 28; buried in an unmarked grave in the segregated Garden of Heavenly Rest, Fort Pierce.

1973   Alice Walker discovers and marks Hurston's grave.

1975   Walker publishes "In Search of Zora Neale Hurston," in *Ms.*, launching a Hurston revival.

Contributors

HAROLD BLOOM is Sterling Professor of the Humanities at Yale University. He is the author of 30 books, including *Shelley's Mythmaking, The Visionary Company, Blake's Apocalypse, Yeats, A Map of Misreading, Kabbalah and Criticism, Agon: Toward a Theory of Revisionism, The American Religion, The Western Canon,* and *Omens of Millennium: The Gnosis of Angels, Dreams, and Resurrection. The Anxiety of Influence* sets forth Professor Bloom's provocative theory of the literary relationships between the great writers and their predecessors. His most recent books include *Shakespeare: The Invention of the Human,* a 1998 National Book Award finalist, *How to Read and Why, Genius: A Mosaic of One Hundred Exemplary Creative Minds, Hamlet: Poem Unlimited, Where Shall Wisdom Be Found?,* and *Jesus and Yahweh: The Names Divine.* In 1999, Professor Bloom received the prestigious American Academy of Arts and Letters Gold Medal for Criticism. He has also received the International Prize of Catalonia, the Alfonso Reyes Prize of Mexico, and the Hans Christian Andersen Bicentennial Prize of Denmark.

ROBERT B. STEPTO is professor of English, African American Studies, and American Studies at Yale University. He is the author of *From Behind the Veil: A Study of Afro-American Narrative* and *Blue as the Lake: A Personal Geography.*

MARY HELEN WASHINGTON is professor of English Language and Literature at the University of Maryland. She has published four books, including *Black-eyed Susans and Midnight Birds: Stories By and About Black Women.*

HAZEL V. CARBY is the Charles C. and Dorathea S. Dilley Professor of African American Studies and Professor of American Studies at Yale. The author of many wide-ranging essays, her books include *Reconstructing Womanhood*, *Race Men*, and *Cultures in Babylon*.

CYNTHIA BOND is a professor at The John Marshall Law School in Chicago. She has a BA in English and Rhetoric from the University of Illinois, Urbana-Champaign, an MFA in poetry from Cornell University, and also a JD from Cornell University.

SIGRID KING is associate professor of English at Carlow University.

JOHN LOWE is professor of English at Louisiana State University. He is the author of *Jump at the Sun: Zora Neale Hurston's Cosmic Comedy*.

SUSAN EDWARDS MEISENHELDER is professor of English at California State University. She is the author of *Hitting a Straight Lick With a Crooked Stick: Race & Gender in the Work of Zora Neale Hurston*.

DEBORAH CLARKE is an associate professor of English and Women's Studies at Penn State. She is the author of *Robbing the Mother: Women in Faulkner*.

RYAN SIMMONS is assistant professor of English and Literature at Utah Valley State College.

SHAWN E. MILLER has contributed essays to *The Southern Literary Journal* and *The Southern Quarterly*.

Bibliography

Awkward, Michael, ed. *New Essays on Their Eyes Were Watching God.* Cambridge: Cambridge University Press, 1991.

Bloom, Harold, ed. *Zora Neale Hurston.* New York: Chelsea House, 1986.

Callahan, John. *In the African-American Grain: Call-and-Response in Twentieth-Century Black Fiction.* Urbana: University of Illinois Press, 2001.

Cronin, Gloria L., ed. *Critical Essays on Zora Neale Hurston.* New York: G. K. Hall, 1998.

Davis, Rose Parkman. *Zora Neale Hurston: An Annotated Bibliography and Reference Guide.* Westport, Conn: Greenwood Press, 1997.

Fulton, DoVeanna. *Speaking Power: Black Feminist Orality in Women's Narratives of Slavery.* Albany: State University of New York Press, 2006.

Gates, Henry Louis, Jr. and K. A. Appiah, eds. *Zora Neale Hurston: Critical Perspectives Past and Present.* New York: Amistad, 1993.

Glassman, Steve and Kathryn Lee Seidel, eds. *Zora in Florida.* Orlando: University of Central Florida Press, 1991.

Harris, Trudier. *The Power of the Porch: The Storyteller's Craft in Zora Neale Hurston, Gloria Naylor, and Randall Kenan.* Athens: University of Georgia Press, 1996.

Hemenway, Robert E. "Zora Neale Hurston and the Eatonville Anthropology." *The Harlem Renaissance Remembered.* Ed. Arna Bontemps. New York: Dodd, Mead and Co., 1972.

———. *Zora Neale Hurston: A Literary Biography.* Urbana and Chicago: University of Illinois Press, 1980.

Holloway, Karla. *The Character of the Word: The Texts of Zora Neale Hurston.* Westport, Conn: Greenwood Press, 1987.

Hooks, bell. "Zora Neale Hurston: A Subversive Reading." *Matatu.* 1989: 5-23.

Howard, Lillie Pearl. *Zora Neale Hurston.* Boston: Twayne, 1980.

Johnson, Barbara. "Metaphor, Metonymy, and Voice in Their Eyes." *Black Literature and Literary Theory.* Henry Louis Gates, Jr., Ed. pp. 205-21. New York: Methuen, 1984.

Jordan, June. "On Richard Wright and Zora Neale Hurston." *Black World 23* (10). August 1974: 4-8.

Lowe, John. *Jump at the Sun: Zora Neale Hurston's Cosmic Comedy.* Urbana: University of Illinois Press, 1994.

Lyons, Mary E. *Sorrow's Kitchen: The Life and Folklore of Zora Neale Hurston.* New York: Scribners, 1990.

McMillan, Sally. "Janie's Journey: Zora Neale Hurston's Framework for an Alternative Quest." *Southern Studies 12* (1-2): 79-94.

Meisenhelder, Susan Edwards. *Hitting A Straight Lick With a Crooked Stick: Race and Gender in the Work of Zora Neale Hurston.* Tuscaloosa: University of Alabama Press, 1999.

Peters, Pearlie Mae Fisher. *The Assertive Woman in Zora Neale Hurston's Fiction, Folklore, and Drama.* New York: Garland, 1997.

Plant, Deborah G. "Metaphors of Self, Language, and the Will-to-Power." *Every Tub Must Sit on Its Own Bottom: The Philosophy and Politics of Zora Neale Hurston.* Urbana and Chicago: University of Illinois Press, 1995.

Stepto, Robert B. *From Behind the Veil: A Study of Afro-American Narrative.* Urbana: University of Illinois Press, 1979.

Sundquist, Eric J. *The Hammers of Creation: Folk Culture in Modern African-American Fiction.* Athens: University of Georgia Press, 1992.

Walker, Alice, ed. *I Love Myself When I'm Laughing: A Zora Neale Hurston Reader.* New York: The Feminist Press, 1979.

———. "In Search of Zora Neale Hurston." *Ms.* March 1975: 74-79, 85-89.

Wall, Cheryl A. "Zora Neale Hurston's Traveling Blues." *Women of the Harlem Renaissance.* Bloomington and Indianapolis: Indiana University Press, 1995.

Warnes, Andrew. "Guantanamo, Eatonville, Accompong: Barbecue and the Diaspora in the Writings of Zora Neale Hurston." *Journal of American Studies 40* (2): 367-89.

Washington, Mary Helen. "The Black Woman's Search for Identity." *Black World* 21, no. 10. August 1972: 68-75.

Web Sites

The Official Zora Neale Hurston Website
    http://www.zoranealehurston.com/index.html

Wikipedia
Zora Neale Hurston
    http://en.wikipedia.org/wiki/Zora_Neale_Hurston

Gale Group
Black History: Zora Neale Hurston
    http://www.galegroup.com/free_resources/bhm/bio/hurston_z.htm

Acknowledgments

Stepto, Robert B. From *Behind the Veil: A Study of Afro-American Narrative*. Copyright 1979, 1991, by the Board of Trustees of the University of Illinois. Used with permission of the University of Illinois Press.

Washington, Mary Helen, "'I Love the Way Janie Crawford Left Her Husbands': Zora Neale Hurston's Emergent Female Hero." From *Invented Lives: Narratives of Black Women, 1860–1960*, Doubleday, 1987, reprinted in *Zora Neale Hurston's Their Eyes Were Watching God: A Casebook*, Oxford University Press, 2000.

Carby, Hazel V. "The Politics of Fiction, Anthropology, and the Folk: Zora Neale Hurston." From *New Essays on Their Eyes Were Watching God*. © Cambridge University Press, 1990.

Bond, Cynthia. "Language, Speech, and Difference in *Their Eyes Were Watching God*." © 1997 by Cynthia Bond. Reprinted in *Zora Neale Hurston: Critical Perspectives Past and Present*. © 1993 by Henry Louis Gates Jr. and K.A. Appiah.

King, Sigrid. "Naming and Power in Zora Neale Hurston's *Their Eyes Were Watching God*." From *African American Review* 24 (Winter 1990): 683–696. © 1990 Indiana State University. Reprinted in *Critical Essays on Zora Neale Hurston*. © 1998 by G.K. Hall and Co.

Lowe, John. From *Jump at the Sun: Zora Neale Hurston's Cosmic Comedy.* Copyright 1994 by the Board of Trustees of the University of Illinois. Used with permission of the University of Illinois Press.

Chapter 3, "Mink Skin or Coon Hide, The Janus-faced Narrative of Their Eyes Were Watching God" from Susan Edwards Meisenhelder, *Hitting a Straight Lick with a Crooked Stick: Race and Gender in the Work of Zora Neale Hurston* (UAP, 1999). Reprinted by permission of The University of Alabama Press.

Deborah Clarke, "The Porch Couldn't Talk for Looking: Voice and Vision in Their Eyes Were Watching God," *African American Review,* Vol. 35, No. 4. Used by permission of the author.

Simmons, Ryan. "'The Hierarchy Itself': Hurston's *Their Eyes Were Watching God* and the Sacrifice of Narrative Authority." From *African American Review,* vol. 36, no. 2. © 2002 Ryan Simmons.

Miller, Shawn E. From *The Southern Literary Journal,* Volume 37, number 1. Copyright © 2004 by the Deparment of English and Comparative Litera-ture of the University of North Carolina at Chapel Hill. Published by the University of North Carolina Press. Used by permisison of the publisher. www.uncpress.unc.edu

Every effort has been made to contact the owners of copyrighted material and to secure copyright permission. Articles appearing in this volume gener-ally appear much as they did in their original publication with few or no edi-torial changes. In some cases foreign language text has been removed from the original essay. Those interested in locating the original source will find information in this section and in the bibliography as well.

Index

Adams, Henry, 170
Aeschylus, 76
African American, 175, 181
    naming and, 58
African American folklore, 194
African American mythology, 108
African American theorists, 150
African American studies, 24, 25
African religious practices, 37
Afro American literature, 8, 41–42, 55,
    59, 152
All the King's Men (Warren), 170
Amistad (film), 151
Anisfield-Wold Award, 38
anthropology, 25, 30–31, 33–37, 40, 151
anthropomorphic images, 53
audience, 137, 138, 142, 178–179, 180, 182
authorship, authority and, 175–176
Autobiography of an Ex-Coloured Man, The
    (Weldon), 6
autonomy, 18, 37, 137, 201, 202
Awkward, Michael, 95, 102, 146, 148,
    169, 175, 177

Baker, Houston A., Jr., 81, 149, 194, 195
Banana Bottom (McKay), 29
Banks, Joe, 91
Barbadians, 37
Bauer, Dale M., 180
bee/flower imagery, 12, 124, 126, 155,
    156–157, 187
    excerpt, 11, 44, 118–119

Benedict, Ruth, 30–31, 40
Benesch, Klaus, 86
Benston, Kimberly, 58–59
biblical references, 43, 80, 82, 90, 92,
    107–108, 111, 174
Black Boy (Wright), 6, 58
black culture, 29
    authenticity, 38, 182
    folktale, 37
    rural consciousness, 27
black humanists, 24, 25
black identity, 32
    male community, 10
    tree imagery and, 119
    undiminished human beings, 97
black intellectuals, 24–26, 28
black literature, 41–42, 55, 108–109
    black discursive practice, 104
black oral tradition, 32, 40, 42
    cultural artifacts and, 55
    described, 16
    power and, 60
    sexual difference and, 49
    women barred from, 10
    See also language
black urban migration, 25, 27, 28,
    37
blackness, concept of, 28, 36
Boas, Franz, 30, 151
book title origin, 68, 133, 150
Bootyny (fictional), 97
Butler, Judith, 149, 159

Cane (Toomer), 6, 7
Carby, Hazel, 182
Caribbean, 32, 37, 40
"Characteristics of Negro Expression,"
    83, 99, 109, 113
Chesnutt, Charles, 147, 195
Chicago Renaissance, 25
Chopin, Kate, 91, 194
chronology, 205–207
Civil Rights "elite," 181
class, 82–83
    confrontation of, 29
    contradiction, 26–27
    expectations, 33, 186
    white class patterns, 96
Color Purple, The (Walker), 39, 160, 172
community, 19, 34
Conjure Woman, The (Chestnutt), 147
"Consciousness of the Court, The" (short
    story), 102
courtroom scene, 15, 16, 34, 51, 68–69,
    179
    defense testimony, 53, 139, 162
    racial conflict in, 136
    white jury, 102, 133–134, 142
cultural suicide, 109
culture, 23, 24
    beliefs and, 37
    industry of, 24–25, 182
    power and, 175

Daisy Blunt (fictional), 46–47
Damballah, West African god, 37, 75
Daniel, Janice, 199
Dark Princess (Du Bois), 176
Davie, Sharon, 161, 168–169
Dee, Ruby, 24
deformation of mastery, 194–195
Deluzian reformation, master-slave
    dialect, 52
Democracy (Adams), 170
dialect writing, 42, 49
    folk content and, 73
    master-slave, 52–53

dialogic novel, 182
domination, 54, 118, 192
    See also male dominance; patriarchy;
        oppression; signifying tradition
Douglas, Mary, 98
Douglass, Frederick, 7, 147
dreams, 43, 61, 201
"Drenched in Light," 107
Du Bois, W.E.B., 6, 88, 163, 168, 170,
    176, 177
Du Plessis, Rachel Blau, 18, 21, 105,
    111, 181, 183
Dust Tracks on a Road: An Autobiography
    (Hurston), 20, 23, 24, 37–38, 50, 76,
    99, 104, 183

Eatonville, Florida, 12, 17, 29, 32, 37,
    59, 60, 170, 183
    all-black, 7, 120, 169
    anthropology and, 30
    courtship of women, 46
    folk in, rejection of, 53
    Harlem Renaissance and, 26
    in *Jonah's Gourd Vine*, 9
    mayor of, 62–63
    move away from, 66
    store in, 44, 45, 171
"Eatonville Anthology, The," 83, 89
Edwards, Lee, 19
egalitarian culture, 17
egalitarian relationship, 186–187
Egyptian symbolism, 107, 108, 124. *See
    also* Osiris/Isis imagery
Ellison, Ralph, 5, 8, 20, 58, 163
ethnography, 30, 35, 36, 49, 163, 164
Everglades, 6, 15, 66, 96, 125, 160. *See
    also* "life on the muck"
experience, inner growth and, 17, 49–50

Fanon, Frantz, 151
Federal Theatre Project, 32, 40
feminism, 14, 150, 180, 186, 188, 191,
    194–199, 202
"Fiery Chariot, The" (play), 32

Fischer, Michael, 30, 36
fishnet imagery, 36, 54
Florida. *See* Eatonville; Everglades
folk community, 9, 10, 26, 31, 32, 37
folk culture
    authenticity of, 26–27
    preservation of, 30–31
folk heritage, 25
folk language, 10, 37. *See also* language
"founding fathers," 46
frame story, 7, 10, 73, 78, 108, 132
free indirect discourse, 20, 49, 73
Freud, Sigmund, 73, 148, 155, 156
From Behind the Veil (Stepto), 20, 40, 168
From Sun to Sun (musical), 31
"fronting," 88–89, 103–104

Gates, Henry Louis, Jr., 19, 23, 32, 73,
    168
    on Fon people, 75
    "free, indirect discourse," 49
    "Speakerly Text," 41–42
gender, 151–152, 153
    central theme, 135, 137
    hierarchical world of, 136
gender roles, 35, 81, 118, 125, 189. *See
    also* hero/heroine
George, Nelson, 39
"Gilded Six Bits, The," 31, 91
grandmother. *See* Nanny
Great Day, The (musical), 31
Guggenheim grant, 35
Gulliver's Travels (Swift), 72, 110

Haiti, 32, 35, 36, 37, 40
Halsey, William, 57
Hambo (fictional), 173
Harlem Renaissance, 25, 26, 87, 143,
    169
Harper and Row, 23, 24
Haurkiewicz, Julie, 189
Hemenway, Robert, 16, 19, 20, 23, 36,
    39, 168, 181
Henderson, Mae, 152

hero/heroine, 17–18, 187
    classic mythological, 21
    female, 6, 10, 16, 18, 21, 202
    male, 18, 140
    romantic, 18, 21
    unnaming and, 58–59
    See also gender roles
Hezikiah (fictional), 14, 91, 112
"Hidden Name and Complex Fate," 58
historical consciousness, 8
Homans, Margaret, 10
hoodoo. *See* voodoo
hooks, bell, 152, 154
horizon imagery, 17, 46, 59, 65, 72, 76,
    154, 176
    as fishnet, 36, 54, 69, 132, 133
    as limit, 67, 68–69
Hughes, Langston, 24, 27, 28, 171
humor, 71–115
    cartoons, 82
    comic speech, 86–87
    'cuttin' the monkey,' 87, 97–98
    Hindu godhead comparison, 108
    interracial, 101
    jokes, 76, 79, 98
    play and, 93
    scornful, 76
    visual images and, 81
hurricane, 66–67, 68, 100–101, 113–114,
    190, 200
    burials following, 101, 160, 128–129
    purification symbolization, 128
Hurston, Zora Neale, 55, 59, 71, 77, 110,
    185
    as anthropologist, 29, 30, 31, 37
    cultural power and, 28, 175
    Everglades and Florida, 15, 37, 183
    family/childhood of, 28, 76, 99, 112
    folk culture and, 26–27, 75
    Harlem Renaissance and, 26, 87, 169
    "industry," 24, 182
    January birth month, 74, 75
    love life, 50, 104, 145
    minister/mayor father of, 62

220

narrative technique of, 137, 162
on segregated train seating, 28–29
travels of, 32, 35, 36, 50
husband. *See* Joe Starks; Logan Killicks; 'Tea Cake'
"hypervisibility," 151

identity, 67, 147, 162
feminine, 59, 153, 155
racial/interracial, 157–158, 159, 161
See also naming; Negro identity
images of devotion, excerpt, 47
intellectual consciousness, 31. *See also* black intellectuals
interiority, 17
intragroup conflict, 140
Invisible Man (Ellison), 5, 6, 8, 58
Isis. *See* Osiris/Isis imagery

Jacobs, Karen, 188
Jamaica, 29, 32, 35, 36, 37, 50
Janie (fictional), 34, 44, 50, 65, 132, 193
abuse of, 14, 64, 84, 87–88, 99, 126
'Alphabet' nickname of, 60, 74
beauty/body of, 10, 74, 131, 153, 154, 159
courtroom defense, 53, 139, 162
friendship with Pheoby, 10
hair of, 13, 18, 80, 124, 155
heroic posture of, 10, 16
identity, 69, 73, 77–78, 137, 157
interiority of, 14, 17, 18, 54
negativity, rejection of, 54
obedience of, 190–191
objectification of, 10, 12, 121
oral speech, 12, 13, 16–17, 64
rebellion of, 12, 15, 32
sexuality of, 11, 12, 44
shooting of Tea Cake, 140, 141, 161
silence of, 14–15, 32, 46, 83, 88, 99, 148, 158, 188
split selves of, 13, 14, 20, 50, 140
third-person narration, 8, 72, 191
voice of, 14–15

Janus myth, 74–76, 92, 117–146, 142
Jim Crow law, 7, 29, 101, 160
Joe ('Jody') Starks (fictional), 7, 12, 18, 20, 120, 192
"big voice," 46, 48, 52, 54, 62, 63, 86, 169
death of, 50, 64, 68, 159, 175
emasculation of, 12, 49, 62, 64, 90, 122, 156, 174
"I god" expression of, 62, 80, 156, 174
lamp-lighting ceremony, 45
as mayor, 62, 82, 196
mule references, 45, 53, 61, 84–85, 135
store in Eatonville, 44, 47, 48–49, 171
John Callahan (fictional), 63, 65, 77, 104
Johnny Taylor (fictional), 11–12, 157
Johnson, Barbara, 13, 20, 48, 158
Johnson, James Weldon, 39–40, 108–109
Jonah's Gourd Vine (Hurston), 18, 20, 23, 32, 140, 152–153
courtroom scene in, 15–16
Hambo, 15, 46, 82
Hattie, 13, 15
Joe Clark, 16
Lucy, 11, 16, 71, 75, 85, 117, 139
publication of, 31
Rev. John Pearson, 9–10, 13, 15–16, 17, 18–19
review of, 40
Jordan, Jennifer, 130–131

Kaplan, Carla, 148, 199
King, Rodney, 149
Kochman, Thomas, 88
Kubitschek, Missy Den, 61, 65

Lakritz, Andrew, 158
language, 10, 46, 52, 54, 59, 179–180
colloquial form, standard English, 19
of dominant discourse, 10
figural, 42, 44, 46, 48, 50, 52, 53
linguistic disjunction, 54–55
linguistic reciprocity, 124

linguistic self-reflexivity, 42
    of men/women, 9, 17
    metonymy, 158
    synecdoche, 33
    as "weapon," 60
    See also black oral tradition; folk
        language; metaphor
Libation Bearers, The (Aeschylus), 76
Library of Congress, 31
"life on the muck," 6, 18, 97, 100, 119,
    125, 188. See also Everglades
Lige Moss (fictional), 45, 87
Lincoln, Abraham, 45–46, 64, 84–85,
    173
Logan Killicks (fictional), 7, 12, 78, 154,
    176
    abusive nature of, 188, 189, 191
    mule references, 61, 63, 96
Lomax, Alan, 31
"Looking for Zora" (article), 181
Lorde, Audre, 149, 150, 155
Lott, Eric, 151
Louisiana, 37

male dominance, 12, 32, 148, 156
    black men in authority, 36, 82
    possessiveness, 99
    sexist views, 98
    See also patriarchy; signifying
        tradition
Marcus, George, 30, 36
marginalized text, 41, 55
marriage, 47–48, 50, 59, 65, 66, 69, 78,
    177, 186, 193
    hierarchical relationship, 173
    See also pear tree imagery
Mason, Mrs. Osgood, 35
materiality, 154
Matt Bonner (fictional), 63, 83, 196
    mule of, 7, 121–122, 173, 188–189,
        191
McKay, Claude, 29
Mead, Margaret, 30, 40
Meese, Elizabeth, 60

metaphor, 60, 103, 118, 119, 121, 135,
    157, 158–159
    internalization of, 44
    See also horizon imagery; language
"Metaphor, Metonymy, and Voice in
    Their Eyes Were Watching God," 20
migration. See black urban migration
minstrelsy, 29–30, 110, 143, 148
Modern Language Association, 20, 23,
    168
Morrison, Toni, 161, 164
Moses, Man of the Mountain (Hurston),
    37, 75
Motor Boat (fictional), 97, 100–101, 128,
    200
"Mouth Almighty," 33, 60, 77, 105, 106
Mr. Turner (fictional), 125–126, 190
Mrs. Annie Tyler (fictional), 16, 66, 74,
    100, 108
Mrs. Bogle (fictional), 197–198
Mrs. Turner (fictional), 97, 98, 99, 125–
    126, 161, 176
"mulatto" novels, 18
mule, 53–54, 83, 188
    black woman as, 61, 118, 119, 135
    "freeing" of, 63–64, 135, 173
    funeral of, 48–49, 188–189, 191
    oration, 173
Mule Bone (Hurston), 111, 171
Mules and Men (Hurston), 23, 24, 29, 83,
    119, 171
    anthropology and, 33, 34, 35
    folklore and, 37
    gender roles and, 36
    "Hoodoo" section, 37
    publication of, 31
    yellow mule episode, 122
multivocal narrative quality, 145
Mulvey, Laura, 155
mythology. See Egyptian symbolism

naming, 57–69
    of God and death, 68
    power and, 61, 62

self-designation, 58
slave renaming, 57, 58
Nanny (fictional), 157, 176–177
    on black women as 'mules,' 61, 83,
        121, 135, 196
    death of, 79
    dreams/prophecies, 65, 100, 108
    hierarchical world of, 136
    naming and, 60–61
    obsession with past, 93, 154
    slavery and, 55, 78
    words to Janie, 42, 118
narrative, building of, 51–52. *See also*
    third-person narration
National Endowment for the
    Humanities, 23
Native Son (Wright), 38
"Negro expression," 78
Negro identity, 28, 29–30, 31
Negro South, 37
Negro spirituals, 26
New Negro, The, 26
Nietzsche, 53
Nobody Knows My Name (Baldwin),
    58
nostalgia, 28, 30
Nunkie (fictional), 99, 126, 127, 138,
    198

objectification, 10, 12, 121, 152
O'Connor, Mary, 172
Odyssey, The, 187
Ong, Walter, 57
oppression, 171, 172, 175, 180, 188
    "double dispossession" of women, 59
    dynamics of, 190–193
    hierarchies, 124
    racial, 30, 53, 124, 129, 135, 149, 158
    sexual, 118, 140
oral tradition. *See* black oral tradition
Orality and Literacy (Ong), 57
Orpheus, 96
Osiris/Isis imagery, 107, 114, 124, 130,
    132, 133, 139, 152

Paradise (Morrison), 161
patriarchy, 18, 36, 60–61, 62, 180, 189,
    195, 198
Patterns of Culture (Benedict), 31
pear tree imagery, 67, 78, 119, 131, 154,
    156
    excerpt, 11, 44, 48
    internalization of, 46
    'marriage' reference, 61, 119
Petry, Ann, 19
phallocentrism, 156
Pheoby Watson (fictional), 10, 60
    character of, 137–138
    as mediator, 33, 34, 40
    response to Janie's story, 136
    sole remark of, 7
"physicalization" of figures, 49
Plant, Deborah G., 177–178
Plato, 148
political consciousness, 15
politics of human dignity, 52, 51
"politics of positioning," 150
polyphonic text, 49
porch talkers, 33, 48–49, 54, 69, 132,
    133
    anthropomorphic myths by, 53
    folktales and, 34
    naming, power and, 59–60
    words as "weapons" metaphor, 52
post civil rights era, 24
power, 52–53, 118, 120, 123, 148,
    196
    black, African drums and, 129
    naming and, 61, 62
    of oral speech, 9, 16
    sexual roles and, 9, 16, 61
    undeployed, 48
    visual, 151
    See also naming
Propp, Vladimir, 17
protagonist, 32, 148, 187. *See also*
    Janie
"protest literature," 78
Quest of the Silver Fleece, The (Du Bois), 6

race, 38, 156
    central theme, 135, 137
    hierarchical world of, 136
    mixed-race heritage, 159
"race records," 26, 27
"racial health," 97
racial identity. *See under* identity
racial oppression. *See under* oppression
Racine, Maria J., 178, 179
racist social order, 38, 60, 66–67
    dominance and, 135, 149, 202
    Indians and, 128
Ramsey, William M., 186, 190, 199, 202
rape. *See* sexual abuse
Raskin, Victor, 83
Reed, Ishmael, 195
remembrance, 43, 59, 201
"Renaissance for a Pioneer of Black
    Pride," 24
renaming. *See* naming
rhetorical strategy, 46–47, 51–52
    communicable meaning and, 51, 55
    See also speakerly tradition
romance, 17–18, 40, 140, 141, 142, 187
Romans. *See* Janus myth
rural folk. *See* black urban migration

Said, Edward, 25
Sam Watson (fictional), 86, 87, 90, 171,
    196
    'King of the Porch,' 107
Scarlet Letter, The, 74
scopophilia, 155, 161
self-discovery, 9
sex-role stereotypes, 186, 187, 201, 202
sexual abuse, 118, 119, 121, 158, 161
sexual difference, 43, 49
sexual oppression. *See under* oppression
sexuality, 11–12, 19, 44, 126, 190
    de-sexing, 49
    sexual awakening, 156–157
    sexualized bodies, 152
    "sexual jealousy," 189, 190
    See also bee/flower imagery

sharecropping, 78
ship imagery, 43, 46, 72, 175–176
"Signify(cant) Correspondences" (essay),
    57
Signifying Monkey, The (Gates), 19, 73
signifying tradition, 42–43, 44–49, 52,
    54, 173
silence
    of blacks, trial scene, 52
    "fronting," 88–89
    paradigm of voice, 32
Silverman, Kaja, 159
Singing Steel (musical), 31
slavery, 78, 96, 118, 148, 158
    dialect and, 52–53
    freedom from, 64
    oral narration and, 55
    renaming and, 57, 58, 61
social contract, 196
social determinants, 181
social identity, 17, 26, 35, 120, 121. *See
    also* class
Sop-de-Bottom (fictional), 14, 97, 127,
    141, 189, 193
    on abuse, 98, 161
    courtroom and, 34, 52, 105, 135, 136
Souls of Black Folk, The (Du Bois), 6, 7
speakerly tradition, 49–50, 51, 73. *See also*
    black oral tradition
Spielberg, Steven, 151
Spillers, Hortense, 60, 163
spirituality, 67–68. *See also* biblical
    references
spirtuals, 26, 27
spittoon, 108, 111, 118, 119, 120, 121,
    171
Spivak, Gayatri Chakravorty, 27, 39
"Sprirtuals and Neospirituals" (essay), 26
"standard english," 49
Stepto, Robert, 14–15, 20, 32, 40, 113,
    148, 168
Stew Beef (fictional), 97, 128
"Story of an Hour, The," 91
subaltern, 25, 27–28, 32, 39

'Tea Cake' Woods (fictional), 13–14, 18, 33, 157
    abuse of Janie, 14, 99, 138
    death of, 18, 34, 50–51, 105, 131, 141
    gambling, 95, 190
    guitar of, 100, 132
    muck immersion, 6, 18, 37
    rabies infection, 50, 96, 101, 104, 130
    use of language, 65–66
    vision of, 200
Tell My Horse (Hurston), 23, 36, 37, 49
third-person narration, 7, 14, 40, 72, 139, 191
Tony Taylor (fictional), 45, 82, 83, 188
Toomer, Jean, 6
train imagery, 11, 17, 20
travelogue, 36
tree imagery, 50, 78, 119. *See also* pear tree imagery
trial. *See* courtroom scene
Truth, Sojourner, 7
Tubman, Harriet, 7

unnaming, 58, 59
urban migration. *See* black urban migration
Urgo, Joseph R., 186, 187, 190, 191, 193, 199, 202

Vergible Tea Cake Woods (fictional), 50, 65, 92. *See also* 'Tea Cake'
violence against women, 99–100, 127, 186. *See also* sexual abuse
vision, 147–163
visual imagery, 148–149
"Visual Pleasure and Narrative Cinema," 155
voice, 137, 147–164, 201
    blackness, body and, 150
    multilevelled, 42
    multivocal narrative quality, 137
    paradigm of, 32

textual, 55
    See also porch talkers
voodoo, 32, 37, 40, 75, 104

Wald, Priscilla, 157, 163
Walker, Alice, 39, 97, 119, 131, 160, 168, 172, 179, 181, 185, 194, 201
Walker, S. Jay, 187, 190
Wallace, Michelle, 151, 156
Warren, Robert Penn, 170
Washburn family (fictional), 60–61, 62, 74, 77–78
Washington, Booker T., 98, 176, 177, 195
Washington, George, 45–46, 64, 84–85, 173
Washington, Mary Helen, 20, 32, 40, 102, 109, 113, 148, 168, 181
Weldon, James, 6
Western tradition, 59, 66, 68
"What White Publishers Won't Print," 150
Wheatley, Phillis, 147
whites, 53, 60, 66–67, 83, 87, 96
    in jury, 51, 52
    male literary canon, 68
    materialism and, 84, 93
    patriarchal system of, 62
    romanticization of lives, 118
    See also Washburn family
Wolff, Maria Tai, 65, 148, 178, 183
Wright, Richard, 5–6, 28, 38, 78
    condemnation, *Their Eyes*, 52, 143, 181, 201
    minstrelsy and, 29–30, 110

"Zora is My Name" (broadcast), 24
"Zora Neale Hurston: A Theatrical Biography" (play), 24
"Zora Neale Hurston and the Speakerly Text," 19
Zora Neale Hurston (Hemenway), 19, 39